C000156548

Collins

Secure Maths
Year 2

a primary maths
intervention programme

Teacher's Pack

Collins

William Collins' dream of knowledge for all began with the publication of his first book in 1819.
A self-educated mill worker, he not only enriched millions of lives, but also founded a flourishing publishing house. Today, staying true to this spirit, Collins books are packed with inspiration, innovation and practical expertise. They place you at the centre of a world of possibility and give you exactly what you need to explore it.

Collins. Freedom to teach.

An imprint of HarperCollins*Publishers*
The News Building
1 London Bridge Street
London
SE1 9GF

Browse the complete Collins catalogue at
www.collins.co.uk

10 9 8 7 6 5 4 3 2 1

ISBN 978-0-00-822143-0

British Library Cataloguing in Publication Data
A catalogue record for this publication is available from the British Library.

Author Paul Hodge
Publishing manager Fiona McGlade
Editor Nina Smith
Development editor Fiona Tomlinson
Project managed by Alissa McWhinnie, QBS Learning
Copyedited by Catherine Dakin
Proofread by Cassie Fox
Answers checked by Steven Matchett
Cover design by Amparo Barrera and ink-tank and associates
Cover artwork by Amparo Barrera
Internal design by 2Hoots publishing services
Typesetting by QBS Learning
Illustrations by QBS Learning
Production by Rachel Weaver
Printed and bound by CPI

Contents

Domain	National Curriculum Attainment Target	Secure Maths Unit number	Page number
Number – number and place value	count in steps of 2, 3, and 5 from 0, and in tens from any number, forward and backward	1	74
	recognise the place value of each digit in a two-digit number (10s and 1s)	2	78
	identify, represent and estimate numbers using different representations, including the number line	3	80
	compare and order numbers from 0 up to 100; use <, > and = signs	4	82
	read and write numbers to at least 100 in numerals and in words	5	86
	use place value and number facts to solve problems	6	88

Domain	National Curriculum Attainment Target	Secure Maths Unit number	Page number
Number – addition and subtraction	solve problems with addition and subtraction: • using concrete objects and pictorial representations, including those involving numbers, quantities and measures • applying their increasing knowledge of mental and written methods	7	90
	recall and use addition and subtraction facts to 20 fluently, and derive and use related facts up to 100	8	94
	add and subtract numbers using concrete objects, pictorial representations, and mentally, including: • a two-digit number and 1s • a two-digit number and 10s • 2 two-digit numbers • adding 3 one-digit numbers	9	98
	show that addition of 2 numbers can be done in any order (commutative) and subtraction of 1 number from another cannot	10	102
	recognise and use the inverse relationship between addition and subtraction and use this to check calculations and solve missing number problems	11	104

Domain	National Curriculum Attainment Target	Secure Maths Unit number	Page number
Number – multiplication and division	recall and use multiplication and division facts for the 2, 5 and 10 multiplication tables, including recognising odd and even numbers	12	106
	calculate mathematical statements for multiplication and division within the multiplication tables and write them using the multiplication (×), division (÷) and equals (=) signs	13	110
	show that multiplication of 2 numbers can be done in any order (commutative) and division of 1 number by another cannot	14	112
	solve problems involving multiplication and division, using materials, arrays, repeated addition, mental methods, and multiplication and division facts, including problems in contexts	15	114
Number – fractions	recognise, find, name and write fractions $\frac{1}{3}$, $\frac{1}{4}$, $\frac{2}{4}$ and $\frac{3}{4}$ of a length, shape, set of objects or quantity	16	116
	write simple fractions, for example $\frac{1}{2}$ of 6 = 3 and recognise the equivalence of $\frac{2}{4}$ and $\frac{1}{2}$	17	120

Domain	National Curriculum Attainment Target	Secure Maths Unit number	Page number
Measurement	choose and use appropriate standard units to estimate and measure length/ height in any direction (m/cm) and mass (kg/g) to the nearest appropriate unit, using rulers and scales	18	122
	choose and use appropriate standard units to estimate and measure temperature (°C) and capacity (litres/ ml) to the nearest appropriate unit, using thermometers and measuring vessels	19	126
	compare and order lengths, mass, volume/capacity and record the results using >, < and =	20	128
	recognise and use symbols for pounds (£) and pence (p); combine amounts to make a particular value	21	130
	find different combinations of coins that equal the same amounts of money	22	132
	solve simple problems in a practical context involving addition and subtraction of money of the same unit, including giving change	23	134
	compare and sequence intervals of time	24	136
	tell and write the time to five minutes, including quarter past/to the hour and draw the hands on a clock face to show these times	25	138
	know the number of minutes in an hour and the number of hours in a day	26	140

Domain	National Curriculum Attainment Target	Secure Maths Unit number	Page number
Geometry – properties of shapes	identify and describe the properties of 2-D shapes, including the number of sides, and line symmetry in a vertical line	27	142
	identify and describe the properties of 3-D shapes, including the number of edges, vertices and faces	28	146
	identify 2-D shapes on the surface of 3-D shapes, [for example, a circle on a cylinder and a triangle on a pyramid]	29	148
	compare and sort common 2-D and 3-D shapes and everyday objects	30	150
Geometry – position and direction	order and arrange combinations of mathematical objects in patterns and sequences	31	152
	use mathematical vocabulary to describe position, direction and movement, including movement in a straight line and distinguishing between rotation as a turn and in terms of right angles for quarter, half and three-quarter turns (clockwise and anti-clockwise)	32	154
Statistics	interpret and construct simple pictograms, tally charts, block diagrams and tables	33	158
	ask and answer simple questions by counting the number of objects in each category and sorting the categories by quantity	34	160
	ask-and-answer questions about totalling and comparing categorical data	35	162

Secure Maths is a structured intervention course for Primary Maths that can be followed in its entirety or dipped into as needed. It is a year-on-year programme, which can be used independently or alongside any programme or scheme.

The purpose of the series is to assist teachers in identifying children who are not on track to meet age-related expectations by the end of the school year, and to provide support to get them back on track, and ensure readiness for the next year or the SAT.

Secure Maths follows the 2014 programme of study and provides an Assess – Teach – Assess cycle.

For each year, there is a Teacher's Pack and Pupil Resource Pack.

Teacher's pack

The Teacher's Pack contains:

- two Diagnostic tests with answers and gap analysis grids
- units of teaching covering each National Curriculum Attainment Target (NCAT), containing background knowledge and teaching activities.

Tests can be delivered by topic/domain or in their entirety.

Diagnostic tests highlight key areas of weakness and gaps in children's knowledge.

Diagnostic test 1

Diagnostic test 1

Number and place value

1. Complete the next three numbers in each sequence.

   a) 0, 2, 4, 6,

   b) 0, 3, 6, 9,

   c) 0, 5, 10, 15,

   d) 30, 40, 50, 60,

   e) 16, 14, 12, 10,

   f) 21, 18, 15, 12,

   g) 40, 35, 30, 25,

   h) 90, 80, 70, 60,

2. Complete the table.

Number (in numerals)	Number (in words)
43	
	seventy-six

The questions in the test are at the end-of-year level expectation for the National Curriculum Attainment Target (NCAT) they are testing.

Answers to the diagnostic tests are provided immediately after the test, and are organised by topic/domain.

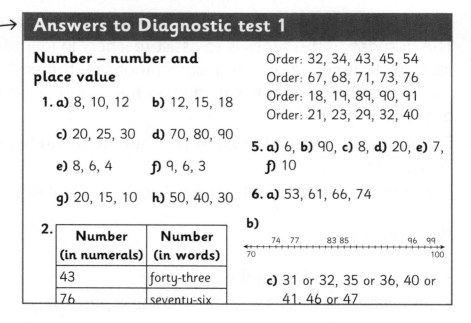

Answers to Diagnostic test 1

Number – number and place value

1. a) 8, 10, 12   b) 12, 15, 18
   c) 20, 25, 30   d) 70, 80, 90
   e) 8, 6, 4   f) 9, 6, 3
   g) 20, 15, 10   h) 50, 40, 30

2.

Number (in numerals)	Number (in words)
43	forty-three
76	seventy-six

Order: 32, 34, 43, 45, 54
Order: 67, 68, 71, 73, 76
Order: 18, 19, 89, 90, 91
Order: 21, 23, 29, 32, 40

5. a) 6, b) 90, c) 8, d) 20, e) 7, f) 10

6. a) 53, 61, 66, 74

b)

```
      74  77      83 85          96  99
  <-+--+---+---+----+--+----------+---+->
  70                                  100
```

c) 31 or 32, 35 or 36, 40 or 41, 46 or 47

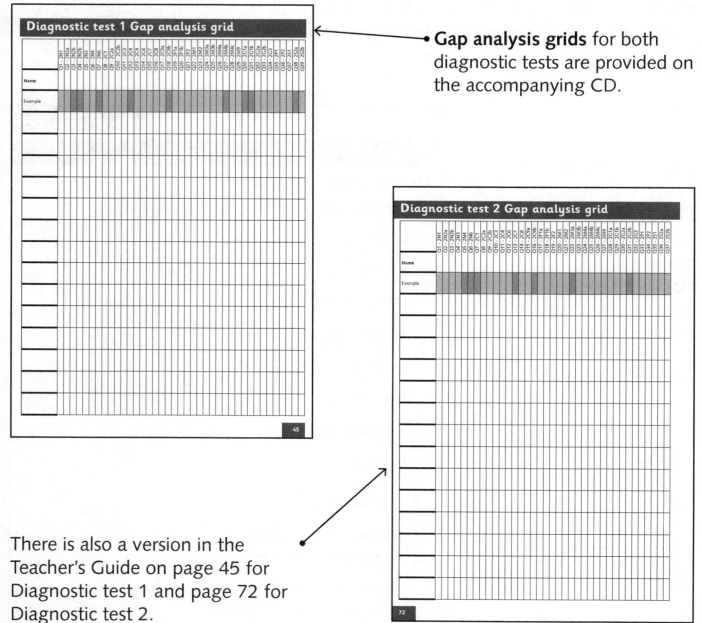

Gap analysis grids for both diagnostic tests are provided on the accompanying CD.

There is also a version in the Teacher's Guide on page 45 for Diagnostic test 1 and page 72 for Diagnostic test 2.

Each unit is linked to the National **Curriculum domain** and attainment target.

Prerequisites for learning list the knowledge children require before teaching of the unit can take place.

Learning outcomes.

Background knowledge provides a clear and concise explanation of the mathematical concept(s) being covered in the unit.

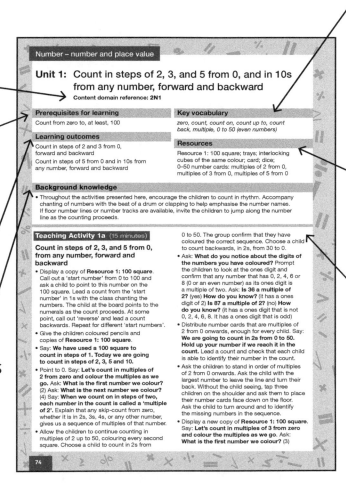

Key vocabulary lists the mathematical words that children need to understand to access the unit.

Resources list any physical resources required for teaching the unit.

Teaching activities are linked to objectives (above) and offer teaching plans for teachers/ TAs. Approximate timing is provided for each activity.

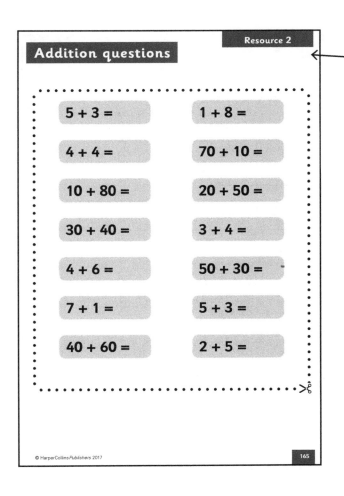

Resource sheets are included to support teaching activities. These are photocopiable pages and can be found from page 164 to 177 of the Teacher's Guide.

Answers to the practice and tests in the accompanying **Pupil Resource Pack** can be found be found from pages 178 to 185 of the Teacher's Guide.

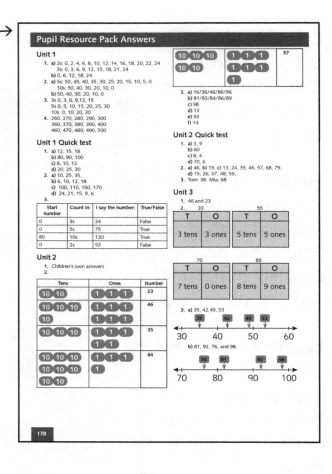

Pupil Resource Pack

The Pupil Resource Pack contains:

• Units, one per National Curriculum Attainment Target (NCAT), each containing:
  – Independent practice
  – Quick test.

Targeted practice linked to the teaching activities in the unit help children reinforce their learning.

Quick tests enable teachers to check that children have mastered the objective and are ready to move on with the rest of the class. These can also be used for evidence.

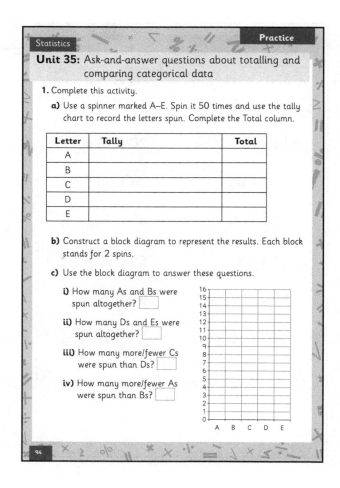

How to use the programme

Assess

Diagnostic tests have been provided to assist you in identifying children in need of intervention, and to ascertain exactly what gaps there are in their knowledge. Tests can be set in their entirety, to get a picture of the children's knowledge of the year's programme of study, or they can be set by topic, to determine how children are faring in a particular domain of the NCAT.

Gap analysis

Use the gap analysis spreadsheet on the accompanying CD to quickly see where the gaps in class, and individual, knowledge are. Each question is testing a content domain, which are linked to units of teaching. By placing a Y against questions that children answered correctly, and an N against questions children answered incorrectly, the spreadsheet will colour code each content domain either green or red. Red indicates a gap in knowledge which may require intervention.

Note: out of necessity, there are some instances where units may cover more than the child's requirements, for example, addition and subtraction where intervention is only required in subtraction. Please be mindful of this, and where possible, use the Diagnostic test in conjunction with other data when identifying intervention requirements. As always, teacher judgement is by far the most powerful diagnostic tool.

Teach

Within each unit of teaching, we have identified specific objectives that the child needs to master in order to meet the requirements of that NCAT. For each objective, there is a choice of activity for the teacher/TA to use with the child or group of children. These provide alternative ways of teaching concepts, and cater for different learning styles. It is important that the intervention activity is different to the main teaching activity, and presents the concept in a different way to the child.

Some units cover just one learning outcome, but most will cover two outcomes and some even cover three outcomes. As each unit covers what would probably be taught over a week in class, some units could take more than one intervention session to cover. For each learning outcome, there are two activities provided. The alternatives are slightly different ways of teaching each concept and can be used in an either/or approach or for further consolidation if children are still insecure after doing one of the activities. Using a limited variety of readily available resources, such as digit cards, dice, number lines and place value grids, helps children to visualise concepts without the distraction of a new resource to get used to.

Activity (a), in many units, is the more efficient, concise method of teaching the outcome and can be used for children who are nearly there, but are making errors. Activity (b) tends to be an alternative or supplementary method that often uses different visual or concrete material support and comes at the learning outcome from a different angle. Activity (b) may often be a better starting point for those children who learn visually and cannot remember the 'rules' or for whom these rules make no sense or for those who have a number of gaps in their mathematics education. Some children could benefit from the related units in a previous year. Using the diagnostic tests of the previous year will help to identify areas where children need to catch up with basic concepts before they can successfully access the curriculum for their own year. Using the diagnostic tests of the previous year with a whole class at the beginning of a year could be useful tool in alerting the teacher to general gaps in understanding to inform future planning.

Practice

As with all learning, it is important for children to practise in order to reinforce the knowledge and skills acquired. Targeted practice is provided in the Pupil Resource Pack for each unit, linked directly to the intervention.

Assess

Quick tests have been provided for each unit, to be completed once the teacher is satisfied that the child has successfully completed the unit of intervention. This is a quick way of confirming that they have mastered the concept in question, and are ready to move on with the rest of the class. Quick tests can also be used as evidence of learning and achievement.

Diagnostic test 1

Number and place value

1. Complete the next three numbers in each sequence.

a) 0, 2, 4, 6,

b) 0, 3, 6, 9,

c) 0, 5, 10, 15,

d) 30, 40, 50, 60,

e) 16, 14, 12, 10,

f) 21, 18, 15, 12,

g) 40, 35, 30, 25,

h) 90, 80, 70, 60,

2. Complete the table.

Number (in numerals)	Number (in words)
43	
	seventy-six
19	
	fifty-eight
90	
	twelve

3. Complete the number sentences using the signs <, > or =.

a) 13 ☐ 12

b) sixteen ☐ 16

c) 45 ☐ 54

d) eighty-seven ☐ seventy-eight

e) 76 ☐ 67

f) 89 ☐ 98

4. Order each set of numbers, from smallest to greatest.

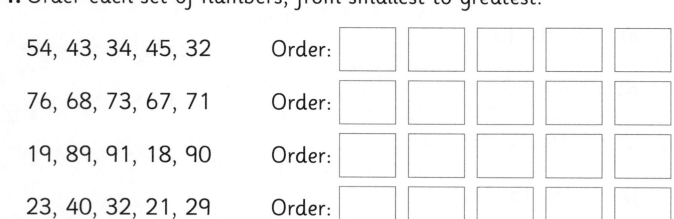

54, 43, 34, 45, 32   Order: ☐ ☐ ☐ ☐ ☐

76, 68, 73, 67, 71   Order: ☐ ☐ ☐ ☐ ☐

19, 89, 91, 18, 90   Order: ☐ ☐ ☐ ☐ ☐

23, 40, 32, 21, 29   Order: ☐ ☐ ☐ ☐ ☐

5. Write the value of each underlined digit.

a) 3<u>6</u>   **b)** <u>9</u>0   **c)** 6<u>8</u>   **d)** <u>2</u>2   **e)** 7<u>7</u>   **f)** <u>1</u>9

☐ ☐ ☐ ☐ ☐ ☐

6. a) Write the number each arrow is pointing to.

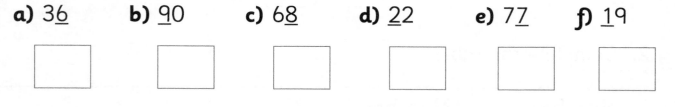

50 ☐ ☐ ☐ ☐ 80

b) Write these numbers on the number line: 96, 74, 83, 77, 99, 85.

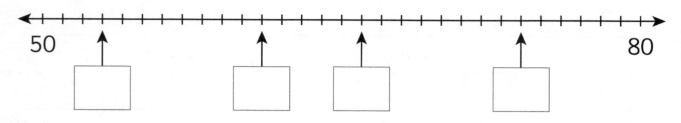

70   100

c) Estimate the number each arrow is pointing to.

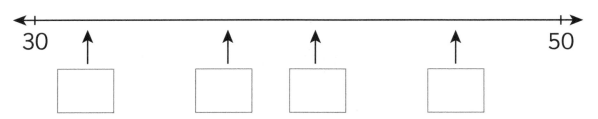

30 ↑ ↑ ↑ ↑ 50

☐ ☐ ☐ ☐

7. Write these calculations in order of value, from smallest to greatest.

a) 30 + 40, 20 + 60, 10 + 20, 10 + 50, 20 + 20

Order: _____ _____ _____ _____ _____

b) 60 − 10, 90 − 60, 40 − 20, 70 − 30, 80 − 70

Order: _____ _____ _____ _____ _____

c) 20 + 25, 10 + 12, 30 + 13, 20 + 1, 10 + 22

Order: _____ _____ _____ _____ _____

d) 55 − 40, 65 − 30, 52 − 20, 63 − 40, 51 − 30

Order: _____ _____ _____ _____ _____

Addition, subtraction, multiplication and division (calculations)

8. Use a fact you know to complete one you may not know.

a) 7 + 2 = ☐   70 + 20 = ☐

b) 4 + 4 = ☐   40 + 40 = ☐

c) 3 + 5 = ☐   30 + 50 = ☐

d) 8 − 3 = ☐   80 − 30 = ☐

e) 9 − 5 = ☐   90 − 50 = ☐

f) 7 − 6 = ☐   70 − 60 = ☐

9. a) Complete the additions.

i) 23 + 5 = ☐   **ii)** 57 + 8 = ☐

iii) 38 + 20 = ☐   **iv)** 47 + 40 = ☐

v) 17 + 22 = ☐   **vi)** 55 + 37 = ☐

vii) 6 + 9 + 4 = ☐   **viii)** 3 + 8 + 7 = ☐

b) Complete the subtractions.

i) 57 − 3 = ☐   **ii)** 82 − 7 = ☐

iii) 63 − 30 = ☐   **iv)** 95 − 70 = ☐

v) 48 − 23 = ☐   **vi)** 72 − 29 = ☐

10. a) Complete the additions.

i)

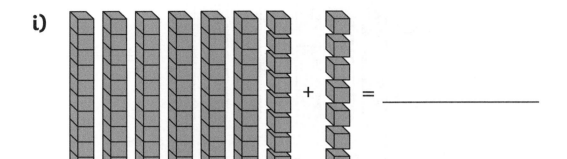 = _____

ii)

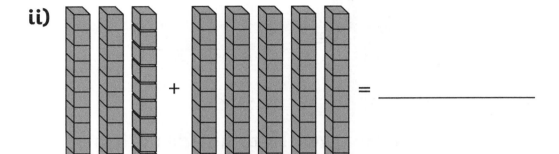 = _____

iii)

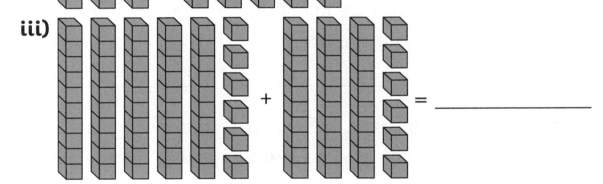 = _____

iv)

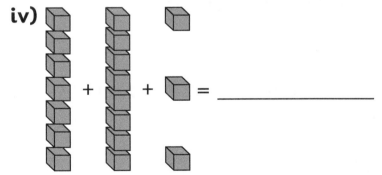 = _____

b) Complete the subtractions.

i)

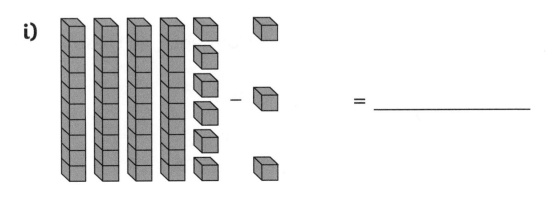 = _____

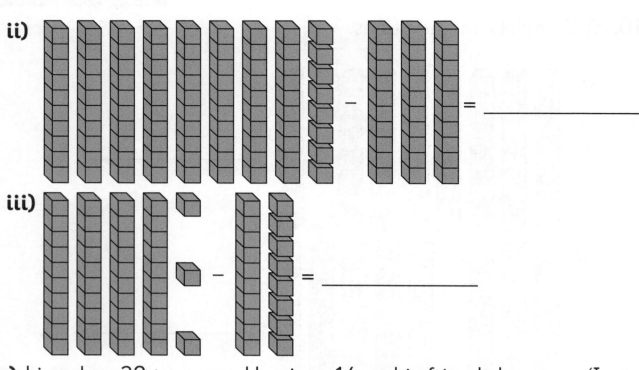

ii) _____ − _____ = _____

iii) _____ − _____ = _____

11. a) Liam has 32 toy cars. He gives 16 to his friend then says 'I have 18 more cars to give away'. Is he right? Use an addition sentence to show your answer.

_____

b) Katie makes 27 cupcakes. When her friend gives her 15 more cupcakes, Kate says 'I now have 43 cupcakes'. Is she right? Use a subtraction sentence to show your answer.

_____

12. a) Together, Freddy and Sienna have £18. Sienna has £4 more than Freddy. How much money does Sienna have? £ ☐

b) Together Ahmed and Lucy have 90 cm of ribbon. Ahmed has 8 cm more ribbon than Lucy. How much ribbon does Ahmed have? ☐ cm

13. What do I need to add to or subtract from each of these numbers to total 70?

a) 45 ☐ **b)** 56 ☐ **c)** 89 ☐ **d)** 67 ☐

e) 94 ☐ **f)** 32 ☐ **g)** 83 ☐ **h)** 12 ☐

14. Answer these.

a) A bird has 2 legs. How many legs do these numbers of birds have?

i) 3 birds ☐　　**ii)** 8 birds ☐　　**iii)** 12 birds ☐

b) A shirt has 5 buttons. How many buttons do these numbers of shirts have?

i) 2 shirts ☐　　**ii)** 6 shirts ☐　　**iii)** 9 shirts ☐

c) A crab has 10 legs. How many legs do these numbers of crabs have?

i) 4 crabs ☐　　**ii)** 7 crabs ☐　　**iii)** 11 crabs ☐

d) Circle the odd numbers in the list.

7　　14　　16　　21　　29　　30　　32
36　　42　　45　　48　　51　　59

15. Write a division sentence for each multiplication sentence, using the same numbers.

a) 9 x 2 = 18　　　　**b)** 7 x 5 = 35　　　　**c)** 12 x 10 = 120

_____　　　　_____　　　　_____

16. Use the array to answer the following questions.

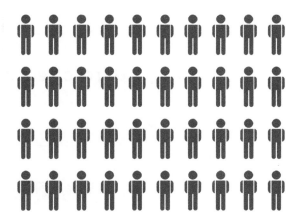

a) Children stand in the playground in 4 rows of 10. How many children are standing in the playground? ☐ children

b) Children stand in the playground in 10 rows of four. How many children are standing in the playground? ☐ children

c) 40 children are split evenly between 10 tables. How many children will there be on each table? [ ] children

d) 40 children are split evenly between four groups. How many children are in each group? [ ] children

17. a) If I know 34 + 43 = 76, what other addition can I write? _____

b) Ria says 'Since 8 subtract 7 makes 1, it follows that 7 subtract 8 is also 1'. Is Ria correct? If not, why? _____

18. Circle the incorrect number sentence. Explain your reasons.

a) 9 x 2 = 18   **c)** 18 ÷ 2 = 9

b) 2 x 9 = 18   **d)** 2 ÷ 18 = 2

Fractions, decimals and percentages

19. a) Shade the fractions. $\frac{1}{4}$ $\frac{1}{2}$

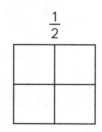

b) Find one third of each set of minibeasts.

a) 6 butterflies [ ]   **b)** 12 caterpillars [ ]

c) 24 beetles [ ]

c) Write the fraction in both words and numbers.

_____

20. Use the array to complete the fraction sentences.

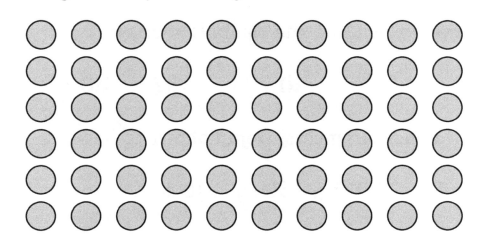

$\frac{1}{2}$ of 60 =

$\frac{1}{4}$ of 60 =

$\frac{3}{4}$ of 60 =

$\frac{1}{3}$ of 60 =

21. $\frac{2}{4}$ of this shape has circles. How else can we describe this fraction?

Measurement

22. a) Fill in the boxes using the symbols < or >.

i) 15 cm ☐ 14 cm   **ii)** 23 l ☐ 32 l   **iii)** 65 kg ☐ 56 kg

b) Order the measurements, from lightest to heaviest.

147 kg, 165 kg, 174 kg, 156 kg, 146 kg

Order: ☐ kg ☐ kg ☐ kg ☐ kg ☐ kg

23. a) Write the unit you would use to measure each item.

Measure	Unit
mass of a pencil	
capacity of a bath	
height of a tree	
temperature of the sea	

b) Draw the pointers on the weighing scales.

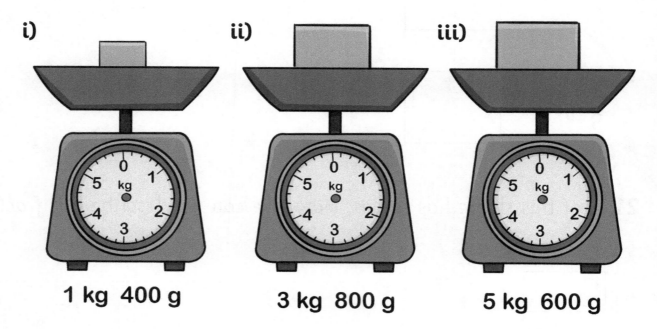

i) 1 kg 400 g   **ii)** 3 kg 800 g   **iii)** 5 kg 600 g

24. Complete the table.

Coins	£	p

25. Write four different combinations of coins that make 72p.

_____

_____

_____

_____

26. a) Write the time shown on each clock.

i)

ii)

_____

_____

iii)

iv)

_____

_____

b) Draw the hands on the clocks to show each time.

i)

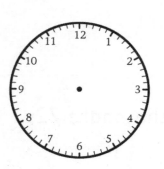

10 past 3

ii)

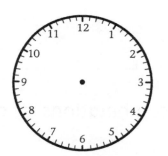

twenty to 7

iii)

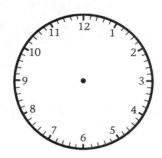

twenty-five past 11

27. a) Work out each time interval in minutes. Then compare the time intervals using the symbols, > or <.

Time interval A: 10 minutes past 2 to 35 minutes past 2

[   ] minutes

Time interval B: twenty past 9 to twenty to 10

[   ] minutes

A [   ] B

Time interval C: quarter to 9 to twenty past 9

[   ] minutes

Time interval D: 5 minutes to 1 to quarter to 2

[   ] minutes

C [   ] D

b) Order these, from earliest time to latest time.

| 10 past 4 | quarter to 4 | 5 past 4 | 5 to 4 | quarter past 3 |

_____ _____ _____ _____ _____

28. a) Danny arrives at the airport at 10 past 7 in the evening. He waits for his flight. If he departs on his flight at 10 past 9 in the evening, how many minutes did he wait? How many hours is this?

[   ] minutes   [   ] hours

b) A driver parks her car at twenty past 8 in the morning on 23rd March. She returns to her car and leaves at twenty past 8 in the morning on 26th March. How many days was the car parked for? How many hours is this?

[   ] days   [   ] hours

29. a) Lucy bought a packet of stickers at a shop. The price of the stickers is under a pound. She paid with 7 coins. Write four possible prices for the stickers.

	p		p		p		p

b) Oliver visits a shop and buys a packet of biscuits for 53p. If he pays with a 50p and a 20p, what change should he get back?

	p

Geometry – properties of shapes

30. Draw two 2-D shapes in each box of the Carroll diagram.

	5 sides or more	Fewer than 5 sides
Has a vertical line of symmetry		
Does not have a vertical line of symmetry		

31. Write the name of at least one 3-D shape that can be sorted into each of the four areas of the Venn diagram.

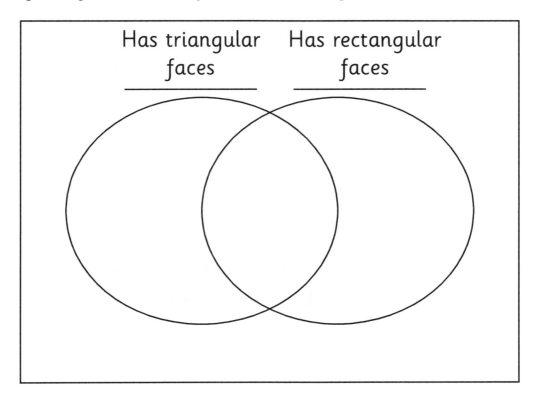

32. Draw and name these shapes.

a) A shape with 6 sides. All the sides are the same length.

Shape: _____

b) A shape with 5 sides. The sides are different lengths.

Shape: _____

c) A shape with 4 sides. All the sides are the same length. The vertices are shaped like the corners of a book.

Shape: _____

d) A shape with 3 sides.

Shape: _____

33. Draw and name these shapes. Draw real-life examples of each shape if you wish.

a) A solid shape with 2 circular bases connected by a curved surface.

Shape: _____

b) A solid shape with 6 square faces, 8 vertices and 12 edges. The faces are all squares.

Shape: _____

c) A solid shape with 1 curved surface and 1 circular base.

Shape: _____

d) A solid shape with a triangular base connected to a point at the top by triangular faces.

Shape: _____

34. Answer these questions.

a) Which 2-D shape makes 6 of the faces on a hexagonal pyramid?

_____

b) Which 2-D shape makes 6 of the faces on a cuboid?

_____

c) Which 2-D shape makes 2 of the faces on a pentagonal prism?

_____

Geometry – position and direction

35. Draw the next three shapes in each sequence.

a)

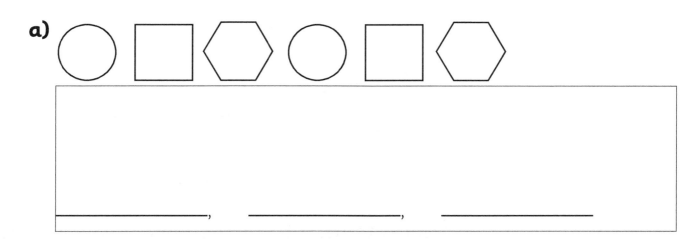

_____ , _____ , _____

b)

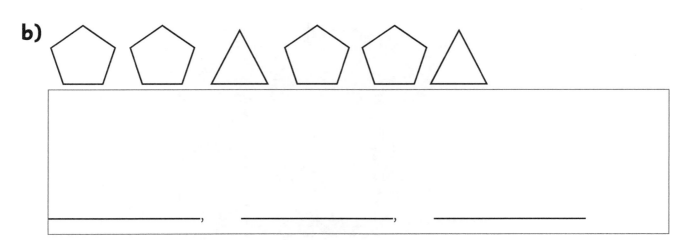

_____ , _____ , _____

c)

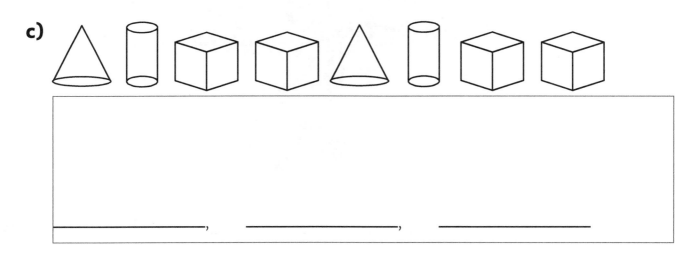

_____ , _____ , _____

d)

_____, _____, _____

36. Answer these.

a) Complete the sentences to describe the position of each object.

The book is _____ the chair. The light

is _____ the boy.

The tower of blocks is _____

_____ of the boy. The window is

_____ the boy.

b) A person stands on a grid that has columns labelled A to G and rows labelled 1 to 7.

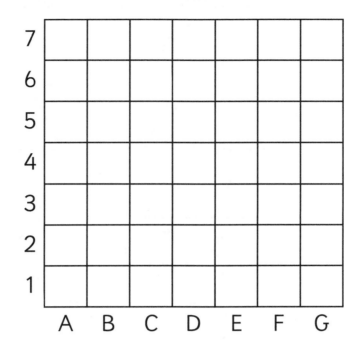

Write an instruction that will take the person from one square to the other.

i) From C3 to F5: _____

ii) From D6 to A1: _____

iii) From B4 to G7: _____

iv) From E5 to B2: _____

Statistics

37. Complete a tally for the number of each shape.

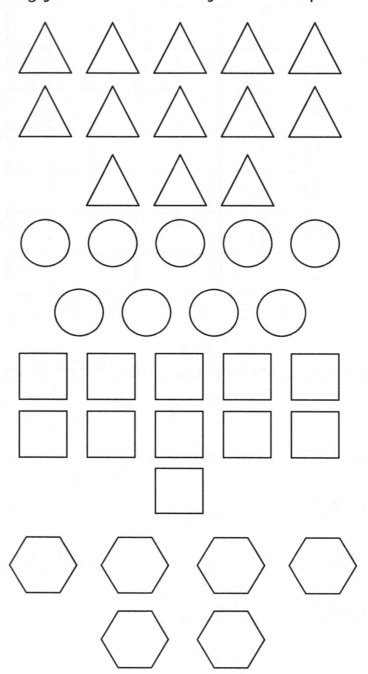

Shape	Tally	Number
circle		
triangle		
hexagon		
square		

a) How many triangles are there?

b) How many squares are there?

38. The pictogram shows the eye colours of children in a class.

= 2 children

Brown	
Blue	
Green	
Grey	

a) How many children have blue eyes?

_____

b) How many children have green eyes?

_____

c) Which eye colour is most common?

_____

d) Which eye colour is least common?

_____

e) Are there more children with green eyes or blue eyes?

_____

f) Are there fewer children with grey eyes or brown eyes?

_____

39. The children in a class were asked, 'What is your favourite milkshake flavour?' The block diagram below shows the responses to the question.

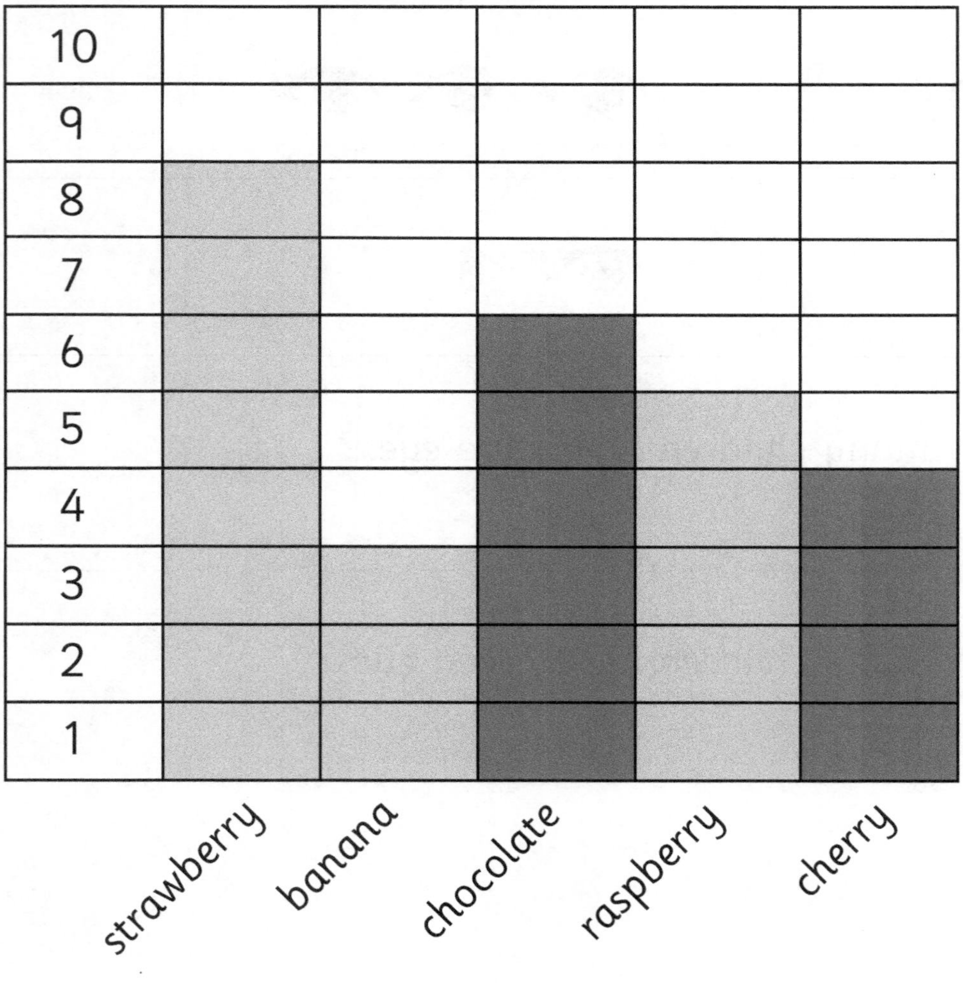

10					
9					
8					
7					
6					
5					
4					
3					
2					
1					
	strawberry	banana	chocolate	raspberry	cherry

a) How many more children prefer strawberry than cherry?

b) How many fewer children prefer banana than chocolate?

c) How many children like strawberry or raspberry?

d) How many children like chocolate or cherry?

Number – number and place value

1. a) 8, 10, 12   b) 12, 15, 18

   c) 20, 25, 30   d) 70, 80, 90

   e) 8, 6, 4   f) 9, 6, 3

   g) 20, 15, 10   h) 50, 40, 30

2.

Number (in numerals)	Number (in words)
43	forty-three
76	seventy-six
19	nineteen
58	fifty-eight
90	ninety
12	twelve

3. a) 13 > 12   b) Sixteen = 16
   c) 45 < 54
   d) Eighty seven > Seventy eight   e) 76 > 67
   f) 89 < 98

4. 32, 34, 43, 45, 54
   67, 68, 71, 73, 76
   18, 19, 89, 90, 91
   21, 23, 29, 32, 40

Order: 32, 34, 43, 45, 54
Order: 67, 68, 71, 73, 76
Order: 18, 19, 89, 90, 91
Order: 21, 23, 29, 32, 40

5. a) 6, b) 90, c) 8, d) 20, e) 7, f) 10

6. a) 53, 61, 66, 74

   b)

   c) 31 or 32, 35 or 36, 40 or 41, 46 or 47

7. a) Order: 10 + 20, 20 + 20, 10 + 50, 30 + 40, 20 + 60

   b) Order: 80 – 70, 40 – 20, 90 – 60, 70 – 30, 60 - 10

   c) Order: 20 + 1, 10 + 12, 10 + 22, 30 + 13, 20 + 25

   d) Order: 55 – 40, 51 – 30, 63 – 40, 52 – 20, 65 – 30

Addition, subtraction, multiplication and division (calculations)

8. a) 7 + 2 = 9
      70 + 20 = 90

b) 4 + 4 = 8
40 + 40 = 80

c) 3 + 5 = 8
30 + 50 = 80

d) 8 − 3 = 5
80 − 30 = 50

e) 9 − 5 = 4
90 − 50 = 40

f) 7 − 6 = 1
70 − 60 = 10

9. a) i) 28, **ii)** 65, **iii)** 58,
iv) 87, **v)** 39, **vi)** 92,
vii) 19, **viii)** 18

b) i) 54, **ii)** 75, **iii)** 33,
iv) 25, **v)** 25, **vi)** 43

10. a) i) 75, **ii)** 79, **iii)** 92, **iv)** 18

b) i) 43, **ii)** 58, **iii)** 25

11. a) Yes, 16 + 18 = 32

b) No, 43 − 15 = 28 not 27

12. a) £11, **b)** 49 cm

13. a) + 25, **b)** + 14, **c)** − 19,
d) + 3, **e)** − 24, **f)** + 38,
g) − 13, **h)** + 58

14. a) i) 6, **ii)** 16, **iii)** 24

b) i) 10, **ii)** 30, **iii)** 45

c) i) 40, **ii)** 70, **iii)** 110

d) 7, 21, 29, 45, 51, 59

15. a) 18 ÷ 9 = 2   or   18 ÷ 2 = 9

b) 35 ÷ 7 = 5   or   35 ÷ 5 = 7

c) 120 ÷ 12 = 10   or
120 ÷ 10 = 12

16. a) 40, **b)** 40, **c)** 4, **d)** 10

17. a) 43 + 34 = 76

b) No, the order of
subtraction matters

18. d) 2 ÷ 18 = 2 No, the order
of division matters

Fractions, decimals and percentages

19. a) $\frac{1}{4}$ $\frac{1}{2}$

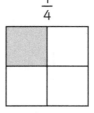   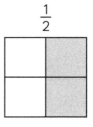

b) a) 2, **b)** 4, **c)** 8

d) $\frac{3}{4}$ Three quarters

20. $\frac{1}{2}$ of 60 = 30

$\frac{1}{4}$ of 60 = 15

$\frac{3}{4}$ of 60 = 45

$\frac{1}{3}$ of 60 = 20

21. $\frac{1}{2}$ of the shape has circles

Measurement

22. i) 15 cm > 14 cm

ii) 23 L < 32 L

iii) 65 kg > 56 kg

b) 146 kg, 147 kg, 156 kg, 165 kg, 174 kg

23. a)

Measure	Unit
the mass of a pencil	g (gram)
the capacity of a bath	L (litre)
the height of a tree	m (metre)
the temperature of the sea	°C (degrees Celsius)

b) Scales should read: **i)** 1kg, 400 g, **ii)** 3 kg 800 g, **iii)** 5 kg, 600 g

24.

Coins	£	p
	1	97
	4	71
	10	71
	23	40

25. Examples:

a) 1 x 50p, 1 x 20p, 1 x 2p

b) 3 x 20p, 1 x 10p, 1 x 2p

c) 7 x 10p, 2 x 1p

d) 2 x 20p, 3 x 10p, 2 x 1p

26. a) i) Quarter to 5
    ii) 5 past 11
    iii) 25 to 12
    iv) 25 past 1

b) Clocks should be set to:
    i) 10 past 3, **ii)** 20 to 7,
    iii) 25 past 11

27. a) Time interval A: 25 minutes
Time interval B:
20 minutes A < B

Time interval C: Quarter to 9 to
Twenty past 9   35 minutes
Time interval D: 5 minutes to
1 to Quarter to 2   50 minutes
C < D

b) Quarter past 3, Quarter
to 4, 5 to 4, 5 past 4,
10 past 4

28. a) 120 minutes   2 hours

b) 72 hours, 3 days

29. a) Examples: 82p, 79p, 88p,
81p

b) 17p

Geometry – properties of shapes

30.

	5 sides or more	Fewer than 5 sides
Has a vertical line of symmetry	pentagon, hexagon	square, rectangle, triangle
Does not have a vertical line of symmetry	arrow shapes	right-angled triangle

31. Example:

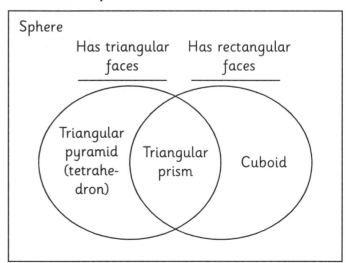

32. a) Regular hexagon,
    b) Irregular pentagon,
    c) Square, **d)** Triangle

33. a) Cylinder, **b)** Cube,
   c) Cone, **d)** Triangular
   pyramid (tetrahedron)

34. a) Triangle, **b)** Oblong (or
   rectangle) **c)** Pentagon

Geometry – position and direction

35. a) Circle, square, hexagon

   b) Pentagon, pentagon,
      triangle

   c) Cone, cylinder, cube

   d) pyramid, prism, pyramid

36. a) The book is under/beneath/
      below the chair. The light
      is above the boy.
      The tower of blocks is
      in front of the boy. The
      window is behind the boy.

   b) i) 3 squares right,
         2 squares up
   ii) 3 squares left,
         5 squares down
   iii) 5 squares right,
         3 squares up
   iv) 3 squares left,
         3 squares down

Statistics

37. Complete a tally for the
   number of each shape.

Shape	Tally	Number
circle	||||| ||||	9
triangle	||||| ||||| |||	13
hexagon	|||||		6
square	||||| |||||		11

   a) 13   **b)** 11

38. a) 11

   b) 6

   c) Blue

   d) Grey

   e) Blue

   f) Grey

39. a) 4   **b)** 3   **c)** 13   **d)** 10

Diagnostic test 1 Gap analysis grid

Name	Q1 - 2N1	Q2 - 2N2a	Q3 - 2N2b	Q4 - 2N2b	Q5 - 2N3	Q6 - 2N4	Q7 - 2N6	Q8 - 2C1	Q9 - 2C2a	Q10 - 2C2b	Q11 - 2C3	Q12 - 2C4	Q13 - 2C4	Q14 - 2C6	Q15 - 2C7	Q16 - 2C8	Q17 - 2C9a	Q18 - 2C9b	Q19 - 2F1a	Q20 - 2F1b	Q21 - 2F2	Q22 - 2M1	Q23 - 2M2	Q24 - 2M3a	Q25 - 2M3b	Q26 - 2M4a	Q27 - 2M4b	Q28 - 2M4c	Q29 - 2M9	Q30 - 2G1a	Q31 - 2G1b	Q32 - 2G2a	Q33 - 2G2b	Q34 - 2G3	Q35 - 2P1	Q36 - 2P2	Q37 - 2S1	Q38 - 2S2a	Q39 - 2S2b
Example																																							

Diagnostic test 2

Number and place value

1. Complete the missing numbers in each sequence.

a) 0, 2, 4, ___, 8, ___, 12, ___, 16

b) 0, 3, 6, ___, ___, 15, 18, ___, 24

c) 0, 5, 10, ___, 20, ___, ___, 35

d) 70, 80, 90, ___, ___, 120, ___

e) 24, 22, 20, ___, 16, ___, 12, ___, 8

f) 30, 27, 24, ___, 18, ___, 12, ___, 6

g) 70, 65, 60, ___, ___, 45, ___, 35

h) 140, 130, 120, ___, 100, ___, ___, 70

2. Draw lines to match the numerals to the words.

41	ninety-seven
53	fourteen
14	seventy-nine
97	thirty-five
35	forty-one
79	fifty-three

3. a) Use <, > and = to make these number sentences correct.

i) 5 tens ☐ 50 ones   **ii)** 3 tens ☐ 29 ones

iii) 7 tens ☐ 72 ones   **iv)** 9 tens ☐ 88 ones

b) Order the following amounts.

5 tens and 2 ones, 46, 44 ones, 5 tens and 1 one, 4 tens and 9 ones

_____ _____ _____

_____ _____

4. Complete the sentences.

a) In the number 72, there are ☐ groups of ten and ☐ ones.

b) The number ☐ is made up of 3 groups of ten and 6 ones.

c) The number 58 shows ☐ in the tens place and ☐ in the ones place.

d) The number ☐ is made up of 9 groups of ten and 0 ones.

5. a) Circle the numbers that are not correctly represented by base ten blocks.

i) 45

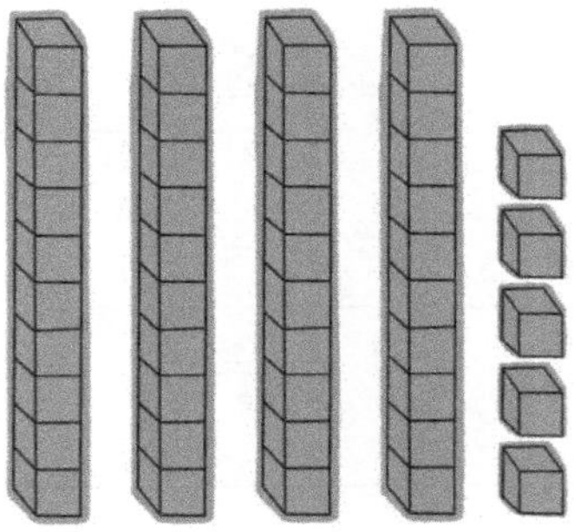

ii) 36

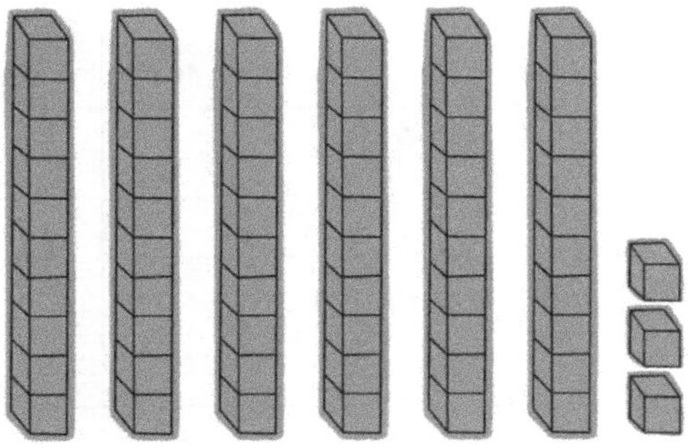

iii) 72 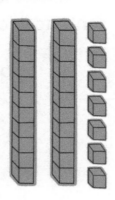 **iv)** 19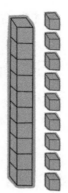

b) Place the number represented by the base ten blocks on each of the number lines.

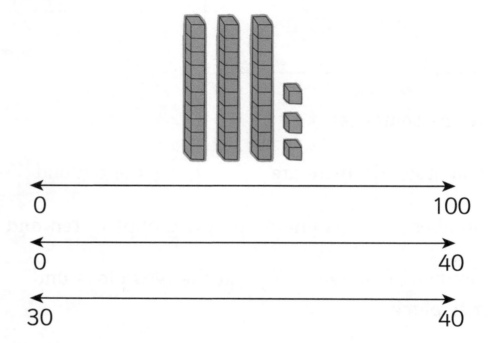

0 ——————————————— 100

0 ——————————————— 40

30 ——————————————— 40

6. Draw coins to make the amounts. The first one has been done for you.

Amount	10p	1p
33p	🪙 🪙 🪙	🪙 🪙 🪙
11p		
67p		
95p		
72p		

Addition, subtraction, multiplication and division (calculations)

7. a) Maisie has 2p. How much more does she need to make the following amounts?

i) 5p ☐ p   **ii)** 10p ☐ p   **iii)** 20p ☐ p

b) Finn has 20p. How much does he need to spend to be left with the following amounts?

i) 17p ☐ p   **ii)** 9p ☐ p   **iii)** 3p ☐ p

8. The numbers in the first two columns are added to make the number in the last column. Work out the missing numbers.

Number	Number	Total
43	4	
6	78	
17	30	
70	29	
36	55	
51		58
	24	74
56		92
4, 9	6	
3, 8	7	
6, 7	4	

9. Complete the missing numbers in each bar model.

22	6

59	
51	

67	
47	

70	28

46	27

93	
65	

10. a) I think of a number. I take away 9 and add 6. My answer is 18. What is my number? ▢

b) I think of a number. I add 36 and take away 11. My answer is 50. What is my number? ▢

11. a) Together, James and Mia have £26. Mia has £8 more than James. How much money does Mia have? £▢

b) Together, Harry and Anika have collected 32 kilograms of rubbish from a beach. If Anika collected 14 kg more rubbish than Harry, how much rubbish did Harry collect? ▢ kg

12. a) I have 16p in my pocket in 2p coins. How many coins do I have? ▢ coins

b) I have 40p in my pocket in 5p coins. How many coins do I have? ▢ coins

c) I have 90p in my pocket in 10p coins. How many coins do I have? ▢ coins

d) Circle the even numbers.

3   8   14   17   29   33   36   40   41   44   55   57   69

13. a) Write these addition sentences as multiplication sentences, then work out the answers.

i)   10 + 10 + 10 + 10 + 10 = _____ = ▢

ii)   5 + 5 + 5 + 5 + 5 + 5 + 5 = _____ = ▢

iii)   2 + 2 + 2 + 2 + 2 + 2 + 2 + 2 + 2 + 2
         = _____ = ▢

b) Lucy wants to buy colour books that are £2 each. How many books will she get for £18? Write the problem as a division sentence.

___

14. a) Complete the fact triangles. The numbers at the base of the triangle multiply to make the number at the top of the triangle.

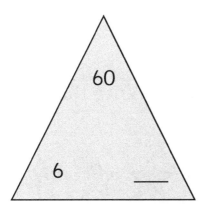
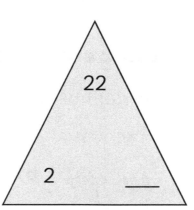
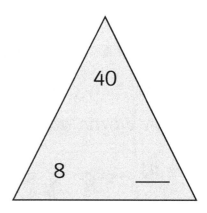

b) i) Beetles have 6 legs. How many beetles have 60 legs?

☐ beetles

ii) Birds have 2 legs. How many birds have 22 legs?

☐ birds

iii) Packets of stickers contain 5 stickers each. How many packets contain 40 stickers? ☐ packets

15. Circle the number statements that are incorrect.

a) 17 + 24 = 41   **b)** 19 − 7 = 12

c) 24 + 17 = 41   **d)** 7 − 19 = 12

e) 23 − 8 = 15   **f)** 71 + 25 = 96

g) 8 − 23 = 15   **h)** 25 + 71 = 96

16. Circle the number statements that are incorrect.

    a) 7 x 5 = 35   **b)** 5 x 7 = 35

    c) 35 ÷ 7 = 5   **d)** 7 ÷ 35 = 5

    e) 16 ÷ 2 = 8   **f)** 2 ÷ 16 = 8

    g) 9 x 10 = 90   **h)** 10 x 9 = 90

Fractions, decimals and percentages

17. What fraction of each array has been circled? Write the fraction in words and in numerals.

a)

b)

c)
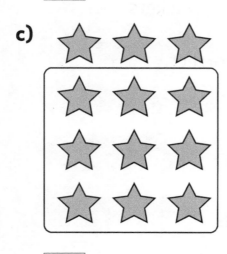

d)
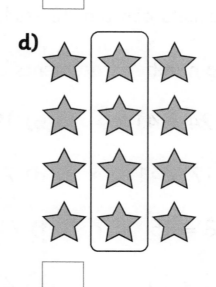

18. Write the fraction sentence described by each array. The first one has been completed for you.

a)

$\frac{1}{4}$ of 16 = 4

b)

___ of ___ = ___

c)

___ of ___ = ___

d)

___ of ___ = ___

19. Lottie eats half the chocolates in a box. Riva eats $\frac{2}{4}$ of the box. What can you say about the number of chocolates eaten by each girl? How do you know?

_____

Measurement

20. a) Circle the statements that are incorrect.

    i) 78 cm > 87 cm   **ii)** 63 kg < 36 kg   **iii)** 95 ml < 97 ml

    iv) $\frac{1}{2}$ of 50 g < $\frac{1}{4}$ of 100 g   **v)** $\frac{3}{4}$ of 40 m > $\frac{1}{3}$ of 60 m

b) Order the measurements, from shortest to longest.

    87 cm, 78 cm, 69 cm, 76 cm, 96 cm, 83 cm

Order: ☐ cm ☐ cm ☐ cm ☐ cm ☐ cm

21. Use a ruler to measure the height of each beanstalk.

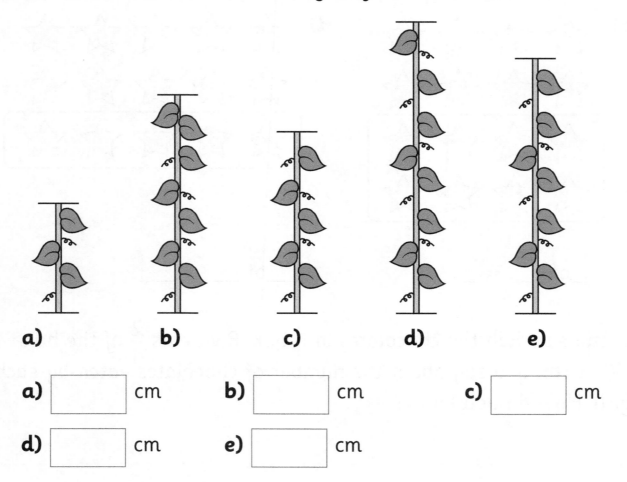

a)   **b)**   **c)**   **d)**   **e)**

a) ☐ cm   **b)** ☐ cm   **c)** ☐ cm

d) ☐ cm   **e)** ☐ cm

22. a) Florence went to the shop to buy a magazine. Which coins could she use to pay so that no change is needed?

b) Arran went to the shop to buy a cupcake. Which coins could he use to pay so that no change is needed?

23. Write four different combinations of coins that make 48p.

_____   _____

_____   _____

24. a) Circle the clocks that show an incorrect time.

i)

ii)

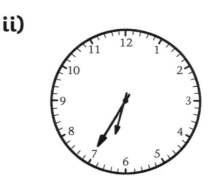

10 past 3   20 to 7

iii)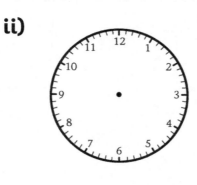

10 to 9

iv)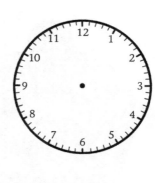

5 past 11

b) Draw the hands on each clock to show the time.

i)

5 past 2

ii)

quarter to 9

iii)

20 past 7

25. Put these clocks in order. Write the letter codes in order, from earlier times to later times.

A

B

C

D

E

Order: _____

26. Complete the number sentences.

a) 1 hour = ⬚ minutes   **b)** ⬚ hours = 120 minutes

c) 5 hours = ⬚ minutes   **d)** 1 day = ⬚ hours

e) 2 days = ⬚ hours   **f)** ⬚ days = 240 hours

27. Complete the money statements.

a) 13p + 26p = ⬚ p   **b)** 20p – 7p = ⬚ p

c) 48p + 24p = ⬚ p   **d)** 50p – 24p = ⬚ p

e) 77p + 18p = ⬚ p   **f)** 70p – 56p = ⬚ p

Choose two of the above statements, one addition and one subtraction. For the addition, write the coins that could be combined together to make the total. For the subtraction, write the coins that could be given as change.

_____

_____

_____

_____

_____

_____

Geometry – properties of shapes

28. Write one similarity and one difference for each pair of shapes.

Shapes	Similarity	Difference
square, regular hexagon		
regular pentagon, irregular pentagon		

29. Write one similarity and one difference for each pair of shapes.

Shapes	Similarity	Difference
cylinder, cone		
cube, square pyramid		

30. Complete the table.

Shape	Name	Number of sides	Number of vertices	Vertical line of symmetry (yes/no)

31. Complete the table.

Shape	Name	Number of faces	Number of vertices	Number of edges

32. Complete the table. The first one has been completed for you.

Shape	Description of faces
triangular prism	2 triangular faces, 3 rectangular faces
triangular pyramid (tetrahedron)	
hexagonal prism	
pentagonal pyramid	

Geometry – position and direction

33. Spot and correct the mistakes.

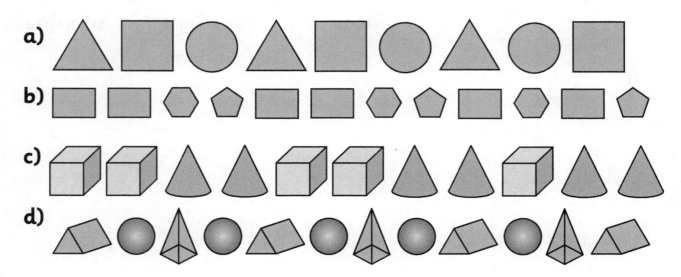

34. a) Each shape has moved from one position to another. Describe each movement in words.

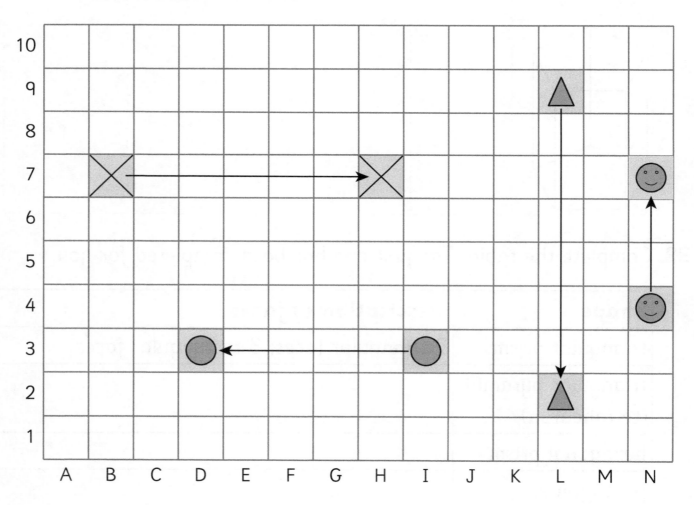

i) cross: _____

ii) circle: _____

iii) triangle: _____

iv) smiley face: _____

b) The pointer on the compass begins at N (North) and moves to the compass points shown here. Describe each movement in two different ways, using **quarter turns, clockwise** and **anticlockwise**.

i)

_____

_____

ii)

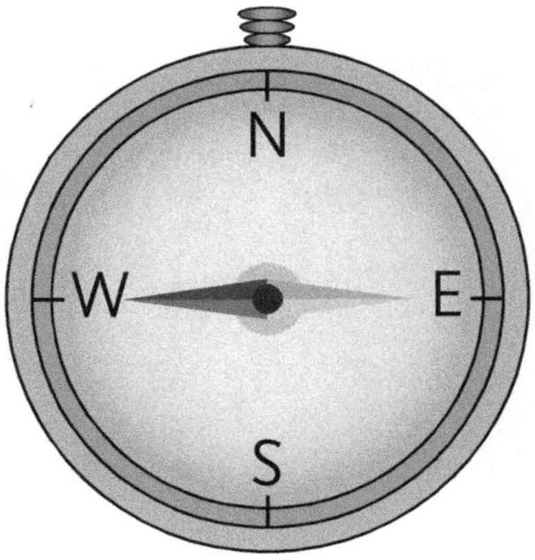

_____

_____

ii)

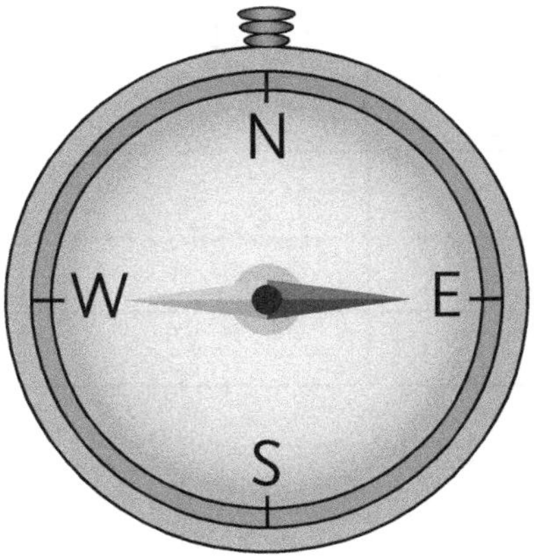

_____

_____

Statistics

35. Complete a tally for the number of sea animals

Animal	Tally	Number
crab		
fish		
octopus		
shark		

Construct a pictogram to present the data. Use the same symbol for each animal. Write a key to say how many of each animal one symbol represents.

a) How many fish are there?

b) How many octopuses are there?

36. The block diagram shows the number of children that prefer each type of book or story.

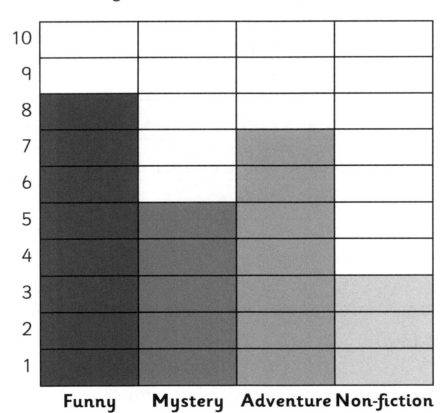

a) How many children prefer a funny story?

b) How many children prefer an adventure story?

c) Which type of story or book was most popular?

_____

d) Which type of story or book was least popular?

_____

e) How many more children prefer a funny story to an adventure story?

f) How many more children prefer a mystery story to a non-fiction book?

37. The pictogram shows the number of people that visited a museum. Use the pictogram to answer the questions.

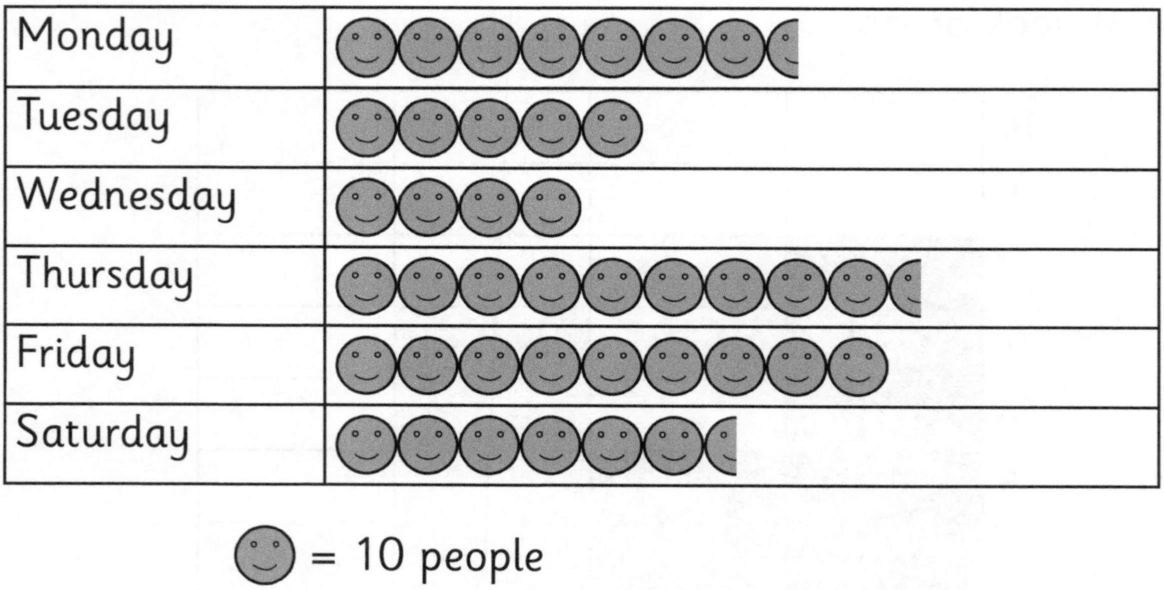

Monday	☺☺☺☺☺☺☺☺☺
Tuesday	☺☺☺☺☺
Wednesday	☺☺☺☺
Thursday	☺☺☺☺☺☺☺☺☺☺
Friday	☺☺☺☺☺☺☺☺☺
Saturday	☺☺☺☺☺☺☺

☺ = 10 people

a) How many more people visited the museum on Thursday than Wednesday?

b) How many fewer people visited the museum on Tuesday than Friday?

c) How many people visited on Monday and Saturday?

d) How many people visited on Tuesday and Thursday?

Number – number and place value

1. a) 6, 10, 14

b) 9, 12, 21

c) 15, 25, 30

d) 100, 110, 130

e) 18, 14, 10

f) 21, 15, 9

g) 55, 50, 40

h) 110, 90, 80

2. 41 forty-one
53 fifty-three
14 fourteen
97 ninety-seven
35 thirty-five
79 seventy-nine

3. a) i) 5 tens = 50 ones
ii) 3 tens > 29 ones
iii) 7 tens < 72 ones
iv) 9 tens >88 ones

b) 44 ones, 46, 4 tens and 9 ones, 5 tens and 1 one, 5 tens and 2 ones.

4. a) 7, 2   **b)** 36
c) 5, 8   **d)** 90

5. a) ii), iii)

b)

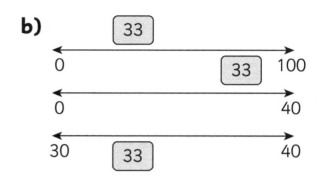

6.

Amount	10p	1p
33p	🪙 🪙 🪙	🪙 🪙 🪙
11p	🪙	🪙
67p	🪙 🪙 🪙 🪙 🪙 🪙	🪙 🪙 🪙 🪙 🪙 🪙 🪙
95p	🪙 🪙 🪙 🪙 🪙 🪙 🪙 🪙 🪙	🪙 🪙 🪙 🪙 🪙
72p	🪙 🪙 🪙 🪙 🪙 🪙 🪙	🪙 🪙

Addition, subtraction, multiplication and division (calculations)

7. a) i) 3p, **ii)** 8p, **iii)** 18p

b) i) 3p, **ii)** 11p, **iii)** 17p

8.

Number	Number	Total
43	4	47
6	78	84
17	30	47
70	29	99
36	55	91
51	7	58
50	24	74
56	36	92
4, 9	6	19
3, 8	7	18
6, 7	4	17

9.

28			59			67	
22	6		51	8		47	20

98			73			93	
70	28		46	27		65	28

10. a) 21, **b)** 25

11. a) £17, **b)** 9 kg

12. a) 8, **b)** 8, **c)** 9, **d)** 8, 14, 36, 40, 44

13. a) i) 5 x 10 = 50, **ii)** 7 x 5 = 35, **iii)** 10 x 2 = 20

b) 18 ÷ 2 = 9

14. a)

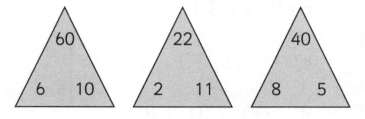

b) i) 10, **ii)** 11, **iii)** 8

15. d), g)

16. d), f)

Fractions, decimals and percentages

17. a) a quarter $\frac{1}{4}$, **b)** a half $\frac{1}{2}$, **c)** three quarters $\frac{3}{4}$, **d)** one third $\frac{1}{3}$

18. b) $\frac{3}{4}$ of 16 = 12, **c)** $\frac{1}{2}$ of 16 = 8, **d)** $\frac{1}{3}$ of 15 = 5

19. As $\frac{2}{4}$ is equal to $\frac{1}{2}$ so the girls have eaten the same amount of chocolates.
As $\frac{1}{2} + \frac{1}{2} = 1$, the girls will have eaten the whole box.

Measurement

20. a) i), ii), iv)

   b) 69 cm, 76 cm, 78 cm, 83 cm, 87 cm, 96 cm

21. a) 3 cm, **b)** 6 cm, **c)** 5 cm, **d)** 8 cm, **e)** 7 cm

22. a) Example: 50p, 20p, 10p, 5p, 2p

   b) Example: 50p, 20p, 20p, 5p, 2p, 2p

23. Examples: 20p, 20p, 5p, 2p, 1p; 10p, 10p, 10p, 10p, 5p, 2p, 1p; 20p, 5p, 5p, 5p, 5p, 5p, 2p, 1p; 10p, 5p, 5p, 5p, 5p, 5p, 5p, 5p, 2p, 1p

24. a) ii), iii)

   b)

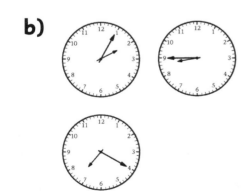

25. Order: C, A, D, E, B

26. a) 60, **b)** 2, **c)** 300, **d)** 24, **e)** 48, **f)** 10

27. a) 39p, **b)** 13p, **c)** 72p, **d)** 26p, **e)** 95p, **f)** 14p

Geometry – properties of shapes

28.

Shapes	Similarity	Difference
square, regular hexagon	Sides of equal length	Different number of sides
regular penta-gon, irregular pentagon	5 sides	Regular pentagon has sides of equal length but an irreg-ular pen-tagon has sides of different lengths

29.

Shapes	Similarity	Difference
cylinder, cone	Both have curved surfaces	The cone has one flat circular surface; the cylinder has two.
cube, square pyramid	Both shapes have examples of square faces	The cube has six square faces; the square pyramid has one square face and four triangular faces

30.

Shape	Name	Number of sides	Number of vertices	Vertical line of symmetry (yes/no)
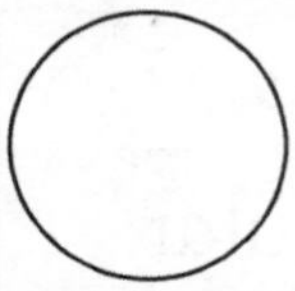 ○	circle	0	0	Yes
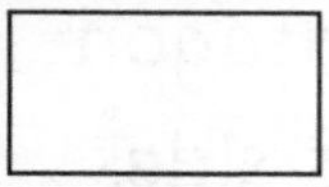 ▭	oblong	4	4	Yes
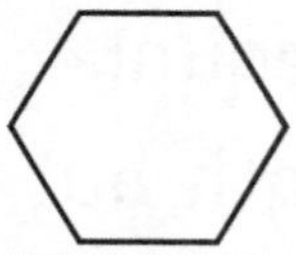 ⬡	pentagon	5	5	Yes
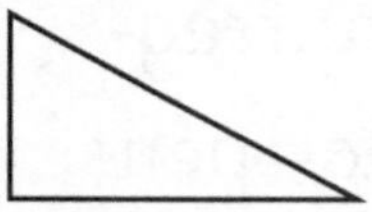 ◺	triangle	3	3	No

31.

Shape	Name	Number of faces	Number of vertices	Number of edges
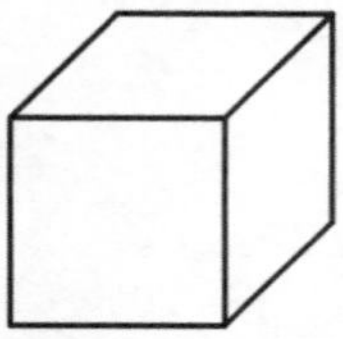 ⬜	cube	6	8	12

	triangular prism	5	6	9
	hexagonal pyramid	7	7	12
	pentagonal prism	7	10	15

32.

Shape	Description of faces
triangular prism	2 triangular faces, 3 rectangular faces
triangular pyramid (tetrahedron)	4 triangular faces
hexagonal prism	2 hexagonal faces, 6 oblong faces
pentagonal pyramid	1 pentagonal face, 5 triangular faces

Geometry – position and direction

33.

a)

b)

c)

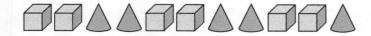

d)

34. a)

i) Cross: Move 6 squares right

ii) Circle: Move 5 squares left

iii) Triangle: Move 7 squares down

iv) Smiley faces: Move 3 squares up

b) i)

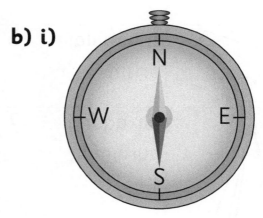

Half turn clockwise
Half turn anti-clockwise

ii)

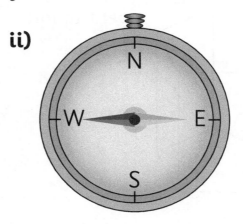

Three quarter turn clockwise
Quarter turn anti-clockwise

iii)

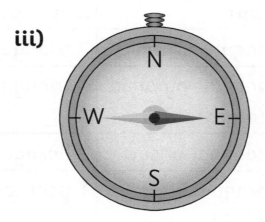

Quarter turn clockwise
Three quarter turn anti-clockwise

Statistics

35.

Animal	Tally	Number
Crab		5
Fish		8
Octopus		15
Shark		12

a) 8

b) 15

36. a) 8, **b)** 7, **c)** funny,
d) non-fiction, **e)** 1 **f)** 2

37. a) 55, **b)** 40, **c)** 140, **d)** 145

Diagnostic test 2 Gap analysis grid

Name	Q1 - 2N1	Q2 - 2N2a	Q3 - 2N2b	Q4 - 2N3	Q5 - 2N4	Q6 - 2N6	Q7 - 2C1	Q8 - 2C2a	Q9 - 2C2b	Q10 - 2C3	Q11 - 2C4	Q12 - 2C6	Q13 - 2C7	Q14 - 2C8	Q15 - 2C9a	Q16 - 2C9b	Q17 - 2F1a	Q18 - 2F1b	Q19 - 2F2	Q20 - 2M1	Q21 - 2M2	Q22 - 2M3a	Q23 - 2M3b	Q24 - 2M4a	Q25 - 2M4b	Q26 - 2M4c	Q27 - 2M9	Q28 - 2G1a	Q29 - 2G1b	Q30 - 2G2a	Q31 - 2G2b	Q32 - 2G3	Q33 - 2P1	Q34 - 2P2	Q35 - 2S1	Q36 - 2S2a	Q37 - 2S2b
Example																																					

Units

Unit 1: Count in steps of 2, 3, and 5 from 0, and in tens from any number, forward and backward

Content domain reference: 2N1

Prerequisites for learning

Count from zero to, at least, 100

Learning outcomes

Count in steps of 2 and 3 from 0, forward and backward

Count in steps of 5 from 0 and in 10s from any number, forward and backward

Key vocabulary

zero, count, count on, count up to, count back, multiple, 0 to 50 (even numbers)

Resources

Resource 1: 100 square; trays; interlocking cubes of the same colour; card; dice; 0–50 number cards: multiples of 2 from 0, multiples of 3 from 0, multiples of 5 from 0

Background knowledge

- Throughout the activities presented here, encourage the children to count in rhythm. Accompany chanting of numbers with the beat of a drum or clapping to help emphasise the number names. If floor number lines or number tracks are available, invite the children to jump along the number line as the counting proceeds.

Teaching Activity 1a (15 minutes)

Count in steps of 2, 3, and 5 from 0, from any number, forward and backward

- Display a copy of **Resource 1: 100 square**. Call out a 'start number' from 0 to 100 and ask a child to point to this number on the 100 square. Lead a count from the 'start number' in 1s with the class chanting the numbers. The child at the board points to the numerals as the count proceeds. At some point, call out 'reverse' and lead a count backwards. Repeat for different 'start numbers'.

- Give the children coloured pencils and copies of **Resource 1: 100 square**.

- Say: **We have used a 100 square to count in steps of 1. Today we are going to count in steps of 2, 3, 5 and 10.**

- Point to 0. Say: **Let's count in multiples of 2 from zero and colour the multiples as we go.** Ask: **What is the first number we colour?** (2) Ask: **What is the next number we colour?** (4) Say: **When we count on in steps of two, each number in the count is called a 'multiple of 2'.** Explain that any skip-count from zero, whether it is in 2s, 3s, 4s, or any other number, gives us a sequence of multiples of that number.

- Allow the children to continue counting in multiples of 2 up to 50, colouring every second square. Choose a child to count in 2s from

0 to 50. The group confirm that they have coloured the correct sequence. Choose a child to count backwards, in 2s, from 30 to 0.

- Ask: **What do you notice about the digits of the numbers you have coloured?** Prompt the children to look at the ones digit and confirm that any number that has 0, 2, 4, 6 or 8 (0 or an even number) as its ones digit is a multiple of two. Ask: **Is 36 a multiple of 2?** (yes) **How do you know?** (it has a ones digit of 2) **Is 87 a multiple of 2?** (no) **How do you know?** (it has a ones digit that is not 0, 2, 4, 6, 8. It has a ones digit that is odd)

- Distribute number cards that are multiples of 2 from 0 onwards, enough for every child. Say: **We are going to count in 2s from 0 to 50. Hold up your number if we reach it in the count.** Lead a count and check that each child is able to identify their number in the count.

- Ask the children to stand in order of multiples of 2 from 0 onwards. Ask the child with the largest number to leave the line and turn their back. Without the child seeing, tap three children on the shoulder and ask them to place their number cards face down on the floor. Ask the child to turn around and to identify the missing numbers in the sequence.

- Display a new copy of **Resource 1: 100 square**. Say: **Let's count in multiples of 3 from zero and colour the multiples as we go.** Ask: **What is the first number we colour?** (3)

Ask: **What is the next number we colour?**
(6) Tell the children to continue counting
in multiples of 3 up to 99, colouring every
third square. Remind the children that each
number in the sequence is a multiple of 3.

- Ask the children to say what they notice about
the pattern and the sequence of multiples.
Establish that multiples of 3 form a diagonal
pattern. Ask the children to add the digits in each
multiple of 3. Ask: **What do you notice?** (the
sums form the repeating pattern 3, 6, 9, 3, 6, 9…)

- Give the children coloured pencils and copies
of **Resource 1: 100 square**. Ask them to colour
in multiples of 3. Choose a child to count in
3s from 0 to 51. The group confirm that they
have coloured the correct sequence. Choose a
child to count backwards, in 3s, from 51 to 0.

- Distribute number cards that are multiples of
3 from 0 onwards, enough for every child. Say:
**We are going to count in 3s from 0. Hold
up your number if we reach it in the count.**
Lead a count and check that each child is
able to identify their number in the count.

- Ask the children to stand in order of multiples
of 3 from 0 onwards. Ask the child with the
largest number to leave the line and turn their
back. Without the child seeing, tap three
children on the shoulder and ask them to place
their number cards face down on the floor.
Ask the child to turn around and to identify
the missing numbers in the sequence.

Teaching Activity 1b (25 minutes)

Count in steps of 2, 3, and 5 from 0, and in 10s from any number, forward and backward

- Arrange cubes (or any other classroom resource
made up of identical units) in a sequence of
multiples of 2 arranged in trays, that is, 0 cubes
(an empty tray), 2 cubes, 4 cubes, 6 cubes, and
so on, up to 20. Place cards alongside each tray.
Point to each tray in order and ask the children
to say the number of cubes to confirm that they
are able to count in steps of 2. As each number
is chanted, write the numeral on the card.

- Ask what the next five numbers in the
sequence will be. (22, 24, 26, 28, 30) Say:
**How do you know these are the next five
numbers?** Establish that counting on in
steps of two gives a sequence of numbers
where each number is a multiple of 2. Explain
that any skip-count from zero, whether it is
in 2s, 3s, 4s, or any other number, gives us
a sequence of multiples of that number.

- Say: **I am going to count back in 2s from
20. Make sure that I don't make any
mistakes.** Count: **20, 18, 16, 12, 10**. Ask
the children to say what was incorrect about
the count. (14 was missed) Repeat for other
forward and backward counts omitting
one of the numbers in the sequence.

- Ask the children to sit in a circle and count
round starting at zero. Every time the number
sequence comes to a multiple of 2, the child
whose turn it is says 'buzz' instead of the
number. For example, an acceptable sequence
would be '0, 1, buzz, 3, buzz, 5, buzz...' Each
child begins the game with two 'lives' and loses
one 'life' if they fail to say 'buzz' at the correct
time, or if they say the word out of sequence. A
child is out of the game if they lose both 'lives'.

- The game ends when a target number is
reached, for example, 40. The winners
are those children still in the game.

- Arrange a set of dice (as large as possible) with
the '3' pattern of spots facing the children,
that is, 0 dice (an empty tray: no spots), 1 dice
(3 spots), 2 dice (6 spots), 3 dice (9 spots), and
so on, up to 27. Place cards alongside each tray.
Point to each tray in order and ask the children
to say the number of spots to confirm that they
are able to count in steps of 3. As each number
is chanted, write the numeral on the card.

- Ask: **What will be the next five numbers
in the sequence?** (30, 33, 36, 39, 42) Say:
**How did you know these are the next five
numbers?** Choose a child to explain how
they determined the next numbers in the
sequence. Establish that, counting on in
steps of three, gives a sequence of numbers
where each number is a multiple of three.

- Say: **I am going to count back in 3s from
27. Make sure that I don't make any
mistakes.** Count: **27, 24, 21, 15, 12**. Ask
the children to say what was incorrect about
the count. (18 was missed) Repeat for other
forward and backward counts, omitting
one of the numbers in the sequence.

- Play a game of 'Buzz' for multiples of 3.
Throughout the game, provide regular
opportunities to model the count in 3s.

Teaching Activity 2a (15 minutes)

Count in steps of 5 from 0, and in 10s from any number, forward and backward

- Display a new copy of **Resource 1: 100 square**. Say: **Let's count in multiples of 5 from zero and colour the multiples as we go**. Ask: **What is the first number we colour?** (5) Ask: **What is the next number we colour?** (10) Tell the children to continue counting in multiples of 5 up to 100, colouring every third square. Remind the children that each number in the sequence is a multiple of 5.

- Ask the children to say what they notice about the pattern and the sequence of multiples. Establish that multiples of 5 form two vertical lines on the 100 square and that any number with a ones digit of 0 or 5 is a multiple of 5.

- Give the children coloured pencils and copies of the 100 square. Ask them to colour in multiples of 5. Choose a child to count in 5s from 0 to 50. The group confirm that they have coloured the correct sequence. Choose a child to count backwards, in 5s, from 50 to 0.

- Distribute digit cards that are multiples of 5 from 0 onwards, enough for every child. Say: **We are going to count in 5s from 0. Hold up your number if we reach it in the count.** Lead a count and check that each child is able to identify their number in the count.

- Ask the children to stand in order of multiples of 5 from 0 onwards. Ask the child with the largest number to leave the line and turn their back. Without the child seeing, tap three children on the shoulder and ask them to place their number cards face down on the floor. Ask the child to turn around and to identify the missing numbers in the sequence.

- Display a new copy of **Resource 1: 100 square**. Say: **Let's count in multiples of 10 from zero and colour the multiples as we go**. Ask: **What is the first number we colour?** (10) Ask: **What is the next number we colour?** (20) Allow the children to continue counting in multiples of 10 up to 100, colouring every tenth square. Remind the children that each number in the sequence is a multiple of 10.

- Ask: **What do you notice about the digits of multiples of 10?** Confirm that any number that has a ones digit of zero is a multiple of 10. Ask: **Is 270 a multiple of 10?** (yes) **How do you know?** (it has a ones digit of 0) **Is 485 a multiple of 10?** (no) **How do you know?** (it has a ones digit that is not 0)

- Ask the children to suggest different multiples of 10. Confirm the multiples.

- Call out a 'start number' that is a multiple of ten. Lead a count forwards in steps of ten, beginning at the start number. At some point, call out 'reverse' and lead a count backwards. Repeat for different 'start numbers', including numbers greater than 100.

- Say: **70, 80, 90, 110, 130, 140, 150**. Ask: **Which number did I miss out?** (120) Repeat for different forward and back sequences of multiples of 10.

- Call out a 'start number' that is not a multiple of ten, for example 21. Point to 21 on the 100 square. Ask: **If we count on ten from here, what is the next number we will come to?** Ask the children to work in pairs and discuss the question.

- Continue to the count up to 21, inviting the groups to say the next number in the sequence. Ask: **What do you notice about the tens and ones digit of the numbers in the sequence?** (the tens digit goes up by 1, but the ones digit stays the same)

- Repeat the count in steps of 10 from other numbers, both forward and backward. Ask the children to say what they think will be the next number in the sequence.

Teaching Activity 2b (15 minutes)

Count in steps of 5 from 0, and in 10s from any number, forward and backward

- Arrange a set of dice (as large as possible) with the '5' pattern of spots facing the children, that is, 0 dice (an empty tray: no spots), 1 dice (5 spots), 2 dice (10 spots), 3 dice (15 spots), and so on, up to 30. Place cards alongside each tray. Point to each tray in order and ask the children to say the number of spots to confirm that they are able to count in steps of 5. As each number is chanted, write the numeral on the card.

- Ask: **What will be the next five numbers in the sequence?** (35, 40, 45, 50, 55) Say: **How did you know these are the next five numbers?** Choose a child to explain how they determined the next numbers in the sequence. Establish that, counting on in steps of five, gives a sequence of numbers where each number is a multiple of five.

- Say: **I am going to count back in 5s from 30. Make sure that I don't make any mistakes.** Count: **30, 25, 20, 15, 5**. Invite the children to say what was incorrect about the count. (10 was missed) Repeat for other forward and backward counts, omitting one of the numbers in the sequence.

- Play a game of 'Buzz' for multiples of 5. Throughout the game, provide regular opportunities to model the count in 5s.

- Arrange a set of identical items such as buttons or beads in a 10 by 10 array. Lead a count in tens from 10 to 100 and backwards. Point to the multiples of ten on a 100 square. Ask: **What do you notice about the digits in the sequence of multiples of ten?** (the ones digit is always zero) Ask the children to count from 100 to 200, and backwards.

- Say: **I am going to count back in 10s from 140. Make sure that I don't make any mistakes.** Count: **140, 130, 120, 100, 90.** Choose a child to say what was incorrect about the count. (110 was missed) Repeat for other forward and backward counts, omitting one of the numbers in the sequence.

- Place buttons or beads on the table in a column. Choose children to add 10 items to the first single bead, 20 to the next, 30 to the next, and so on. Lead a count in steps of ten from 11, pointing to each row of beads as the count proceeds: 11, 21, 31, and so on. Ask: **What do you notice about the tens and ones digit of the numbers in the sequence?** (the tens digit goes up by 1 but the ones digit stays the same)

- Repeat for items with different starting numbers, for example 3, arranged in steps of ten: 3, 13, 23, 33, 43. Ask the children to say the next three numbers in the sequence (53, 63, 73).

Unit 2: Recognise the place value of each digit in a two-digit number (10s, 1s)

Content domain reference: 2N3

Prerequisites for learning

Be familiar with numbers 0–100

Key vocabulary

tens, ones, digit, numerals

Learning outcomes

Recognise the place value of each digit in a two-digit number (10s, 1s)

Resources

base ten blocks; place value mat; 0–9 spinner

Background knowledge

- The decimal number system is an example of a place value system where the position of each digit determines its value. The value of each place is 10 times greater than the place to the right. For instance, a digit in the tens column has a value ten times the value of the ones place. Thus, a number like 73 has a 7 in the tens place and a 3 in the ones place. The digit 7, in the tens place, does not represent 7 – it represents 70.

- If a child understands that 73 is actually 70 + 3, they can manipulate this number more easily, making it easier to add or subtract numbers, as well as helping with multiplication calculations later.

Teaching Activity 1a (20 minutes)

Recognise the place value of each digit in a two-digit number (10s, 1s)

- Give pairs of children a tray of base ten blocks and a place value mat with cells marked Tens (T) and Ones (O).

- Introduce the children to base ten blocks. Point to the cubes and rods and explain that the cubes represent ones and the rods represent tens.

- The children create one rod using ones. Ask: **How many cubes make up a rod?** (10)

- Write on the board: 48. Ask the children to represent the number with base ten blocks. Ensure that they use the correct number of rods and cubes to represent each place value. (4 rods for 4 tens and 8 cubes for 8 ones) To show the number 66, six rods and six ones are needed.

- Point to the digit 4 in 48. Ask: **How many tens does this digit represent?** (4) **What is the value of the 4 tens?** Confirm that the children understand that the value of 4 tens is 40.

- Point to the digit 8 in 48. Ask: **How many ones does this digit represent?** (8) **What is the value of the 8 ones?** Confirm the children understand that the value of 8 ones is 8.

- Explain that the position of each digit in a number determines its place value. Point to 4 in 48 and say: **The 4 is in the tens position and therefore, we read the number as 4 tens not 4. Its value is 40.** Point to 8 in 48 and say: **The 8 is in the ones position and therefore, the value is 8.**

- Write on the board: 29, 54, 83, 90. Ask each group to model a different number in base ten blocks.

- Point to a digit and ask the pair who modelled the number to say the value of the digit. They should refer to their model for help.

- Point to 90. Say: **When we write 90, we write a nine followed by a zero and not just nine. Why do we need the zero?** Discuss and establish that the zero acts as a place holder. Say: **We need to know that there are zero tens. Without a zero in the ones column, the number would read nine ones and not nine tens.**

Teaching Activity 1b (20 minutes)

Recognise the place value of each digit in a two-digit number (10s, 1s)

- Draw two houses side by side on the board. Label the house to the left '10' and the house to the right '1'. Draw ten oblongs in each house to represent tables.

- Say: **Imagine that you are the teacher running a lunchtime computer club. You have two rooms with ten computers each.** Explain that each oblong in the 'Ones' hut is a computer station that can seat one child and each oblong in the 'Tens' hut is a computer station that can seat ten children. Say: **Children arrive at the 'ones' hut first then enter the 'tens' hut if they are allowed.**

- Continue to tell a story in which you arrive at the computer room to find that there are seven children waiting. You welcome them and show them to their computer stations in the 'ones' hut. Ask: **How many stations is this?** (7) Write '7' below the 'ones' hut.

- Say: **Then five more children arrive. How will you provide computer stations for these children?** Discuss and introduce the phrase 'make a ten'. Establish that adding three more children will fill all the stations in the 'ones' hut. Say: **To find room for the remaining two children, we move all ten children in the 'ones' hut to the 'tens' hut.**

- Remind them that each station in this hut is for ten children only. Ask: **How many stations will the children need in the 'tens' hut?** (one) Say and record: **We move the ten children from the 'ones' hut to one station in the 'tens' hut.** Ask: **How many stations of ten do we have in the 'tens' hut?** (one) Write '1' below the 'tens' hut. Say and record: **Now we place the remaining three children in the 'ones' hut. How many stations do we need?** (3) Write '3' below the ones hut.

- Say: **We have one set of ten children in the 'tens' hut and three children in the 'ones' hut, making thirteen children altogether.** Point to the digits and say: **One set of ten and three ones is 13.** Ask: **What does the 1 in 13 stand for?** (one set of ten) **How many children is that?** (10) **And the 3?** (three ones) **How many children is that?** (3)

- Draw another pair of 'tens' and 'ones' huts. Tell a story in which the computer club has become very popular and the next day, 36 children turn up at the huts waiting to come in. Ask: **How will you find stations for all of these children?** Remind the children of the phrase 'make a ten' and ask: **How many sets of ten children can we make from 36?** (3) **Where should we put these children?** (3 stations in the 'tens' hut) Record the occupation of three tables in the 'tens' hut and write a '3' below. Ask: **How many children are there that still need stations?** (6) **Where should we put these children?** (6 tables in the 'ones' hut)

- Say: **We have three sets of ten children in the 'tens' hut and six children in the 'ones' hut, making sixteen children altogether.** Point to the digits and say: **Three sets of ten and six ones is 36.** Ask: **What does the 3 in 36 stand for?** (three sets of ten) **How many children is that?** (30) **And the 6?** (six ones) **How many children is that?** (6)

- Repeat finding stations for different numbers of children, for example, 59 (5 tables in the 'tens' hut and 9 tables in the 'ones' hut) and 74 (7 tables in the 'tens' hut and 9 tables in the 'ones' hut).

- If time, ask children to work in pairs and to draw their own 'tens' and 'ones' huts. Use a 0–9 spinner to create a two-digit number. Record the number on the board and ask the children to find room in their huts for this number of children. Ask pairs to share how they distributed the children across the huts and what the digits recorded below each hut represent. Repeat for two more random numbers.

Unit 3: Identify, represent and estimate numbers using different representations, including the number line

Content domain reference: 2N4

Prerequisites for learning

Recognise and write numbers to 100
Understand place value

Learning outcomes

Identify, represent and estimate numbers using different representations, including the number line

Key vocabulary

place value, estimate

Resources

base ten blocks; place value mats; 0–9 digit cards

Background knowledge

- To be able to manipulate numbers easily, children need to understand different representations of numbers. This prepares them for multiplication and division operations, as well as understanding and comparing fractions and decimals.
- Numbers can be represented in a variety of forms. For example, 79 can be represented using:
  - numerals: 79
  - words: seventy-nine
  - a decimal model, such as base ten blocks
  - expanded form: 70 + 9
  - measures: 79p (money), 79 kg (mass), 79 ml (capacity), 79 cm (length).
- Try to introduce as many of these different forms during the course of the lesson.

Teaching Activity 1a (15 minutes)

Identify, represent and estimate numbers using different representations, including the number line

- Put a tray of base ten blocks and a place value mat in front of the children. Arrange a set of 0–9 digit cards alongside.
- Remind the children how a number can be represented in base ten blocks. Place seven rods in the tens column of the place value chart and four cubes in the ones column.
- Ask questions, such as:
  - **How many sets of ten are there in the tens column?** (7) Place a '7' digit card below the tens column. Ask: **What is the value of the seven tens?** Prompt the children by reminding them that there are seven sets of ten. Establish that the value of a 7 digit in the tens column is 70, as 7 sets of 10 make 70.

- **How many ones are there in the ones column?** (4) Place a '4' digit card below the ones column. Ask: **What is the value of the four ones?** Establish that the value of a 4 digit in the ones column is 4 as four ones make four.
- Write on the board: 86. Point to the 8. Say: **The digit 8 represents 8 tens and has the value 80.** Point to the 6. Say: **The digit 6 represents 6 ones and has the value 6.**
- Write: 86 = 80 + 6. Say: **We can write a number as the sum of its place values. For 86, that is 80 and 6**. Explain that we call this the expanded form of a number.
- Place five rods in the tens column of the place value chart and nine cubes in the ones column. Ask: **What number is represented by the cubes?** Discuss and establish that there are 5 sets of ten in the 'tens' column.

- Place a '5' digit card below the tens column. Establish that there are 9 ones in the 'ones' column. Place a '9' digit card below the ones column. Say: **We have the number 59.** Write on the board: '59 = ___ + __'. Ask: **Who can write 59 in expanded form, as the sum of its place values?** Ask a child to complete the number sentence on the board. (59 = 50 + 9)

- Ask the children to work in pairs and give them base ten blocks, digit cards and place value mats.

- Write on the board: 65, 40, 99. Ask the children to represent each number with base ten blocks. They model the number on the mat and place corresponding digit cards below each column. Invite the children to share their models and confirm that each is correct.

Teaching Activity 1b (20 minutes)

Identify, represent and estimate numbers using different representations, including the number line

- Draw a number from 20 to 50 on the board. Mark and label the intervals of ten, not the ones.

- Write: 36. Ask: **Where do you think 36 belongs on the number line: between 20 and 30, between 30 and 40, or between 40 and 50?** (30 and 40) **How do you know?** Establish that since 36 has 3 tens it must belong to the set of numbers that lie between 30 and 40.

- Ask a child to circle 30 and 40 on the board. Ask: **Do you think 36 will be closer to 30 or 40?** (40) **Why?** Discuss answers.

- Ask another child to estimate and mark the position of 36 on the number line. Ask: **Why did you place 36 here?** Confirm that the position is a good estimate.

- Mark and label the position of 35 on the number line. Say: **Since 5 is halfway between 0 and 10, we know that 35 must be halfway between 30 and 40.** Ask: **Is 36 closer to 35 or 40?** (35) **How do you know?** (6 is closer to 5 than 10) Confirm that 36 lies just to the right of 35 on the number line.

- Draw a number from 70 to 100 on the board. Mark and label the intervals of ten, not the ones.

- Write: 92. Ask: **Where do you think 92 belongs on the number line: between 70 and 80, between 80 and 90, or between 90 and 100?** (90 and 100) **How do you know?** Establish that, since 92 has 9 tens, it must belong to the set of numbers that lie between 90 and 100.

- Ask a child to the board to circle 90 and 100. Ask: **Do you think 92 will be closer to 90 or 100?** (90) **Why?** Discuss answers. Ask another child to estimate and mark the position of 92 on the number line.

- Ask: **Why did you place 92 here?** Accept and confirm that the position is a good estimate.

- Mark and label the position of 95 on the number line. Say: **Since 5 is halfway between 0 and 10, we know that 95 must be halfway between 90 and 100.** Ask: **Is 92 closer to 90 or 95?** (90) **How do you know?** (2 is closer to 0 than 5) Confirm that 92 lies to the right of 90 on the number line, closer to 90 than 95.

- Draw a number from 40 to 60 on the board. Mark and label the intervals of ten, not the ones.

- Mark an arrow approximately above 55 on the number line and ask: **What number is represented by this arrow?** (55) **How do you know?** (it is halfway between 50 and 60)

- Mark arrows approximately above 44, 48 and 59 on the number line and ask: **What numbers are represented by these arrows?** Remind the children to use the multiples of ten and halfway numbers such as 45 and 55 to help them.

- Ask the children to work in pairs to write their estimates. Ask them to share their estimates and confirm the position of the numbers on the number line.

Unit 4: Compare and order numbers from 0 up to 100; use <, > and = signs

Content domain reference: 2N2b

Prerequisites for learning

Recognise numbers from 0 up to 100

Demonstrate a good understanding of place value

Understand the terms 'greater than', 'less than' and 'equal to'.

Learning outcomes

Compare numbers from 0 up to 100

Compare numbers using <, > and = signs

Order numbers from 0 up to 100

Key vocabulary

compare, order, less than, greater than, equal to, place value

Resources

place value mats; base ten blocks; mini whiteboards and pens

Background knowledge

• In the course of the lesson, emphasise that knowing how to compare and order numbers is a skill we use every day. Use examples, such as knowing whether you have enough money to buy an item or not, knowing which of the recorded times for completing a race is the quickest, or knowing which container holds the most. Explain that finding the answers to these questions is achieved by comparing and ordering numbers.

Teaching Activity 1a (10 minutes)

Compare numbers from 0 up to 100

• Draw a number line from 30 to 60 on the board, marked out and labelled in ones.

• Below the line, write the numbers: 43 and 34. Ask a child to mark the position of the two numbers on the number line.

• Choose another child to confirm the positions on the number line.

• Ask: **Which number is greater, 43 or 34?** (43) **How do you know?** Discuss and establish that since numbers further to the right of the number line are greater than numbers to the left, then 43 is greater than 34.

• Ask: **Which number is smaller?** (34) **How do you know?** (34 is further to the left of the number line and therefore, smaller than 43)

• Model the correct use of comparative language, for example: '43 is more than 34', '34 is less than 43'.

• Repeat the above activity for 87 and 78. Choose children to compare the two numbers using the phrases 'more than' or 'less than'. Expect: '87 is more than 78' or '78 is less than 87'.

• Ask: **If you were to arrange the two numbers in order, which number would come first?** (78) **Why?** (it is less than 87 / it is smaller than 87) **Which number would come after 78?** (87) **Why?** (it is more than 78 / it is greater than 78)

Teaching Activity 1b (10 minutes)

Compare numbers from 0 up to 100

• Put a place value mat and a tray of base ten blocks in front of the children. Remind them that a rod represents 10 and a cube represents 1.

• In the first row of the place value chart, arrange five rods in the Tens column and four cubes in the Ones column. Ask: **What number is represented by the blocks?** (54) **How do you know?** Establish that, since there are 5 sets of ten in the tens column and 4 ones in the ones column, the number is 54. Write 54 on the board.

• In a second row of the place value chart, arrange four rods in the Tens column and five cubes in the Ones column. Ask: **What number is represented by the blocks?** (45) **How do you know?** Establish that, since there are 4 sets of ten in the tens column and 5 ones in the ones column, the number is 45. Write 45 on the board.

- Point to 54 and 45. Ask: **Which is greater, 54 or 45?** (54) **How do you know?** Discuss the children's ideas. Point to the rods in the tens column of the place value chart. Ask: **Which number, 54 or 45, has the greater number of tens?** (54) Say: **Since 5 tens is greater than 4 tens, 54 must be the greater number.** Ask: **Which is smaller, 54 or 45?** (45) **How do you know?** Establish that, since 4 tens is less than 5 tens, 45 must be the smaller number.

- Say: **Compare the two numbers, using the phrases 'more than' or 'less than'.** Choose children to compare the numbers. Model the correct use of comparative language: **54 is more than 45, 45 is less than 54.**

- Ask: **If you were to arrange the two numbers in order, which number would come first?** (45) **Why?** (it is less than 54 / it is smaller than 54) **Which number would come after 45?** (54) **Why?** (it is more than 45 / it is greater than 45)

Teaching Activity 2a (15 minutes)

Compare numbers using <, > and = signs

- Write the symbols <, > or = on the board. Confirm that the children recognise the 'equals' symbol, then ask if any of them recognise the first two symbols. Ask the children to say where they have seen them before and what they might be used for.

- Say: **These are called 'inequality symbols' and they are used to compare two numbers to say which number is greater and which number is smaller.** Point to the symbol <. Say: **This symbol means 'is less than'.**

- Write: 3 < 7. Say: **The symbol shows that the number on the left is smaller, or less than, the number on the right. In this case, we are making the statement that 3 is less than 7.**

- Point to the symbol >. Say: **This symbol means 'is greater than'.** Write: 8 > 4. Say: **The symbol shows that the number on the left is greater, or more than, the number on the right. In this case, we are making the statement that 8 is greater than 7.**

- Point to the symbols and say to the children that a good way to remember the difference between the symbols is that the open end, not the pointed end, always points to the larger number. Alternatively, explain that the symbol 'points' to the smaller number.

- Write on the board: 43 [ ] 34. Choose a child to come to the board to insert the correct symbol of inequality between the numbers. Expect: 43 > 34. Demonstrate the alternative way of writing the inequality with the numbers in reversed order (34 < 43).

- Draw a number line from 80 to 90 marked out and labelled in ones.

- Below the line, write the numbers: 88 and 86. Ask a child to mark the position of the two numbers on the number line.

- Choose a child to confirm the positions on the number line.

- Ask: **Which number is greater, 88 or 86?** (88) **How do you know?** Establish that, since numbers further to the right of the number line are greater than numbers to the left, then 88 is greater than 86.

- Ask: **Which number is smaller?** (86) **How do you know?** (86 is further to the left of the number line and therefore smaller than 88)

- Choose a child to make a statement that compares to the two numbers. Prompt them to use the language of comparison, for example: 'less than', 'greater than', 'more than', 'smaller than'. Ask the children for alternative ways to compare the numbers in their statements.

- Ask: **If you were to arrange the two numbers in order, which number would come first?** (86) **Which would come next?** (88).

- Point to the symbols of inequality. Choose a child to come to the board to write a statement that compares the two numbers using the correct symbol. Expect: 88 > 86 (or 86 < 88).

- Give pairs of children paper or a mini whiteboard. Write 65 and 56 on the board. Ask the children to draw a number line and mark the positions of 65 and 56. Confirm that the groups are able to represent the numbers on the number line, then ask them to write a number statement that compares the two numbers. Choose a pair to share the statement and 'read' it to the class. Expect: '65 > 56 (or 56 < 65)'; '65 is greater than 56'; or '56 is less than 65'.

- Repeat for other pairs of numbers, for example: 35 and 33 (35 > 33), 67 and 76 (76 > 67).

Teaching Activity 2b (15 minutes)

Identify, represent and estimate numbers using different representations, including the number line

- Write the symbols <, > or = on the board. Confirm that the children recognise the 'equals' symbol, then ask if any of them recognise the first two symbols. Ask the children to say where they have seen them before and what they might be used for.

- Say: **These are called inequality symbols and they are used to compare two numbers to say which number is greater and which number is smaller.** Point to the symbol <. Say: **This symbol means 'is less than'.** Write: 12 < 16. Say: **The symbol shows that the number on the left is smaller, or less than, the number on the right. In this case, we are making the statement that 12 is less than 16.**

- Point to the symbol >. Say: **This symbol means 'is greater than'.** Write: 19 > 13. Say: **The symbol shows that the number on the left is greater, or more than, the number on the right. In this case, we are making the statement that 19 is greater than 13.**

- Point to the symbols and say to the children that a good way to remember the difference between the symbols is that the open end, not the pointed end, always points to the larger number. Alternatively, explain that the symbol 'points' to the smaller number.

- On the board, write: 54 [ ] 45. Choose a child to come to the board to insert the correct symbol of inequality between the numbers. Expect: 54 > 45 or 45 < 54. Whichever symbol the child inserts, demonstrate the alternative way of writing the inequality with the numbers in reversed order.

- Put a place value mat and a tray of base ten blocks in front of the children. Remind them that a rod represents 10 and a cube represents 1.

- In the first row of the place value chart, arrange eight rods in the Tens column and seven cubes in the Ones column. Ask: **What number is represented by the blocks?** (87) Write 87 on the board. In a second row, arrange eight rods in the Tens column and two cubes in the Ones column. Ask: **What number is represented by the blocks?** (82) Write 82 on the board.

- Point to 87 and 82. Ask: **Which is greater, 87 or 82?** (87) **How do you know?** Discuss and then point to the rods in the tens column of the place value chart. Ask: **What do you notice about the number of tens in both numbers?** (they are the same. Both have 8 tens)

- Say: **The number of tens does not tell us which number is greater. To compare the numbers, we move to the column to the right, the ones column and compare the number of ones.**

- Ask: **Which is greater, 7 ones or 2 ones?** (7 ones) Establish that, since 7 ones is greater than 2 ones, 87 must be greater than 82 (or 82 is smaller than 87).

- Choose a child to compare the numbers using the phrases 'more than' or 'less than'. Model the correct use of comparative language: '87 is more than 82', '82 is less than 87'.

- Write on the board: 87 [ ] 82. Choose a child to insert the correct symbol of inequality between the numbers. Remind the children of the difference between the two symbols. Expect: 87 > 82. Demonstrate the alternative way of writing the inequality with the numbers in reversed order (82 < 87).

- Give pairs of children place value mats and base ten blocks. Write 66 and 59 on the board. Ask the children to model the numbers in base ten blocks, then make a statement to their partner that compares the two numbers. Choose a pair to share their statements. Expect: '66 is greater than 59' or '59 is less than 66'. Ask the children to write the statement in numbers, using the correct symbol of inequality. Expect: 66 > 59 or 59 < 66.

- Repeat for other pairs of numbers, for example: 77 and 75 (77 > 75), 38 and 40 (40 > 38).

Teaching Activity 3a (10 minutes)

Order numbers from 0 up to 100

- Write on the board: 47, 37, 43, 39. Ask: **How would we arrange these numbers in order, from the smallest number to the greatest?** Give the children time to discuss the question. Draw a number line from 30 to 50 marked out in ones. Choose children to mark and label the position of each number on the time line. Ask: **Which number is the greatest?** (47) **How do you know?** (it is the furthest to the right of the number line) **Which number is the smallest?** (37) **How do you know?** (it is furthest to the left of the number line)

- Choose children to write the numbers on the board in order, from the smallest to the greatest. (37, 39, 43, 47)

- Repeat for other sets of numbers, for example: 93, 86, 98, 84 (84, 86, 93, 98).

Teaching Activity 3c (10 minutes)

Order numbers from 0 up to 100

- Write on the board: 67, 54, 52, 39. Ask: **How would you arrange these numbers in order, from the smallest number to the greatest?** Give the children time to discuss the question. Model each number in base ten blocks in different rows of the place value mat.

- Ask: **Which of the numbers is the smallest?** (39) **How do you know?** (3 tens is less than 5 tens) Write '39' on the board to begin the order.

- **Which numbers are the next smallest?** (54 and 52) **How do you know?** (5 tens is smaller than 6 tens (67)) **What do you notice about the number of tens in 54 and 52?** (they are the same) **Who can tell me how we decide which number is smaller?**

- Establish that we move to the place value column to the right and compare the ones. Ask: **Which is smaller 4 ones or 2 ones?** (2) Say: **Since 2 ones is smaller than 4 ones, we know 52 is smaller.** Choose a child to write 52 and 54 in the correct order following 39.

- Say: **This means that 67 is the greatest number.** Write '67' to the right of the ordered numbers. Say: **We have our order: 39, 52, 54, 67.**

- Repeat for other sets of numbers, for example: 93, 86, 98, 84 (84, 86, 93, 98).

Unit 5: Read and write numbers to at least 100 in numerals and in words

Content domain reference: 2N2a

Prerequisites for learning

Be familiar with numbers up to 100

Write numerals 0–9 clearly, with correct orientation and formation

Apply understand of place value to read two-digit numbers

Learning outcomes

Read and write numbers to at least 100 in numerals and in words

Key vocabulary

twenty, thirty... ninety, digit, numeral

Resources

arrow cards; mini whiteboards and pens; Resource 1: 100 square

Background knowledge

- During the lesson, it is important to reintroduce the 'teen' numbers. These numbers may confuse children as the ten is spoken as 'teen' following the ones, the opposite to most two-digit tens and ones numbers.

- Look out for children that confuse numbers such as 'sixty' and 'sixteen'. Revisit the number names and emphasise the differences between them when spoken.

Teaching Activity 1a (15 minutes)

Read and write numbers to at least 100 in numerals and in words

- Display a 100 square and colour the squares 1 to 20. Ask: **Who can remember the number names from 1 to 20?** Lead a chant of the number names up to 20, pointing to each numeral as it is spoken.

- Write out the numbers 1 to 10 in a row on the board and the numbers 11 to 20 aligned below.

- Choose children to write the number names for one to ten on the board and a selection of numbers from 11 to 20.

- Establish that the 'teen' numbers sixteen, seventeen and nineteen, amount to combining –teen with the appropriate number prefix. Say: **For example, by combining 'six' and 'teen', we get 'sixteen'.** Explain that the suffix '–teen' means 'ten more'. Say: **So 'sixteen' literally means 'six and ten'.** Explain that the numbers 13, 14, 15 and 18 follow a similar pattern to 16, 17 and 19, except that the prefix is slightly altered.

- Colour the multiples of ten on the 100 square. Point to each number in turn and say: **Ten, twenty, thirty, forty, fifty, sixty, seventy, eighty, ninety, one hundred.**

- Ask: **What do you notice about the number names of multiples of ten?** Discuss that multiples of ten between 20 and 90 have a –ty ending that is equivalent to 'tens'.

- Write the multiples of tens in a column below 20 on the board. Circle 60, 70, 80 and 90. Explain that the names of these numbers come from combining –ty with the number of tens. Choose children to write the number names on the board (sixty, seventy, eighty, ninety).

- Write the names for 20, 30, 40 and 50. Discuss how the names follow a similar pattern to 60, 70, 80 and 90, except that the prefix is slightly altered.

- Point to each multiple of ten in random order and ask the children to say the number name.

- Choose a child to write 21 to 29 in the correct row on the board. Lead a chant of the number names from 21 to 29, pointing to each number in turn.

- Repeat for 31 to 39.

- Ask: **What do you notice about how we name the numbers after 20 compared to the teen numbers?** Establish that numbers between 20 and 99 are said with a tens-before-ones structure, for example: 'twenty' is said first in 'twenty-seven', and 2 is written first in 27 (2 tens, 7 ones).

Teaching Activity 1a (20 minutes)

Read and write numbers to at least 100 in numerals and in words

- Give out sets of arrow cards. If the children are not familiar with the resource, demonstrate that the cards can overlap. Then line up the arrows to form multi-digit numbers or arrange the cards horizontally or vertically to represent numbers in expanded notation.

- Build a few two-digit numbers. Say: **Show me 11, 12, 17, 23… 48**. Remind the children that when they build 48, the 40 is still there. Say: **It's 40 + 8. Forty is 4 tens; 48 is 4 tens plus 8**. Support this understanding by modelling the same number with base ten blocks, for example, 48 represented as 40 + 8.

- Draw a large 10 by 10 grid on the board. This will be the frame for a 100 square. Write 10 at the end of the first row. Say: **We are going to make a 100 square and fill in some of the numbers. Each time, we make a number with our arrow cards we will add it to the square.**

- Lead a count in tens from 10 to 100. The children say the next number in the sequence and make the number using their arrow cards: 20, 30…100. Ask the children to hold up the numbers to confirm they are correct. Write the number both in numerals and in words in the correct part of the grid.

- Ask: **What do you notice about the number names of multiples of ten?** Discuss that between 20 and 90, the names have a –ty ending that is equivalent to 'tens'.

- Circle 60, 70, 80 and 90. Explain that the names of these numbers come from combining –ty with the number of tens.

- Circle 20, 30, 40 and 50. Discuss how the names follow a similar pattern to 60, 70, 80 and 90 except that the prefix is slightly altered.

- Point to each multiple of ten in random order and ask the children to make the number with their arrow cards and say its name.

- Point to 20. Say: **Make the number that comes after 20.** Confirm the children make 21. Write 21 in the number square. Repeat for 22 up to 29, write the number in numerals and in words each time.

- Ask: **What do you notice about how we name the numbers after 20?** Establish that numbers are said with a tens-before-ones structure, for example: 'twenty' is said first in 'twenty-one', and 2 is written first in 21 (2 tens, 1 one).

- Complete the first two rows of the 100 square by writing and naming the numbers 1 to 19.

- If time, give out mini whiteboards and call out random numbers from 1 to 99. Ask the children to make the number with their arrow cards. They write the number both in numerals and in words, then hold up their boards to confirm they are correct.

Unit 6: Use place value and number facts to solve problems

Content domain reference: 2N6

Prerequisites for learning

Recognise and write numbers to 100

Demonstrate a good understanding of place value and ordering numbers

Learning outcomes

Use place value and number facts to solve problems

Key vocabulary

greater, smaller, greatest, smallest, more, less

Resources

arrow cards

Background knowledge

- The teaching activities in this unit help children develop strong number sense through use of logical questioning to identify the digits of a 'secret' number. The questioning relies on understanding of place value and strategies for ordering numbers.

- During the activity, reinforce the concept that the value of any digit in a number is a combination of the face value of the digit and the place.

Teaching Activity 1a (15 minutes)

Use place value and number facts to solve problems

- Display a 100 square. Say: **In this lesson, we are going to use our knowledge of place value to solve problems.**

- Tell the children a 'guess the number' story: **Toby has a small bottle of yoghurt. He looks on the bottle to see how much it contains. He notices that the amount is a two-digit number of millilitres. The number has seven set of tens and five ones. How much yoghurt does the container hold?**

- Ask the children to discuss the problem in pairs. Establish that a two-digit number that has seven tens and five ones must have a tens digit of 7 and a ones digit of 5. Choose a child to write the amount on the board. Expect: 75 millilitres.

- Say: **Toby decides to buy a smaller container. Tell me a number that is smaller than 75.** (any number from 1–74) Ask: **How do you know this number is less than 75?** Choose a pair to explain the method they use to compare numbers. Say: **Toby decides to buy a larger container. Tell me a number that is greater than 75.** (any number over 75)

- Tell the children another 'guess the number' story: **Lucy is thinking of a two-digit number. The digit in the tens place is 4 less than the digit in the ones place. The sum of the digits is 10. What is the two-digit number?**

- Give the children time to discuss the strategies they would use to solve the problem. Say: **We know that the tens digit is 4 less than the ones digit.** Establish that a good way to solve the problem is to list all the possible two-digit numbers where the tens digit is 4 less than the ones digit and then find which of these numbers has a digit sum of 10. Ask a child to write a two-digit number on the board, where the tens digit is 4 less than the ones digit.

- Choose other children to list all the possible numbers. Expect: 15, 26, 37, 48, 59. Ask: **Which of these numbers has a digit sum of 10?** (37) Say: **We have our 'secret number'. Lucy was thinking of the number 37.**

- Tell the children another 'guess the number' story: **William wrote down the amount of money he is taking to the shop to spend. The digit in the ones place is 6 less than the digit in the tens place. The sum of the digits is 8. If the sum is less than one pound, how much money does William have to spend?**

- Give children time to discuss the strategies they would use to solve the problem. Say: **We know that the ones digit is 6 less than the tens digit**. Establish that a good way to solve the problem is to list all the possible two-digit numbers where the ones digit is 6 less than the tens digit and then find which of these numbers has a digit sum of 8.

- Ask a child to write a two-digit number on the board, where the tens digit is 6 less than the ones digit. Choose other children to list all the possible numbers. Expect: 60, 71, 82, 93.

- Ask: **Which of these numbers has a digit sum of 8?** (71) Say: **We know that William has 71p to spend.**

- On the board, write: William (71p), Bryony (86p), Kyle (68p), Lydia (69p), Cameron (76p). Say: **William compares the amount he has to spend with that of his friends. Who has the most money? The least? How would you find out?** Establish that a good way to solve the problem is to arrange the numbers in order, from the smallest number to the greatest.

- Ask: **How would you do this?** Accept and discuss the strategies suggested by the children. Establish and work through two methods: ordering the numbers on the number line, and using a place value chart. Determine the order and answer the questions. (greatest amount: 86p; least amount: 68p)

Teaching Activity 1b (15 minutes)

Use place value and number facts to solve problems

- Give pairs of children arrow cards and ask them to make a two-digit number, for example, 47.

- Hold up the number for the children to see. Say: **I am thinking of a secret number. My number has two more tens than this number but three less ones. What number am I thinking of?**

- Discuss and say: **Hold up your numbers.** Confirm that the children have made 64. Intervene and address any misconceptions in understanding of place value.

- Make another two-digit number, for example, 72. Say: **I am thinking of a secret number. My number has five less tens than this number but seven more ones. What number am I thinking of?**

- Discuss and say: **Hold up your numbers.** Confirm that the children have made 59.

- Ask the children to take turns to make two-digit numbers with their arrow cards and pose similar questions to their partner, for example, say: **I have made the number 45. My secret number has four more tens but four less ones. What is my number?** (81)

- Hold up two sets of arrow cards, one that models the number 38 and the other that models the number 46. Say: **I am thinking of a number that is between 38 and 46. The sum of the digits of the number is 7. What is my secret number?**

- Discuss and say: **Hold up your numbers.** Confirm that the children have made 43. Ask: **How did you work out the answer?** Choose a pair to explain the method they used. Establish that a good method is to make the numbers that lie between 38 and 46 on the number line and find the sum of each number's digits until a sum of 7 is found.

- Use arrow cards to make two, two-digit numbers, for example, 24 and 37. Hold the numbers behind your back so that the children cannot see them, and say: **I have made two secret two-digit numbers. The sum of the tens digits of both numbers is 18 and the difference in the ones digit of both numbers is 9. What are my secret numbers?**

- Discuss and say: **Hold up your numbers.** Confirm that the children have made the numbers 90 and 99. Choose a pair to explain how they worked out the answer.

- Write on the board: 89, 76, 84, 81, 67. Say: **These are the scores of five children that played a video game. Which score is the highest? Lowest? Which score is in the middle?**

- Ask: **How would you answer this problem?** Establish that a good way to find the answers is to arrange the numbers in order, from the smallest number to the greatest.

- Ask: **How would you do this?** Discuss the strategies suggested by the children. Establish and work through two methods: ordering the numbers on the number line, and using a place value chart. Determine the order and answer the questions (67, 76, 81, 84, 89; highest score: 89; lowest score: 67; middle score: 81).

Unit 7: Solve problems with addition and subtraction: using concrete objects and pictorial representations, including those involving numbers, quantities and measures; applying their increasing knowledge of mental and written methods

Content domain reference: 2C4

Prerequisites for learning

Use knowledge of number facts and place value to solve simple problems with addition and subtraction

Demonstrate a good understanding of the language of addition and subtraction

Learning outcomes

Use concrete objects and pictorial representations, including those involving numbers, quantities and measures, to solve simple problems with addition and subtraction

Apply knowledge of mental and written methods to solve simple problems with addition and subtraction

Key vocabulary

add, plus, total, altogether, subtract, take away, minus

Resources

Resource 1: 100 square; base ten blocks

Background knowledge

- Encourage children to draw pictures to illustrate the problem they are solving. This helps them visualise the problem and translate the words into a number sentence.
- Prior to the lesson, discuss synonyms for addition and subtraction and create a word list to support the children during the activities.

Teaching Activity 1a (20 minutes)

Use concrete objects and pictorial representations, including those involving numbers, quantities and measures, to solve simple problems with addition and subtraction

- Say: **Let's pretend that we are chefs working at a restaurant. As part of our job, we need to add and subtract weights and volumes.**
- Draw and label two sacks, 10 kg and 20 kg, on the board. Say: **The restaurant has had a delivery of two bags of potatoes, one 10 kg bag and one 20 kg bag. What is the total mass of the two bags?** Give the children time to discuss the question with a partner.

- Say: **Let's think about the question. We are asked to find the total mass of the two bags. Is that an addition or a subtraction question?** Establish that finding the total of two amounts involves adding the amounts together. Write '20 kg' and '10 kg' with a space between on the board.
- Say: **We are going to write the question as a number problem to solve. Which symbol do we need to place between 20 kg and 10 kg to make an addition problem?**

- Choose a child to write the symbol. Expect: 20 kg + 10 kg. Say: **The addition symbol tells us that we add the amounts, but we if we want to make this a number sentence with an answer, then we need to include another symbol. Which symbol is that?** (an 'equals' sign is needed) After '10 kg', write '='. Say: **Now we need to complete the number statement by finding the total and writing it after the equals sign.**

- Ask: **What is 10 add 20?** (30) Ask: **How did you work this out?** Establish that a quick method is to begin at 20 and count on 10 to make 30.

- Change the masses of the bags to 22 kg and 13 kg. Say: **Two more bags are delivered to the restaurant, this time, bags of carrots. How much do the bags weigh altogether?** Give the children time to discuss the problem with their partner. Explain that the word 'altogether' has the same meaning as 'total'.

- Choose a child to write the problem as a calculation to solve. Expect: 22 + 13 =. Establish that 22 + 13 is preferable to 13 + 22 when solving a problem mentally. Say: **It is easier to hold the larger number in your head and count on to add the smaller number.**

- Give the children base ten apparatus and ask them to use them to add the numbers. Ask: **How did you solve the problem?** Establish that the place values of each number can be added separately: 20 + 10 = 30; 2 + 3 = 5.

- Say: **The answer has three tens and five ones. What is the number?** (35) **What is the total mass of the two bags?** (35 kilograms) Write on the board: 35 kg.

- Say: **Over a week, we use 24 kg of carrots in our cooking. What amount of carrots is left? Is this an addition or subtraction problem?** Establish that use of the word 'left' in the question tells us that this is a subtraction problem. Write '24' next to '35' with a space in between.

- Say: **We are going to write the question as a number problem to solve. Which symbol do we need to place between 35 and 24 to make this a subtraction problem?** Choose a child to write the symbol. Expect: 35 – 24 =. Say: **The subtraction symbol tells us that we need to calculate the answer to 35 minus 24.**

- Ask the children to use the base ten apparatus to subtract the numbers. Ask: **How did you solve the problem?** Choose a pair to explain how they found the total. Establish that the place values of each number can be subtracted separately: 30 – 20 = 10; 5 – 4 = 1. Ask: **The answer has one ten and one. What is the number?** (11) **What mass of carrots is left?** (11 kilograms)

- If time, tell other subtraction stories based on supplies to the restaurant and ask the children to construct number problems to find the amount that remains.

Teaching Activity 1b (20 minutes)

Use concrete objects and pictorial representations, including those involving numbers, quantities and measures, to solve simple problems with addition and subtraction

- Say: **Let's pretend that we work in a shop that sells fabric and other materials.** Explain that they will need to work out the total length of two pieces of material or to shorten single pieces.

- Say: **Mrs Jones wants 30 centimetres of red material and 20 centimetres of green material. As we charge by the centimetre, we need to find the total length of material Mrs Jones needs.**

- Draw two oblongs on the board to represent each piece of material and label them '30 cm' and '20 cm'. Ask children what the total of each piece will be. Say: **Let's think about the question. We are asked to find the total length of the two pieces. Is that an addition or a subtraction question?** Establish that we add to find the total of two amounts.

- Write on the board: '20 centimetres' and '30 centimetres' with a space between.

- Say: **We are going to write the question as a number problem to solve. Which symbol do we need to place between 20 and 30 to make an addition problem?** Choose a child to write the symbol. Expect: 30 + 20.

- Say: **The addition symbol tells us that we need to add the amounts but we also need to include another symbol to make this a number statement that gives an answer.** Write '=' after '20'. Ask: **What symbol is this?** (equals) **What does it mean?** (it tells us that the amounts on each side of the sign are the same. Both sides are balanced)

- Ask: **What is 30 add 20?** (50) Ask: **How did you work this out?** Establish that a quick method is to begin at 30 and count on two steps of ten to make 50.

- Display a 100 square or number line and demonstrate counting on by two steps of 10.

- Change the lengths of the two pieces of material to 34 cm and 43 cm. Say: **Mr Smith wants the same colour of material but in two different lengths, 34 cm of red and 43 cm of green. How much is that altogether?** Explain that the word 'altogether' has the same meaning as 'total'.

- Choose a child to write the problem as a calculation to solve. Expect: 43 + 34 =. Establish that 43 + 34 is preferable to 34 + 43. Say: **It is easier to hold the larger number in your head and count on to add the smaller number.**

- Display a 100 square and point to 43. Say: **Lets add the three tens first that are in 34.** Lead the children in a chant of steps of 10 from 43, tracing a finger down the column for each step: 53, 63, 73. Mark the approximate position of 73 on the number line and indicate the three jumps of ten.

- Say: **Now we will add the ones.** Point to 73 on the 100 square and count on four: 74, 75, 76, 77. Mark the approximate position of 77 on the number line and indicate the four jumps of one.

- Ask: **What is 43 add 34?** (77) **What is the total length of material?** (77 centimetres)

- Write on the board: 96 cm. Say: **Mrs Daniels has selected some pink material. We have 96 centimetres left but Mrs Daniels only wants 54 cm. How much of the material should we cut? Is this an addition or subtraction problem?** Establish that use of the phrase 'cut off' tells us that this is a subtraction problem.

- Discuss how to solve the problem and establish that the amount of material to cut is equivalent to the 96 cm we have minus the 54 cm we need to keep.

- Write '54 cm' to the right of '96 cm' with a space in between on the board. Say: **We are going to write the question as a calculation to solve. Which symbol do we need to place between 96 and 54 to make this a subtraction problem?** Choose a child to write the correct symbol between the numbers. Expect: 96 – 54 =. Say: **The subtraction symbol tells us that we need to take the second number from the first number.**

- Display a 100 square and point to 96. Say: **Lets subtract the three tens first.** Lead the children in a chant in steps of 10 backward from 96, tracing a finger down the numbers in the column: 86, 76, 66, 56, 46. Mark the approximate position of 46 on the number line and indicate the five backward jumps of ten.

- Say: **Now we will subtract the ones.** Point to 46 on the 100 square and count back four: 45, 44, 43, 42. Mark the approximate position of 42 on the number line and indicate the four jumps backward of one.

- **What is 96 subtract 54?** (42) **How much material do we need to cut?** (42 centimetres)

- If time, tell other subtraction stories based on requests to reduce the length of material and ask the children to construct number problems to solve.

Teaching Activity 2a (15 minutes)

Apply knowledge of mental and written methods to solve simple problems with addition and subtraction

- Ask the children to work in pairs. Say: **In this lesson, we are going to solve problems that involve minibeasts.**

- Draw a flower with two leaves on the board. Explain that ladybirds like to rest on the leaves of the flower. Write 33 on one leaf and 25 on the other leaf. Say and record: **How many ladybirds are there altogether?**

- Ask: **Is this an addition or subtraction problem?** Agree that the word 'altogether' tells us that this is an addition problem.

- Say: **Next, we gather all the information we need and write the word problem as a calculation to solve.** Ask: **What do we need to find out?** (the number of ladybirds on one leaf add the number of ladybirds on the other leaf) Say: **Who can write this as a number problem to solve?** Choose a child to write the addition problem. Expect: 33 + 25 =. Point to the '+' sign. Say: **Remember, this symbol tells us that we need to add the numbers together.**

- Say: **Work out 33 plus 25 on paper. Which method will you use?** Discuss a range of written strategies for addition, for example: horizontal addition (partitioning), using a 100 square. Say and record: **Add the tens together.** (30 + 20 = 50) **Then add the ones together.** (3 + 5 = 8) **Find the total.** (50 + 8 = 58)

- Give children time to complete the calculation. Ask: **What is the answer to the problem?** (there are 58 ladybirds altogether)

- Draw another two-leaf flower. Say: **Let's solve another ladybird problem. This time, we are told that 87 ladybirds are sitting on both leaves. Of these 87 ladybirds, 62 are sitting on the leaf to the left. How many ladybirds are sitting on the leaf to the right?**

- Ask: **Is this an addition or subtraction problem?** Agree that, since we know the total number of ladybirds on both leaves, and the number sitting on one leaf, to work out the number on the other leaf will involve a subtraction.

- Say: **Next, we gather all the information we need and write the word problem as a calculation.** Ask: **What do we need to find out?** (the number of ladybirds on both leaves, subtract the number on one leaf)

- Say: **Who can write this as a calculation to solve?** Choose a child to write the subtraction problem. Expect: 87 – 62 =. Say: **Work out 87 subtract 62 on paper. Which method will you use?** Discuss examples of written strategies for subtraction, for example, using a number line. Say and record: **Start at 87 – jump back in tens six times. Then jump back in ones once.** Alternatively, say and record: **Start at 62. Jump forward in tens twice to 82 then forward five ones to 87. Total jumps = 20 + 5 = 25.**

- Give children time to complete the calculation. Ask: **What is the answer to the problem?** (there are 25 ladybirds on the other leaf)

- If time, tell other addition and subtraction minibeast stories and ask the children to write them as calculations to solve.

Teaching Activity 2a (15 minutes)

Apply knowledge of mental and written methods to solve simple problems with addition and subtraction

- Draw a bookshelf with two shelves on the board. Say: **Pretend that you work in a library. Your job is to work out how many books are in the library and how many books have been borrowed.**

- Write '44' on one shelf and '32' on the other. Ask: **How many books are there altogether?**

- Say: **Is this an addition or subtraction problem?** Explain that the word 'altogether' is similar to total or sum and tells us that we need to add.

- Say: **Next, we gather all the information we need and write the word problem as a calculation.** Ask: **What do we need to find out?** (the total number of books on both shelves) Choose a child to write the addition calculation to solve. Expect: 44 + 32 =.

- Say: **Work out 44 add 32 on paper. Which method will you use?**

- Discuss written strategies for addition that use a 100 square for support, including:

- ◆ Horizontal addition (partitioning), using a 100 square. Say and record: **Collect the tens together.** (40 + 30 = 70) **Then collect the ones together** (4 + 2 = 6) **Find the total.** (70 + 6 = 76)

- ◆ Use a number line. Say and record: **Start at 44. Jump forward three steps of 10** (32 = 30 + 2) **to 74, then jump forward two steps of 1 to 76.** (76)

- ◆ Give children time to complete the calculation. Ask: **What is the answer to the problem?** (there are 76 books altogether)

- Draw another pair of shelves. Say: **Let's solve another book problem. We know that the shelves have a total of 76 books. However, the next day, when we count them, we only have 23 books. How many books have been borrowed?**

- Say: **Is this an addition or subtraction problem?** Establish that, since the number of books have been reduced, and we are given the number before the reduction, this is a subtraction problem.

- Say: **Next, we gather all the information we need and write the word problem as a calculation.** Ask: **What do we need to find out?** (the total number of books before some were borrowed minus the number that remain) Say: **Who can write this as a calculation to solve?** Choose a child to write the subtraction problem. Expect: 76 – 23 =.

- Say: **Work out 76 subtract 23 on paper. Which method will you use?** Discuss written strategies for subtraction that use a 100 square for support, including:

- ◆ Horizontal subtraction (partitioning), using a 100 square. Say and record: **Collect the tens together and subtract.** (70 – 20 = 50) **Then collect the ones together and subtract.** (6 – 3 = 5) **Find the total.** (50 + 3 = 53)

- ◆ Use a number line. Say and record: **Start at 76. Jump back two steps of 10. Then jump back three steps of 1.**

- ◆ Say and record: **Start at 23. Jump five steps of 10 to 73 then three steps of 1 to 76. Total jumps = 50 + 3 = 53.**

- Give the children time to complete the calculation. Ask: **What is the answer to the problem?** (53 books were borrowed)

- If time, tell other addition and subtraction stories set in a library and ask the children to write them as calculations to solve.

Unit 8: Recall and use addition and subtraction facts to 20 fluently, and derive and use related facts up to 100

Content domain reference: 2C1

Prerequisites for learning

Use the symbols +, – and = to record addition and subtraction facts

Know addition and subtraction facts to 10 and some facts to 20

Learning outcomes

Recall and use addition and subtraction facts to 20 fluently

Derive and use related facts up to 100

Key vocabulary

add, plus, make, total, altogether, subtraction, subtract, take away, minus, leaves, less, equals

Resources

Resource 2: Addition questions; base ten apparatus; number cards; place value mats; mini whiteboards and pens

Background knowledge

- In preparation for this activity, ensure the children know addition and subtraction facts up to 10 from memory or by using a strategy.

Teaching Activity 1a (20 minutes)

Recall and use addition and subtraction facts to 20 fluently

- Draw a number line from 0 to 20 on the board. Say: **Let's practise adding and subtracting numbers up to 20 so that we become confident working with these numbers.**

- Draw a circle and five cupcakes. Point to the drawing and say: **Five cupcakes are placed on a tray.** Write 7 next to the tray. Say: **7 more cupcakes are placed on the tray. How many cupcakes is that altogether? Is this an addition or subtraction problem?** Establish that the word 'altogether' tells us that we are adding numbers to find a total.

- Ask: **Who can write this number problem as a calculation?** Choose a child to write the calculation on the board. Expect: 5 + 7 (or 7 + 5). Ask: **Is there another way of writing the addition?** Expect: 7 + 5 (or 5 + 7). Ask: **Why are we able to write the addition in any order?** (you can add numbers in any order and still get the same answer)

- Say: **Let's calculate the answer with the help of a number line.** Point to the two numbers in the addition problem. Ask: **Which order should we use and why?** (starting with the greater number rather than the smaller number requires less counting on)

- Point to 7 on the number line and count on 5. Ask: **What is the answer?** (12)

- Ask: **Is there another way to add on 5?** Point to 7. Say: **We can bridge to 10 by adding on 3.** Draw a jump from 7 to 10. Say: **Then we add on the remaining 2.** Draw a jump from 10 to 12.

- Give out mini whiteboards to pairs of children. Tell other addition stories that involve cupcakes and ask the children to write the problems as calculations to solve. The children draw a number line and use it to calculate the answer.

- Encourage both 'counting on' and 'bridging to ten' methods. Include problems that start with ten cupcakes and various one-digit numbers that are added. Point out that the tens digit in the answer remains the same, whilst the ones digit is the same as the number added. Choose pairs to share the methods they use.

- Draw a circle (to represent a tray) and 14 cupcakes on the board. Point to the drawing and say: **14 cupcakes are placed on a tray.** Write 14 next to the tray. Say: **8 cupcakes are taken from the tray and eaten.** How many cupcakes will be left? Ask: **Is this an addition or subtraction problem?** Establish that, since the number of cupcakes is reduced, the problem involves subtraction.

- Ask: **Who can write this subtraction question as a calculation to solve?** Choose a child to write the number problem on the board. Expect: 14 − 8. Ask: **Why did you not write this as 8 subtract 14?** Agree that whereas addition can be done in any order, the order for subtraction matters. Say: **Reversing the order of the numbers creates a different problem that we cannot answer. We cannot take away 14 cakes when there only 8 cakes on the tray.**

- Point to 14 on the number line and count back 8. Ask: **What is the answer?** (6)

- Ask: **Is there another way to use the number line to solve this problem?** Say: **We can think of the problem in another way: What do we need to add to 8 to make 14?** Explain we can think of the problem as finding the difference between two numbers. Say: **We start at 8 and count on in ones or jump in steps to 14. The amount we count on or jump is the difference between 8 and 14.** Point to 8. Say and record: **We can bridge to 10 by adding on 2.** Draw a jump from 8 to 10. Say: **Then we jump 4 to get to 14. The total of the jumps is 2 + 4 = 6. The difference between 8 and 14 is 6. In other words, 14 take away 8 is 6.** Write: 14 − 8 = 6.

- Discuss the difference between subtracting (finding the answer by counting back on the number line) and finding the difference (counting on where the answer is the number of jumps).

- Give out mini whiteboards to pairs of children. Tell other cupcake subtraction and addition stories and ask the children to write the problems as calculations to solve. The children draw a number line and use it to calculate the answer.

- Encourage the children to use either 'counting back' or 'counting on to find the difference' methods and include problems that start with 20 cupcakes and have various one-digit numbers subtracted. Point out that the tens digit in the answer is one less whilst the ones digit is the difference between 10 and the one-digit number. Choose pairs to share the methods they use.

Teaching Activity 1b (20 minutes)

Recall and use addition and subtraction facts to 20 fluently

- Say: **Let's practise adding and subtracting numbers up to 20 so that we become confident working with these numbers.**

- Arrange six pencils in a tray. Point to the pencils and say: **Six pencils are placed in a tray.**

- Place the number card 9 next to the tray. Say: **If 9 more pencils were placed in the tray, how many pencils will there be altogether?** Ask: **Is this an addition or subtraction problem?** Establish that the word 'altogether' tells us that we are adding numbers to find a total.

- Ask: **Who can write this addition question as a calculation?** Choose a child to write the calculation on the board. Expect: 6 + 9 (or 9 + 6). Ask: **Is there another way of writing the addition?** Expect: 9 + 6 (or 6 + 9). Ask: **Why are we able to write the addition in any order?** (you can add numbers in any order and still get the same answer)

- Give pairs of children base ten apparatus. Say: **We will use base ten blocks to work out the answer.** Point to the two numbers in the addition problem. Ask: **Which order should we use and why?** (it is easier to keep a larger number in our head and then add a smaller number)

- Give the children time to calculate the answer then choose a pair to demonstrate the method they used.

- Collect together 9 cubes. Say: **Now we add on 6.** Add one cube and say: **We can exchange the ten cubes for one rod.** Replace the ten cubes with one rod and then add the remaining 5 as single cubes. Ask: **How many tens do we have?** (1) **How many ones?** (5) **What is the answer?** (15) On the board, write: 9 + 6 = 15.

- Tell other addition stories involving pencils in a tray and ask the children to write the problems as calculations to solve on mini whiteboards. Encourage the children to use the base ten blocks to work out the answers. Include problems that start with ten pencils and various one-digit numbers that are added. Point out that the tens digit in the answer remains the same whilst the ones digit is the same as the number added. Choose pairs to share the methods they use.

- Arrange 16 pencils in a tray. Point to the pencils and say: 16 pencils are placed in a tray.

- Place the number card 9 next to the tray. Say: **If 9 pencils were to be taken, how many pencils would be left? Is this an addition or subtraction problem?** Establish that since the number of pencils is reduced, the problem involves subtraction.

- Ask: **Who can write this subtraction question as a calculation?** Choose a child to write the calculation on the board. Expect: 16 – 9. Ask: **Why did you not write this as 9 subtract 16?** Agree that, whereas addition can be done in any order, the order for subtraction matters. Say: **Reversing the order of the numbers creates a different problem that we cannot answer. We cannot take away 16 pencils when there only 9 pencils in the tray.**

- The children use the base ten blocks to work out the answer. Ask: **What is the answer?** (7) **How did you work it out?** Choose a pair to demonstrate the method they used.

- Ask: **Is there another way to solve this problem?** Say: **We can think of the problem in another way by asking the question: What do we need to add to 9 to make 16?** Explain we can think of the problem as finding the difference between two numbers. Collect together 9 cubes and add cubes one at a time until 16 is reached.

- Ask: **How many cubes did I add on?** (7) Say: **The difference between 9 and 16 is 7. In other words, 16 take away 9 is 7.** Write: 16 – 9 = 7. Discuss the difference between subtracting (finding the answer by counting back on the number line) and finding the difference (counting on where the answer is the number of jumps).

- Tell other subtraction stories related to pencils in a tray and ask the children to write the problems as calculations to solve. Encourage the children to use base ten blocks to work out the answers and to use either 'counting back' or 'find the difference' methods. Include problems that start with 20 pencils and have various one-digit numbers subtracted. Point out that the tens digit in the answer is one less, whilst the ones digit is the difference between 10 and the one-digit number. Choose pairs to share the methods they use.

Teaching Activity 2a (15 minutes)

Derive and use related facts up to 100

- Put a place value chart or mat in front of the children. Place a single cube in the ones column. Ask: **How many cubes are in the ones column?** (1) **What is the value of the one cube?** (1) **What number is represented by the cube?** (1)

- In a row below, place a single rod in the tens column. Ask: **How many tens are there?** (1) **What is the value of the one ten?** (10) **What number is represented by the one red?** (10)

- Compare the one cube and the one rod. Ask: **How many times bigger is 10 than 1?** (10 times) **Write the numbers 10 and 1 on the board.**

- Place two cubes in the ones column. Ask: **What is the value of the two cubes?** (2) **What number is represented by the cubes?** (2)

- In a row below, place two rods in the tens column. Ask: **How many are there?** (2) **What is the value of the two tens?** (20) **What number is represented by the two rods?** (20)

- Compare the two cubes and the two rods. Ask: **How many times bigger is 20 than 2?** (10 times) Write the numbers 20 and 2 on the board.

- Repeat the above activity for 30 and 40. Point to the numbers on the board. Say: **By multiplying one-digit numbers by 10 we make multiples of ten.** Point to the multiples and say: 10, 20, 30. Ask: **What is the next multiple of ten?** (40) **Which one-digit number is multiplied by ten to make 40?** (4) Repeat for numbers 5 to 9 and build the sequence of multiples of ten to 90.

- Say: **Knowing multiples of ten and how they are made by multiplying one-digit numbers by ten can help us to solve many number problems.**

- Write on the board: 4 + 3 = and 40 + 30 =.

- Point to 4 + 3. Ask: **What is the answer?** (7) Point to 40 + 30. Ask: **What do you notice about this addition?** (The numbers are multiples of ten) Point to 40. Ask: **Which one-digit number multiplied by ten makes 40?** (4) Point to 30. Ask: **Which one-digit number multiplied by ten makes 30?** (3)

- Say: **The value of the numbers 40 and 30 are ten times the value of 4 and 3. How would you use the answer to 4 add 3 to answer 40 add 30?** Say: **Since 40 is ten times larger than 4 and 30 is ten times larger than 3, the answer to 40 + 30 is ten times larger than the answer to 4 + 3.** Ask: **What is 40 add 30?** (70)

- Choose a child to come to the board to complete the two number sentences. (4 + 3 = 7, 40 + 30 = 70)

- Say: **When we use a number fact we know, 4 + 3 = 7, for example, to answer a fact we don't yet know, such as 40 + 30, we call this a 'related fact'.**

- Write on the board: 50 + 40 =. Ask: **Which related fact would you use to answer this problem?** Choose a child to come to the board to write the related fact. Expect: 5 + 4 = 9. Ask: **How does this help us to answer 50 add 40?** (since 50 is ten times larger than 5 and 40 is ten times larger than 4, we know that the answer to 50 + 40 is ten times larger than the answer to 5 + 4) Ask the child to complete the number sentence (50 + 40 = 90).

- Write: 50 – 20. Say: **We can use related facts to answer subtraction problems.** Ask: **Which related fact would you use to answer this problem?** Choose a child to come to the board to write the related fact. Expect: 5 – 2 = 3. Ask: **How does this help us to answer 50 subtract 20?** (since 50 is ten times larger than 5 and 20 is ten times larger than 2, we know that the answer to 50 – 20 is ten times larger than the answer to 5 – 2) Ask the child to complete the number sentence (50 – 20 = 30). Repeat for similar subtraction problems.

Teaching Activity 2b (15 minutes)

Derive and use related facts up to 100

- Give pairs of children base ten apparatus and a copy of **Resource 2: Addition questions**.

- Choose a pair to hold up blocks that represent a two-digit add two-digit addition problem, for example, 30 add 40. Ask: **How would you use base ten blocks to work out the answer?** Expect the children to arrange 3 rods to represent 30 and 4 rods to represent 40. They combine the rods. Ask: **How many rods is that?** (7) **What is the value of the seven rods?** (70) Ask the children to complete the addition statement. (30 + 40 = 70)

- Ask the pairs to cut out the addition questions cards and use the base ten blocks to work out the answers.

- Ask: **The statements can be arranged in pairs. How would you group them?** Give the children time to discuss the problem and group the statements. Choose a pair to explain how they paired the statements.

- Establish that the statements that share the same digits can be paired. Place '5 + 3 = 8' alongside '50 + 30 = 80' and '2 + 5 = 7' next to '20 + 50 = 70'. Ask: **Why do you think I have paired these statements?** Establish that the numbers in the addition calculation and the answer are ten times bigger than the corresponding numbers in the one-digit addition problem.

- Point to 50 in the 50 + 30 and 5 in 5 + 3. Say: **50 is ten times bigger than 5.** Point to 3 in 5 + 8 and 30 in 50 + 30. Say: **30 is ten times bigger than 3.** Point out that the answer to 50 + 30 is ten times bigger than the answer to 5 + 3.

- Say: **The numbers in the problem 50 add 30 are ten times the value of the numbers in the problem 5 + 3.** Establish that, since 50 is ten times larger than 5 and 30 is ten times larger than 3, the answer to 50 + 30 will be ten times larger than the answer to 5 + 3. Confirm that the answer to 50 + 30 is ten times the answer to 5 + 3.

- Choose groups to show the other statements they have paired and explain how the numbers are related.

- Say: **When we use a number fact we know, 5 + 3 for example, to answer a fact we don't yet know, for instance 50 + 30, we call this a 'related fact'.**

- On the board, write: 60 + 30 =. Ask: **Which related fact would you use to answer this problem?** Choose a child to come to the board to write the related fact. Expect: 6 + 3 = 9.

- Ask: **How does this help us to answer 60 add 30?** (since 60 is ten times larger than 6 and 30 is ten times larger than 3, we know that the answer to 60 + 30 is ten times larger than the answer to 6 + 3) Ask the child to complete the number sentence. (60 + 30 = 90)

- Write: 70 – 40. Say: **We can use related facts to answer subtraction problems.** Ask: **Which related fact would you use to answer this problem?** Choose a child to come to the board to write the related fact. Expect: 7 – 4 = 3. Ask: **How does this help us to answer 70 subtract 40?** (since 70 is ten times larger than 7 and 40 is ten times larger than 4, we also know that the answer to 70 – 40 is ten times larger than the answer to 7 – 4) Ask the child to complete the number sentence (70 – 40 = 30). Repeat for similar subtraction problems.

Unit 9: Add and subtract numbers using concrete objects, pictorial representations, and mentally, including: a two-digit number and 1s; a two-digit number and 10s; 2 two-digit numbers; adding 3 one-digit numbers

Content domain reference: 2C2b

Prerequisites for learning

Have a rapid recall of addition facts to 20
Have a secure understanding of place value
Able to add multiples of ten and ones

Learning outcomes

Add and subtract numbers: a two-digit number and 1s and a two-digit number and 10s

Add and subtract two, two-digit numbers

Add three, one-digit numbers

Key vocabulary

add, plus, make, total, altogether, subtraction, subtract, take away, minus, leaves, less, equals

Resources

Resource 1: 100 square, base ten apparatus

Background knowledge

• Before beginning the activity, give the children practice at counting forwards and back using a 100 square where the counting crosses the tens barrier. This will give them experience of counting across the rows of the 100 square in preparation for more challenging addition and subtraction problems. Point out how the tens digit changes as the counting crosses the tens barrier.

Teaching Activity 1a (25 minutes)

Add and subtract numbers: a two-digit number and 1s and a two-digit number and 10s

• Write on the board: 43 + 5 = 48, 5 + 43 = [ ]. Say: **What is the answer to the second addition calculation?** (48) **How did you work this out so quickly?** (we are told 43 add 5 is 48. Since the order in which we add numbers does not matter, we know that 5 add 43 will also be 48) Remind the children that addition can be done in order.

• Write on the board: 60 + 7 = [ ]. Say: **What is the answer?** (67) **How did you work this out so quickly?** Remind the children that it is easy to add a single-digit number to a multiple of ten. Say: **When we add a one-digit number to a multiple of ten, only the ones digit changes to that of the single-digit number.**

• Give pairs of children copies of **Resource 1: 100 square** and write on the board: 23 + 5. Say: **Use your 100 square to add the numbers. Which number is it best to begin**

the count at? (23) **Why?** (adding a smaller number to a bigger number involves less counting on) Give the children time to count on 5 squares. Ask: **What is the answer?** (28)

• Write: 33 + 5. Ask: **What is the answer?** (38) Repeat for 43 + 5 (48) Ask: **What do you notice about the answers to three addition problems?** (all the answers have a ones digit of 8)

• Write: 53 + 5. Ask: **Without using the 100 square, can you tell me what the answer is?** (58) **How did you know?** (the answer follows the same pattern as other 'add 5' additions) Establish that, for addition problems such as this where the tens barrier is not crossed, the tens digit remains the same and the ones digit is the sum of the ones digits in both numbers.

• Write on the board: 48 + 6. Say: **Use your 100 square to work out the answer.** Choose a pair to demonstrate how they used the number square to count on. Establish that working out the answer involves crossing the tens barrier and involves a move to the next row of the number square. Ask: **What is the answer?** (54)

How does the tens digit of the answer compare to that of the two-digit number added? (the digit increases by one)

- Repeat for 58 + 6 and 68 + 6. (64, 74) Ask: **What do you notice about the answers?** Establish that the tens digit increases by one and the ones digit is always 4. Ask: **Why do you think we get this pattern?** Use the 100 square to demonstrate that, when we add six to a number with a ones digit of 8, we bridge 2 to the tens barrier and then cross it by four units. Ask the children to predict the answers to 78 + 6 and 88 + 6 (84, 95).

- Write on the board: 17 + 10, 17 + 20, 17 + 30. Ask the children to use the number square to work out the answer to each problem. Ask: **What are the answers?** (27, 37, 47) **What do you notice about the position of the answers on the 100 square?** (they are all in the same column) Establish that whilst the ones digit stays the same, the tens digit of the answer increases by the number of tens added.

- Write on the board: 18 – 4, 28 – 4, 38 – 4. Say: **Use the 100 square to answer these problems. Is there a pattern to the answers?** Choose a pair of children to state the answers and describe the pattern. (all the answers have a ones digit of 4: 14, 24, 34)

- Write: 48 – 4. Ask: **Without using the 100 square, can you tell me what the answer is?** (44) **How did you know?** (the answer follows the same pattern as other 'subtract 4' subtractions) Establish that, for subtraction problems such as this where the tens barrier is not crossed, the tens digit remains the same and the ones digit is the difference of the ones digits in both numbers.

- Write on the board: 34 – 7. Say: **Use your 100 square to work out the answer.** Choose a pair to demonstrate how they used the number square to count back. Establish that working out the answer involves crossing the tens barrier and involves a move to the previous row of the number square. Ask: **What is the answer?** (27) **How does the tens digit of the answer compare to that of the two-digit number in the subtraction?** (the digit is one less)

- Repeat for 44 – 7 and 54 – 7 (37, 47). Ask: **What do you notice about the answers?** Establish that the tens digit increases by one and the ones digit is always 7. Ask the children to predict the answers to 64 – 7 and 74 – 7 (57, 67).

Teaching Activity 1b (25 minutes)

Add and subtract numbers: a two-digit number and 1s and a two-digit number and 10s

- Write on the board: 38 + 7 = 45, 7 + 38 = [ ]. Say: **What is the answer to the second addition?** (48) **How did you work this out so quickly?** (38 add 7 is 45 so 38 add 7 will also be 45) Remind the children that addition can be done in order. Say: **We can change the order in an addition and still get the same answer.**

- Write on the board: 80 + 6 = [ ]. Say: **What is the answer?** (86) **How did you work this out so quickly?** Remind the children that it is easy to add a single-digit number to a multiple of ten. Say: **When we add a one-digit number to a multiple of ten, only the ones digit changes to that of the number added.**

- Write on the board: 22 + 7. Ask: **Who can come to the board to draw a number line that will help us find the answer?** Choose a child to draw the number line. Expect: A number line marked out in numbers from 20 to 30.

- Ask: **Which number is it best to begin the count at?** (22) **Why?** (adding a smaller number to a bigger number involves less counting on) Ask the child to count on 7 squares. Ask: **What is the answer?** (29)

- Write: 32 + 7. Ask: **What is the answer?** (39) Repeat for 32 + 7. (39) Ask: **What do you notice about the answers to three addition problems?** (all the answers have a ones digit of 9)

- Write: 42 + 7. Ask: **Without using the number line, can you tell me what the answer is?** (49) **How did you know?** (the answer follows the same pattern as other 'add 7' additions) Establish that, for addition problems like this one where the tens barrier is not crossed, the tens digit remains the same, whereas the ones digit is the sum of the ones digits in both numbers.

- Give the children whiteboards. Write on the board: 58 + 5. Say: **Draw a number line that will help you work out the answer. Think about whether you need to extend the number line beyond 60.**

- Choose a child to demonstrate how they used the number line to count on. Establish that working out the answer involves crossing the tens barrier and extending the number line beyond 60. Ask: **What is the answer?** (63) **How does the tens digit of the answer compare to that of the two-digit number added?** (the digit increases by one)

- Repeat for 68 + 5 and 78 + 5. (73, 83) Ask: **What do you notice about the answers?** Establish that the tens digit increases by one and the ones digit is always 3. Ask: **Why do you think we get this pattern?** Use the number line to demonstrate that, when we add 5 to a number with a ones digit of 8, we bridge 2 to the tens barrier and then cross it by three units. Ask the children to predict the answer to 88 + 5. (93)
- Give out base ten apparatus. Write on the board: 16 + 10, 16 + 20, 16 + 30. Ask the children to model and answer the calculations using base ten blocks. Ask: **What are the answers?** (26, 36, 46) **What do you notice about the answers?** Establish that, whilst the ones digit of the answer stays the same the tens digit increases by the number of tens added.
- Write on the board: 17 – 5, 27 – 5, 37 – 5. Say: **Use a number line or base ten blocks to solve these calculations. Is there a pattern to the answers?** (all the answers have a ones digit of 2: 12, 22, 32)
- On the board, write: 35 – 8. Say: **Draw a number line that will help you answer the problem. You may need to extend the number line back beyond 30.** Establish that the subtraction involves crossing the tens barrier and a move back along the number line beyond 30. Ask: **What is the answer?** (27) **How does the tens digit of the answer compare to that of the two-digit number in the subtraction?** (the digit is one less)
- Repeat for 42 – 8, 52 – 8, 62 – 8 (34, 44, 54) Ask: **What do you notice about the answers?** Establish that the tens digit increases by one and the ones digit is always 4. Ask: **Why do you think we get this pattern?** Use the 100 square to demonstrate that, when we subtract 8 from a number with a ones digit of 2, we subtract 2 to the previous tens barrier and count back by six units to reach 4. Ask the children to predict the answers to 72 – 8 and 82 – 8. (64, 74)

Teaching Activity 2a (15 minutes)

Add and subtract two, two-digit numbers

- Say: **We are now going to practise adding two, two-digit numbers using a 100 square.**
- Give pairs of children copies of **Resource 1: 100 square**. Write on the board: 14 + 43. Ask: **How would you use your 100 square to work out the answer to this addition problem?**
- Discuss the strategy of counting on. Ask: **Which number should we begin with, 43 or 14?** (43) Start at 43 and lead the children in counting forward 14. Ask: **What is the answer?**

(57) **Do you think counting on 14 was the best strategy? If not, can you suggest a different way to add 14?** Praise any child who suggests partitioning 14 by place value, and adding the tens and ones separately.

- Choose a child to come to the board to write 14 in the expanded form (14 = 10 + 4). Confirm that 14 can be split into one ten and four units.
- Point to 43 on the 100 square. Say: **Let's add 14 in two steps: first the ten, then the four units.** Ask: **How can we use the number square to add ten quickly?** (the next number down in any column on the 100 square is always ten more than the previous number) Move your finger from 43 to 53. Confirm that 53 is ten more than 43.
- Say: **Now we count on 4.** Move a finger four steps of one to reach 57. Say: **Splitting 14 into 10 and 4, and adding each part separately, we save time compared to counting on 14 steps of one.**
- Say: **We are now going to practise adding two, two-digit numbers that will need us to cross the tens boundary.**
- On the board, 17 + 48. Ask: **Which number should we start with?** (48) **How would you add on 17 without counting on in 17 steps of one?** (partition 17 by place value into one ten and seven units)
- Point to 48 on the 100 square. Ask: **How do we add the ten quickly?** (move down one row in the same column to reach 58) Say: **Now we add the seven units. Count on two steps of one to reach 60.** Ask: **How many more do we need to add?** (5) **Where do we continue the count?** (at the beginning of the next row) Count on five steps of one to reach 65. Ask: **What is the answer?** (65)
- Repeat for subtraction problems where the tens barrier is not crossed, for example, 56 – 12, 78 – 24, then for problems where the tens barrier is crossed, for example, 53 – 16, 75 – 27.

Teaching Activity 2b (15 minutes)

Add and subtract two, two-digit numbers

- Say: **We are now going to practise adding two, two-digit numbers using base ten apparatus.**
- Give pairs of children base ten blocks. Write on the board: 15 + 33. Say: **Use base ten blocks to work out the answer to this addition problem.** Establish that we can model each number as tens and ones then group the tens then the ones. Demonstrate the addition and ask: **How many tens do we have now?** (4) **How many ones do we have now?** (8) **What is the number?** (48)

- Say: **We are now going to practise adding two, two-digit numbers that will need us to cross the tens boundary.**

- On the board, write 56 + 27. Choose children to model each number using base ten blocks. Ask the children to combine the tens (rods). Ask: **How many tens is that?** (7) Say: **Now combine the ones (cubes). How many ones is that?** (13) Explain that, to help the addition, we can exchange 13 ones for one ten and three ones. Ask the children to group ten ones from 13 and exchange them for one ten (rod). Ask: **How many tens do we have now?** (8) **How many ones?** (3) Ask: **What is the answer?** (83)

- Repeat for other additions where the tens barrier is crossed, for example: 28 + 44, 57 + 35. Ask the children to model the addition using base ten blocks and to exchange the result of the ones addition for tens and ones. Ask: **What are the answers?** (72, 92)

- Ask children to use base ten blocks for subtraction problems where the tens barrier is not crossed, for example, 48 – 13, 67 – 25.

- Write: 55 – 17. Ask the children to model the numbers 55 and 17 with base ten blocks. Ask: **If we were to subtract the tens then the ones, will there be a problem completing the subtraction?** Establish that subtracting the tens (50 – 10) will leave four tens but there will be a problem completing the subtraction 5 – 7. Point to one of rods in the 4 tens. Say: **To help us continue with the subtraction, we can exchange one of the tens for ten ones.**

- Replace ten cubes for one rod. Ask: **How many ones do we have now?** (10 + 5 = 15) Say: **Now we subtract the 7 ones from the 15 ones. Ask: What does that leave?** (8 ones) Point to the 3 tens. **How many tens do we have?** (3) **How many ones do we have?** (8) **What is the answer?** (38)

Teaching Activity 3a (10 minutes)

Add three, one-digit numbers

- Write on the board: 2, 4, 3. Say: **We are now going to add three, one-digit numbers using different strategies.**

- Ask: **Which is the biggest number?** (4) Say: **As before, it is a good idea to begin with the biggest number.** Point to 2 and 3. Ask: **Should we add 2 then 3 separately or can we do something with these numbers before we add 4?** Establish that 2 and 3 add to 5 and 5 is an easy number to work with in addition problems. Ask: **What is 4 + 5?** (9)

- Say: **2 and 3 are examples of compatible numbers.** Explain that they add to make a number that is easy to use in calculations. Ask: **Can you think of any other compatible numbers?** Say: **What about 4 and 6?** Establish that 4 and 6 are compatible numbers as they add to make 10. Ask: **Are there any other numbers that make ten?** (1, 9; 2, 8; 3, 7; 4, 6; 5, 5)

- Say: **When we add three or more numbers together, it is a good idea to begin with the largest number, but it is also good to look for numbers that are compatible.**

- Write: 3, 4, 7. Ask: **How should we begin the addition, with the largest number 7 or another suggestion?** Accept comments. Praise any child who identifies 3 and 7 as compatible numbers that add to make 10. Say: **We can add 3 and 7 to make 10, then add the 4 to make 14.**

- Repeat for other sets of three numbers, for example: 8, 1, 4 (13); 6, 8, 4 (18).

Teaching Activity 3b (10 minutes)

Add three, one-digit numbers

- Write on the board: star (4p), balloon (3p), kite (6p). Say: **The prices of stickers sold by a shop are given on the board. If you wanted to buy all three stickers, what would be the total price? How would you work this out?**

- Remind the children that one efficient method is to begin with the biggest number then count on. Ask: **What is the biggest number?** (6) Say: **We could begin at 6 on the 100 square or number line, then count on 4, then count on 3, but is there a quicker method?**

- Prompt the children by asking if there are two numbers in the set that are easy to add. Praise any child who identifies that 4p and 6p add to make 10p and 10 is an easy number to work with in addition problems. Say: **We add 4 and 6 to make then 10, then add the 3 to make 13.** Ask: **What is the answer?** (13p)

- Say: **4 and 6 are examples of compatible numbers.** Explain that they add to make a number that is easy to use in calculations. Ask: **Can you think of any other compatible numbers?** Accept suggestions.

- Say: **What about 2 and 3?** Establish that 2 and 3 are compatible numbers as they add to make 5, another easy number to use in calculations. Ask: **Are there any other numbers that make five?** (1, 4) **What about ten?** (1, 9; 2, 8; 3, 7, 4, 6, 5, 5)

- Say: **When we add three or more numbers together, it is a good idea to begin with the largest number but it is also good to look for numbers that are compatible.**

Unit 10: Show that addition of 2 numbers can be done in any order (commutative) and subtraction of 1 number from another cannot

Content domain reference: 2C9a

Prerequisites for learning

Recall addition and subtraction facts to 20
Understand and record addition and subtraction facts using the symbols +, – and =

Learning outcomes

Show that addition of 2 numbers can be done in any order (commutative) and subtraction of 1 number from another cannot

Key vocabulary

add, plus, make, total, altogether, subtraction, subtract, take away, minus, leaves, less, equals

Resources

plastic or metal hangers; plastic or wooden clothes pegs

Background knowledge

• A secure understanding of the commutative property of addition is very important for progress in problem-solving. Understanding that to answer $5 + 87$, you can actually do $87 + 5$. This makes computation and problem-solving much easier.

Teaching Activity 1a (15 minutes)

Show that addition of 2 numbers can be done in any order (commutative) and subtraction of 1 number from another cannot

• Write on the board: $3 + 6 =$, $6 + 3 =$. Say: **We have two addition statements where the order of the numbers to be added is different. Let's investigate whether they give the same answer or not.**

• Place nine clothes pegs on a metal or plastic hanger. Hold the hanger up and ask the children to count the number of pegs. Agree that there are nine pegs.

• Point to $3 + 6 =$. Choose a child to move the pegs on the hanger to model the addition. Expect three pegs on one side of the hanger and six pegs on the other side. Ask: **What do three pegs add six pegs make?** (9 pegs) Complete the statement: $3 + 6 = 9$.

• Point to $6 + 3 =$. Choose a child to move the pegs on the hanger to model the addition. Expect six pegs on one side of the hanger and three pegs on the other. Ask: **Did we use the same number of pegs?** (yes) **What do six pegs and three pegs make?** (9 pegs) Complete the statement: $6 + 3 = 9$.

• Establish that the order of addition does not matter. Say: **We get the same answer, no matter the order of the numbers added.**

• Repeat the above activity for the addition statements $11 + 4 =$, $4 + 11 =$. Confirm that the answer is 15 no matter the order in which 4 and 11 are added.

• Write on the board: $10 – 7 =$, $7 – 10 =$. Place 10 pegs on the hanger.

• Ask: **Does the order matter for subtraction?** Discuss and say: **Let's find out if a subtraction problem can be completed in any order.**

• Point to $10 – 7 =$. Choose a child to remove pegs on the hanger to model the subtraction. Expect seven pegs to be removed. Ask: **How many pegs are left?** (3 pegs) Complete the statement: $10 – 7 = 3$.

• Point to $7 – 10 =$. Ask: **Will the answer be 3 again? If not, why?** Establish that it is not possible to take 10 pegs away from 7 pegs because there are not enough pegs. Say: **There would need to be at least 10 pegs to be able to subtract and 13 pegs for the answer to be 3.**

• Say: **We have found that addition can be done in any order, but subtraction cannot.**

Teaching Activity 1a (15 minutes)

Show that addition of 2 numbers can be done in any order (commutative) and subtraction of 1 number from another cannot

- Write on the board: 2 + 5 =, 5 + 2 =. Say: **We have two addition statements where the order of the numbers to be added is different. Let's investigate whether they give the same answer or not.**

- Draw a number line on the board from 0 to 10 marked in ones.

- Point to 2 + 5 =. Choose a child to use the number line to count on 5 from 2. Ask: **What is the answer?** (7) Complete the statement: 2 + 5 = 7.

- Point to 5 + 2 =. Choose a child to use the number line to count on 2 from 5. Ask: **What is the answer?** (7) Complete the statement: 5 + 2 = 7.

- Establish that the order of addition does not matter. Say: **We get the same answer, no matter the order of the numbers added.**

- Repeat the above activity for the addition statements 16 + 3 =, 3 + 16 =. Confirm that the answer is 19 no matter the order in which 3 and 16 are added.

- Ask: **When counting on, which number is it best to start with – the smaller or the larger number?** (larger) **Why?** (less counting on is required)

- Write on the board: 12 – 8 =, 8 – 12 =. Draw a number line from 0 to 20 marked out in ones.

- Ask: **Does the order matter for subtraction?** Discuss and say: **Let's find out if a subtraction problem can be completed in any order.**

- Point to 12 – 8 =. Choose a child to begin at 12 on the number line, then count back 8. Ask: **What is the difference between 12 and 8?** (4) Complete the statement: 12 – 8 = 4.

- Point to 8 – 12 =. Ask: **Will the answer be 4 again? If not, why?** Establish that counting back 12 from 8 gives an answer that crosses the zero barrier to numbers that are less than zero. Say: **Numbers less than zero are called negative numbers. These are different from positive numbers.** Say: **Since 8 – 12 does not give the same answer as 12 – 8 we know that the order of subtraction does matter.**

- Repeat the above activity for the addition statements 15 – 9 =, 9 – 15 =. Confirm that the answer is different, depending on the order of the numbers in a subtraction problem.

- Say: **We have found that addition can be done in any order, but subtraction cannot.**

Unit 11: Recognise and use the inverse relationship between addition and subtraction and use this to check calculations and solve missing number problems

Content domain reference: 2C3

Prerequisites for learning

Recall addition and subtraction facts to 20

Understand and record addition and subtraction facts using the symbols +, – and =

Learning outcomes

Recognise, write and use inverse calculations to check the answers to addition problems

Recognise, write and use inverse calculations to check the answers to subtraction problems

Key vocabulary

add, plus, make, total, altogether, subtraction, subtract, take away, minus, leaves, less, equals

Resources

interlocking cubes

Background knowledge

- Since addition and subtraction are inverse operations (the mathematical 'opposite' of the other), it is important that children work on problems that involve both calculations, rather than the operations being taught separately.

Teaching Activity 1a (15 minutes)

Recognise, write and use inverse calculations to check the answers to addition problems

- Write on the board: 9 + [ ] = 15. Say: **This is an example of a missing number problem.** Explain that the box represents the number we need to find. Ask: **Who can say this problem in words?** Choose a child to 'read' the problem. Expect: '9 add something makes 15' or 'What do we need to add to 9 to make 15?'

- On the board, draw the bar model as below.

15	
9	

- Say: **This is an example of a 'bar model'; we write the total in the top row of the diagram and the parts in separate boxes in the bottom row.**

- Point to the diagram. Say: **We know that 9 add the missing number makes 15. Is there a way of thinking of the problem as a subtraction?**

- Draw a number line on the board from 0 to 20 marked out in ones. Point to 9. Ask: **How would we use the number line to work out how many more we need to add to 9 to make 15?**

- Choose a child to come to the board to count on from 9 to 15. Ask: **What is the answer?** (6) Say: **We can think of the answer in two ways: we know 9 add 6 makes 15, but we also know that the difference between 15 and 9 is 6.** Write on the board: 15 – 9 = 6.

- Insert '6' in the lower right box of the bar model.

- Point to the two calculations on the board. Say: **9 + 6 = 15 and 15 – 9 = 6 are examples of inverse operations.** Explain that an inverse operation is an operation that reverses the effect of another operation. Say: **Addition and subtraction are inverse operations. In maths, we can think of them as the opposite of each other. We add 9 to 6 to make 15, but we can undo this by taking 9 away from 15 to get back to the 6 that was added.**

Teaching Activity 1b (15 minutes)

Recognise, write and use inverse calculations to check the answers to addition problems

- Write on the board: 'Six boys and eight girls stand in a circle. How many children are standing in the circle altogether?' (14)

- Choose a child to come to the board to write the calculation as a number sentence. Expect: 6 + 8 = 14. Ask: **Is there another way we can write the calculation.** Expect: 8 + 6 = 14. Remind the children that addition can be done in any order.

- Draw the diagram below on the board.

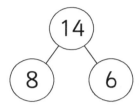

- Say: **Looking at the diagram, we can see that 8 plus 6 makes 14 and 6 plus 8 makes 14.**

- On the board, write: 14 – [ ] = 8. Say: **This is an example of a missing number problem. We have to find the number that goes in the box.** Ask: **Who can say this number problem in words?** Ask a child to 'read' the problem. Expect: '14 subtract/take away/ minus a number/something leaves 8'.

- Point to the number bond diagram. Say: **How could we use this diagram to answer the problem?** Establish that, as we know 8 plus 6 makes 14, we also know that 14 minus 8 leaves 6. Model this with interlocking cubes.

- Combine 8 red cubes with 6 blue cubes. Say: **8 red cubes add 6 blue cubes make 14 cubes altogether.** Remove the 6 cubes. Ask: **How many are left?** (8 cubes) Say: **14 minus 6 makes 8.** Complete the number statement on the board: 14 – 6 = 8.

- Point to the two calculations on the board. Say: **8 + 6 = 14 and 14 – 6 = 8 are examples of inverse operations.** Explain that an inverse operation is an operation that reverses the effect of another operation. Say: **Addition and subtraction are inverse operations. In maths, we can think of them as the opposite of each other. We add 6 to 8 to make 14, but we can undo this by taking 6 away from 14 to get back to the 8 that was added.**

Teaching Activity 2a (15 minutes)

Recognise, write and use inverse calculations to check the answers to subtraction problems

- Say: **Let's look at a missing number problem that involves a subtraction.** Write on the board: 24 – [ ] = 17. Ask: **Who can say this problem in words?** Choose a child to 'read' the problem. Expect: '24 take away/minus/less something leaves 17'.

- Point to 24 – [ ] = 17. Ask: **Which number is the whole amount that will go in the top bar of the model?** (24) **Which numbers are the parts that go in the bottom bar?** (17 and the missing number)

- Ask a child to the board to draw the bar model. Expect the diagram below:

24	
17	

- Say: **Using a mental method or number line, work out the answer to the problem.** Expect: 7. Say: **We can check the answer by using the inverse operation.** Ask: **What is the opposite of subtraction?** (addition)

- Point to the bar model. Say: **The model tells us that, if 7 is the correct answer, then 7 plus 17 should make 24.**

- Choose a child to come to the board to write the inverse operation. Expect: 17 + 7 = 24. Ask: **Is this correct?** (yes) **How do you know?** (partition 17 by place value: 10 + 7. Add the ones of both numbers, 7 and 7 makes 14. Recombine the tens and ones: 10 + 14 = 24)

Teaching Activity 2b (15 minutes)

Recognise, write and use inverse calculations to check the answers to subtraction problems

- Say: **Let's look at a missing number problem that involves a subtraction.** Write on the board: 33 – [ ] = 21. Ask: **Who can say this problem in words?** Choose a child to 'read' the problem. Expect: '33 take away/minus/ less something/a number leaves 21'.

- Ask: **How would you use a number line to calculate the answer to this problem?** Draw a number line on the board from 20 to 40 marked in ones. Label the numbers 21 and 33 on the number line. Ask: **How many do we have to count back from 33 to leave 21?** On the board, write: 33 – 12 = 21.

- Say: **This is a subtraction. What would be the inverse operation?** (addition) Ask: **Who can come to the board to write the inverse operation?** Expect: 21 + 12 = 33. Model this with interlocking cubes to support those children who need help with understanding the concept of an inverse operation.

Unit 12: Recall and use multiplication and division facts for the 2, 5 and 10 multiplication tables, including recognising odd and even numbers

Content domain reference: 2C6

Prerequisites for learning

Recognise and write number facts using the symbols × and =

Understand the concept of sharing

Be able to count in 2s, 5s and 10s

Learning outcomes

Recall and use multiplication and division facts for the 2 multiplication table

Recall and use multiplication and division facts for the 5 multiplication table

Recall and use multiplication and division facts for the 10 multiplication table

Recognise odd and even numbers

Key vocabulary

multiply, multiple, multiplication table, times table, divide, share, number fact

Resources

counters; beads; cubes

Background knowledge

- When introducing division, it is important to use two structures, 'sharing equally between' and 'grouping into equal sets'. To understand this fully, think of the following examples:

  ◆ 'Matt has 12 cupcakes and shares them between 3 of his friends. How many cupcakes does each friend get?' (4) In this example, the answer lies in the value of each equal share (4) [Sharing]

  ◆ 'Grace has 12 cupcakes. She wants to put them onto plates of 3. How many plates will she have?' (4) In this example, the answer lies in the number of equal groups. [Grouping]

Teaching Activity 1a (20 minutes)

Recall and use multiplication and division facts for the 2 multiplication table

- Arrange counters in 12 rows of 2 on a large piece of paper. Say: **We are going to count in 2s.** Lead a chant in multiples of 2, pointing to each group of two counters as the count proceeds. Ask a child to record the multiple of 2 alongside each row of counters: 2, 4, 6, 8… 24.

- Point to the numbers alongside the rows. Remind the children that each number is a multiple of 2.

- At the end of the first row, write: $1 \times 2 = 2$. Ask: **Who can tell me what this number sentence means?** Remind the children that '×' is the symbol for multiplication.

- Say: **When we multiply a number, we join together equal groups of that number. For 1×2, we are thinking about one equal group of 2.** Explain that we can read the number sentence as 1 times 2 equals 2 as the word 'times' means 'lots of' or 'groups

of'. Ask: **What other words do we use that mean to multiply?** Discuss the terms 'lots of', 'sets of', 'groups of', 'multiplied by' and 'times' as alternative terms for multiplication.

- Write a multiplication sentence for each multiple of 2 and ask the children to 'read' the sentence, for example: 'Two times two equals four' ($2 \times 2 = 4$), 'Three times two equals six' ($3 \times 2 = 6$), and so on, up to '12 times two equals twenty-four' ($12 \times 2 = 24$)

- Say: **The twelve multiplication sentences make up what we call the '2 times table'.** Explain that it is important for the children to eventually learn these facts off by heart. Say: **Knowing multiplication facts will help you to work quickly through the steps involved when problem solving.**

- Say: **I am going to call out questions about the 2 times table and I want you to use the facts on the board to answer them.** Explain that you will use different words to describe multiplication.

- Call out 2 times table questions: **What is 4 times 2?** (8) **What is 2 multiplied by 6?** (12) **What is 8 lots of 2?** (16) **What do 12 groups of 2 make?** (24)

- Arrange beads in three groups of two. Ask: **How many equal groups of counters are there?** (3) **How many counters are in each group?** (2) **What is the total number of counters?** (6) **What multiplication sentence could we write for this model?** Choose a child to come to the board to write the sentence. Expect: 3 × 2 = 6. Repeat for four groups of two beads. Ask a child to write the multiplication sentence that describes the array. (4 × 2 = 8)

- Ask four children to stand up. Say: **If we were to share these eight beads between four children, how many beads would each child get?** Choose a child to share the counters with the four children. Remind them of the need to share beads equally so that each person gets the same number. Ask: **What is the answer?** (2)

- Say: **We have found that each person gets two beads when eight beads are shared between four people. This is the same as saying that 8 divided by 4 is 2.** Explain that the phrase 'divided by' means to take a group of things and split them into equal groups. Introduce the word 'division'. Say: **When we divide objects into equal groups we call this division.**

- Write on the board: 8 ÷ 4 = 2. Point to the division sign. Say: **This is the sign for division. We read this number sentence as 8 divided by 4 equals 2.**

- Point to the eight beads. Say: **We can think of division in two different ways. We have found that eight can be divided into four groups of two. But we could also think of this division as finding out how many groups of two there are in eight.**

- Explain to the children that you are going to remove the beads two at a time. Say: **Help me count the number of groups of two counters.** Remove two counters at a time until all of the counters are removed then count the total number of groups. Ask: **How many groups of two counters are there?** (4). Say: **This means that eight shared into groups of two makes four groups.**

Teaching Activity 1b (20 minutes)

Recall and use multiplication and division facts for the 2 multiplication table

- Draw a number line from 0 to 24 marked in 1s. Say: **We are going to use the number line to count in 2s.** Lead a chant skip-counting in 2s along the number line. Circle the multiples of two as the count proceeds.

- Point to the circled numbers. Remind the children that each number is a multiple of 2.

- Below the number line, write: 1 × 2 = 2. Ask: **Who can tell me what this number sentence means?** Give the children time to discuss the question then accept answers. Remind the children that 'x' is the sign for multiplication. Say: **When we multiply a number, we join together equal groups of that number. For 1 × 2, we are thinking about one equal group of 2.** Explain that we can read the number sentence as 1 times 2 equals 2 as the word 'times' means 'lots of' or 'groups of'. Ask: **What other words do we use that mean 'to multiply'?** Discuss the terms 'lots of', 'sets of', 'groups of', 'multiplied by' and 'times' as alternative terms for multiplication.

- Write multiplication sentences for each multiple of 2 and ask the children to 'read' them: 'Two times two equals four' (2 × 2 = 4), 'Three times two equals six' (3 × 2 = 6), and so on, up to '12 times two equals twenty-four' (12 × 2 = 24).

- Say: **The twelve number sentences make up what we call the '2 times table'.** Explain that it is important for the children to eventually learn these facts off by heart. Say: **Knowing multiplication facts will help you to work quickly through the steps involved when problem solving.**

- Say: **I am going to call out 2 times table questions and I want you to use the facts on the board to answer them.** Explain that you will use different words to describe multiplication.

- Ask questions: **What is 4 times 2?** (8) **What is 2 multiplied by 6?** (12) **What is 8 lots of 2?** (16) **What do 12 groups of 2 make?** (24)

- Draw a space hopper at 0 on the number line. Say: **The space hopper is going to travel from 0 to 8 in jumps of two. How many jumps will it take to reach 8?** Mark out jumps of two from 0 to 8. Ask: **How many jumps did it take?** (4) **Were you right?**

- Say: **We know that four jumps of two from zero will reach 8.** Choose a child to write this as a multiplication on the board. Expect: 4 × 2 = 8.

- Say: **We can think of this set of jumps in a different way. How many jumps of two did it take the space hopper to move from 0 to 8?** (4) Say: **This means that if we split the distance from 0 to 8 into four equal lengths, then each length will be 2 units. This is the same as saying that 8 divided by 4 is 2.** Explain that the phrase 'divided by' means to take a group of things and split them into equal groups. Introduce the word 'division'. Say: **When we divide objects into equal groups we call this division.**

- Write on the board: 8 ÷ 4 = 2. Point to the division sign. Say: **This is the sign for division. We read this number sentence as 8 divided by 4 equals 2.**
- Point to the four jumps of 2 on the number line. Say: **We can think of division in different ways. We have found that eight can be divided into four groups of two. But we could also think of this division as finding out how many groups of two there are in eight.**

Teaching Activity 2a (10 minutes)

Recall and use multiplication and division facts for the 5 multiplication table

- Arrange counters in 12 rows of 5. Lead a count in 5s and write multiplication facts alongside each row of 5 counters: 1 × 5 = 5, 2 × 5 = 10 ...12 × 5 = 60. Say: **The twelve multiplication sentences make up what we call the '5 times table'.** Remind the children that it is important to eventually learn these facts off by heart.
- Call out 5 times table questions for the children to answer, for example: **What is six times 5?** (30) **What is 5 multiplied by 8?** (40) **What is 12 lots of 5?** (60).
- Arrange beads in six groups of five and write a multiplication sentence to describe the arrangement. (6 × 5 = 30) Share the beads between six children and write a number sentence to describe the division. (30 ÷ 6 = 5) Remove the beads in groups of five, one group at a time, and discuss how the division can also be interpreted as '30 shared into equal groups of five makes six groups'.

Teaching Activity 2b (10 minutes)

Recall and use multiplication and division facts for the 5 multiplication table

- Continue the multiplication and division activities above for the 5 multiplication table. Lead a count in 5s along the number line from 0 to 60 and write the corresponding multiplication facts below: 1 × 5 = 5, 2 × 5 = 10 ...12 × 5 = 60. Say: **The twelve number sentences form what we call the '5 times table'.** Remind the children that it is important to eventually learn these facts off by heart. Call out questions about the 5 times table for the children to answer, for example: **What is six times 5?** (30) **What is 5 multiplied by 8?** (40) **What is 12 lots of 5?** (60).
- Draw a space hopper at 0 on the number line. Say: **The space hopper is going to travel from 0 to 35 in jumps of five. How many jumps will it take to reach 35?**. Mark out jumps of five from 0 to 35. Ask: **How many jumps did it take?** (7) **Were you right?**
- Say: **We know that seven jumps of five make thirty-five.** Choose a child to write this as a multiplication on the board. Expect: 7 × 5 = 35.
- Say: **We can think of this set of jumps in a different way How many jumps of five did it take the space hopper to move from 0 to 35?** (7) Say: **This means that if we split the distance from 0 to 35 into seven equal lengths then each length would be 5 units. This is the same as saying that 35 divided by 7 is 5.** Write on the board: 35 ÷ 7 = 5. Ask the children to 'read' the division sentence (35 divided by 7 equals 5).

Teaching Activity 3a (10 minutes)

Recall and use multiplication and division facts for the 10 multiplication table

- Arrange counters in 12 rows of 10. Lead a count in 10s and write multiplication facts alongside each row of 10 counters: 1 × 10 = 10, 2 × 10 = 20 ...12 × 10 = 120. Say: **The twelve number sentences make up what we call the '10 times table'.** Remind the children that it is important to eventually learn these facts off by heart. Call out 10 times table questions for the children to answer, for example: **What is seven times 10?** (70) **What is 10 multiplied by 3?** (30) **What is 12 lots of 10?** (120)
- Arrange beads in four groups of ten and write a multiplication sentence to describe the arrangement. (4 × 10 = 40) Share the beads between four children and write a number sentence to describe the division. (40 ÷ 4 = 10) Remove the beads in groups of ten, one group at a time, and discuss how the division can also be interpreted as '40 shared into equal groups of ten makes four groups'.

Teaching Activity 3b (10 minutes)

Recall and use multiplication and division facts for the 2 multiplication table

- Lead a count in 10s along the number line from 0 to 120 and write the corresponding multiplication facts below: 1 × 10 = 10, 2 × 10 = 20 ...12 × 10 = 120. Say: **The twelve number sentences form what we call the '10 times table'.** Remind the children that it is important to eventually learn these facts off by heart. Call out 10 times table questions for the children to answer, for example: **What is eight times 10?** (80) **What is 10 multiplied by 11?** (110) **What is 9 lots of 10?** (90).

- Draw a space hopper at 0 on the number line. Say: **The space hopper is going to travel from 0 to 80 in jumps of ten. How many jumps will it take to reach 80?** Mark out jumps of ten from 0 to 80. Ask: **How many jumps did it take?** (8) **Were you right?**

- Say: **We know that eight jumps of ten make eighty.** Choose a child to write this as a multiplication on the board. Expect: 8 × 10 = 80.

- Say: **We can think of the jumps in a different way. How many jumps of ten did it take the space hopper to move from 0 to 80?** (8) Say: **This means that if we split the distance from 0 to 80 into eight equal lengths, then each length will be 10 units. This is the same as saying that 80 divided by 8 is 10.** On the board, write: 80 ÷ 8 = 10. Ask the children to 'read' the division sentence (80 divided by 8 equals 10).

Teaching Activity 4a (10 minutes)

Recognise odd and even numbers

- Write a definition of each type of number on the baord: 'An even number is a number that can be divided evenly into groups of two', 'An odd number is a number that *cannot* be divided evenly into groups of two'

- Ask the children to work in pairs and give each group a tray of cubes. Allocate a number to each group, for example: 11, 16, 9, 14, 19, 18.

- Say: **You are going to find out whether the number you have is odd or even.** Explain to the children that are going to count out the number of cubes, then work out whether the cubes can be divided evenly into groups of two.

- Give the children time to work on the problem. When all the groups have finished, say: **Put your hand up if you were able to divide your cubes evenly into equal groups of two cubes.** Confirm the groups that were able to do so. Ask: **Which number did you have? Is this number odd or even?** (even) **Write all the even numbers on the board.** (14, 16, 18)

- Say: **Put your hand up if you were not able to divide your cubes evenly into equal groups of two cubes**. Confirm the groups that were not able to do so. Ask: **Which number did you have? Is this number odd or even?** (odd) **Write all the odd numbers on the board.** (9, 11, 19)

- Repeat for a different set of numbers, for example: 20, 13, 17, 12, 15. Write the even numbers on the board (12, 20) then the odd numbers (13, 15, 17).

- Ask: **What do you notice about the ones digit of the even numbers?** (the digits are either 0, 2, 4, 6 or 8) Explain that any number that is a multiple of 2, or has a ones digit of 0, 2, 4, 6 or 8, is an even number. Ask: **What do you notice about the ones digit of the odd numbers?** (the digits are either 1, 3, 5, 7 or 9) Explain that any number that has a ones digit of 1, 3, 5, 7 or 9 is an odd number.

- Point to the number square and ask the children to identify numbers as odd or even, explaining how they know.

- Play a 'secret number' game using clues of the following types: **I am thinking of the greatest even number between 39 and 49. What is it?** (48) **I am thinking of the smallest odd number between 90 and 100. What is it?** (91)

Teaching Activity 4b (10 minutes)

Recognise odd and even numbers

- Attach a number square to the board. Choose a child to come to the board and count from zero in twos. Ask them to colour every multiple of two up to 50 red.

- Ask: **What do all of these numbers have in common?** (they are all multiples of 2) **What do you notice about the ones digit of the numbers?** (the digits are either 0, 2, 4, 6 or 8)

- Say: **The numbers have something else in common, they are all even numbers.** Explain that any number that is a multiple of 2, or has a ones digit of 0, 2, 4, 6 or 8, is also an even number.

- Ask: **What do you think will be the next even number in the sequence?** (52) Point to 57 and say: **Is this an even number?** (no) **Why not?** (it does not have a ones digit of 0, 2, 4, 6 or 8)

- Choose a child to come to the board and count from 1 in twos. Ask them to colour every number in the sequence red: 1, 3, 5, 7, 9, 11 …49.

- Ask: **What do you notice about the ones digit of the numbers?** (the digits are either 1, 3, 5, 7 or 9) Say: **The numbers have something else in common, they are all odd numbers. Explain that any number with a ones digit of 1, 3, 5, 7 or 9 is also an odd number. Ask: What do you think will be the next even number in the sequence?** (51)

- Point to the number square and ask the children to identify numbers as odd or even, explaining how they know.

- Play a 'secret number' game using clues of the following types: **I am thinking of the greatest even number between 39 and 49. What is it?** (48) **or I am thinking of the smallest odd number between 90 and 100. What is it?** (91)

Unit 13: Calculate mathematical statements for multiplication and division within the multiplication tables and write them using the multiplication (×), division (÷) and equals (=) signs

Content domain reference: 2C7

Prerequisites for learning

Recognise and write number facts using the symbols ×, ÷ and =

Understand the concept of sharing

Be able to count in 2s, 5s and 10s

Learning outcomes

Calculate and write mathematical statements for multiplication and division using the correct signs

Key vocabulary

multiply, multiple, multiplication table, times table, divide, share, number fact

Resources

sets of natural objects, such as pine cones, stones or feathers, beads and strings

Background knowledge

- Before the lesson, ask the children to model a basic multiplication fact as an array using counters. Check that they know how to line up the counters in straight rows and that their model is constructed accurately. For example, 8 × 2 would be 8 rows of 2 (rows go from left to right so there would be 2 counters in each row across and 8 counters in each row going down).
- The children need to be able to construct their arrays accurately and use it to say or write the multiplication fact that it models.

Teaching Activity 1a (15 minutes)

Calculate mathematical statements for multiplication and division within the multiplication tables and write them using the multiplication (×), division (÷) and equals (=) signs

- Gather a collection of natural objects such as pine cones, stones or feathers. Say: **We are going to use these objects to make arrays — sets of objects that are arranged in rows and columns**.
- Choose a set of objects, for example, pine cones. Place the cones in 6 rows of 2. Ask: **How many cones are there?** (12) **How did you work this out?**

- Ask the children to explain how they calculated the total. Say: **We could count the cones individually, but this would take a lot of time. Another method would be count in 2s.** Point to one row at a time and count in 2s: 2, 4, 6, 8, 10, 12. Ask: **What would be a quicker method?** Praise any child who suggests using multiplication. Remind the children that multiplication is a quick method for adding equal sets.
- Ask: **Who can come to the board and write a multiplication that would help us calculate the number of pine cones?** Choose a child to write the multiplication. Expect: 6 × 2.
- Ask: **How do we read this sentence?** (six times two) Say: **We must work out what is six times or two or six lots of two. What is the answer?** (12) Write on the board: 6 × 2 = 12.
- Say: **Let's continue to work with the 2 times table but this time, using number facts to solve a division problem.**

- Write the division sign (÷) on the board. Ask: **Who can remember what this sign is?** (division sign) Remind the children that we use the sign when we want to write a number sentence that describes dividing a set of objects into equal sets.

- Arrange two strings and two beads. Say: **If I were to share the beads equally between the two strings, how many beads would there be on each string?** (1) Choose a child to demonstrate the sharing. Say: **Two beads divided between two strings means that there will be one bead on each string. In other words, two shared between two is one each.**

- Write the division fact: $2 \div 2 = 1$ on the board. Choose a child to read the fact. (two divided by two is one)

- Arrange two strings and four beads. Say: **If I were to share the beads equally between the two strings, how many beads would there be on each string?** (2) Choose a child to demonstrate the sharing. Say: **Four beads divided between two strings means that there will be two beads on each string. In other words, four shared between two is two each.**

- Write the division fact: $4 \div 2 = 2$ on the board. Choose a child to read the fact. (four divided by two is two)

- Repeat the above bead division activities for 6, 8, 10, 12, 14, 16, 18, 20, 22 and 24 beads, dividing the beads between the two strings. Write the division fact for each bead model on the board and ask the children to read the fact ($6 \div 2 = 3$, $8 \div 2 = 4$ …$24 \div 2 = 12$)

Teaching Activity 1b (25 minutes)

Calculate mathematical statements for multiplication and division within the multiplication tables and write them using the multiplication (×), division (÷) and equals (=) signs

- Say: **We are going to write multiplication sentences to describe amounts of money.**

- Place five 10p coins on the table. Ask: **How many coins do we have?** (5) **What is the value of each coin?** (10 pence) **How much money do we have altogether?** (50p) **How did you work this out?**

- Ask the children to explain how they calculated the total amount. Say: **We could find the total amount by counting in 10s.** Point to one coin at a time and count the combined value in 10s: 10p, 20p, 30p, 40p, 50p. Ask: **What would be a quicker method?** Praise any child who suggests using multiplication.

- Ask: **Who can come to the board and write a multiplication that would help us calculate how much the coins are worth?** Choose a child to write the multiplication. Expect: 5 × 10p. Ask: **How do we read this sentence?** (five times ten pence) Say: **We must work out what is five times ten pence or five lots of ten pence. What is the answer?** (50p) Complete the multiplication: $5 \times 10p = 50p$.

- Say: **Let's continue to work with the 10 times table but this time, using number facts to solve a division problem.**

- Place 10 books beside a bookshelf with 10 shelves. Say: **If I were to share the books equally between the 10 shelves, how many books would there be on each shelf?** (1) Choose a child to demonstrate the sharing. Say: **10 books divided between 10 shelves means that there will be one book on each shelf. In other words, 10 shared between 10 is one each.**

- Write the division fact: $10 \div 10 = 1$ on the board. Choose a child to read the fact. (10 divided by 10 is one)

- Place 20 books beside the 10 shelves. Say: **If I were to share the books equally between the ten shelves, how many books would there be on each shelf?** (2) Choose a child to demonstrate the sharing.

- Say: **20 books divided between 20 shelves means that there will be two books on each shelf. In other words, 20 shared between 10 is two each.**

- Write the division fact: $20 \div 10 = 2$ on the board. Choose a child to read the fact. (20 divided by 10 is two)

- Repeat the above books sharing activities for 30 and 40, dividing the books between the two shelves. Write the division fact for each book model on the board and ask the children to read the fact ($30 \div 10 = 3$, $40 \div 10 = 4$).

Unit 14: Show that multiplication of two numbers can be done in any order (commutative) and division of one number by another cannot

Content domain reference: 2C9b

Prerequisites for learning

Recognise and write number facts using the symbols x, ÷ and =

Be familiar with the concept of arrays

Know multiplication and related division facts for the 2, 5 and 10 multiplication tables

Key vocabulary

array, multiply, multiple, multiplication table, times table, divide, share, number fact, does not equal

Resources

counters; card

Learning outcomes

Show that multiplication of 2 numbers can be done in any order (commutative) and division of 1 number by another cannot

Background knowledge

- Some children may hold the notion that division is commutative, for example, that 4 ÷ 2 is equal to 2 ÷ 4, despite being taught otherwise. The misconception that division sentences always involve the smallest number dividing into the largest, and confusion of how to read division sentences, tend to contribute to this.

Teaching Activity 1a (15 minutes)

Show that multiplication of 2 numbers can be done in any order (commutative) and division of 1 number by another cannot

- Say: **We are going to arrange counters in rows and columns to describe a multiplication sentence.**

- Give pairs of children a tray of counters and a large piece of card. Say: **On your piece of card, arrange the counters in five rows of two counters.** Ask: **How many counters are in each row?** (2) **How many rows are there?** (5) **How many counters are there in total?** (10) Choose children to describe how they worked out the answer.

- Say: **Who can tell me the multiplication sentence that describes this array?** (5 times/lots of/groups of 2 equals/makes 10 or 2 multiplied by 5 equals/makes 10)

- Choose a child to write the multiplication sentence described by the array. (5 × 2 = 10)

- Say: **I want you to turn your card a quarter turn to the right or left.**

- Ask: **How many counters are in each row now?** (5) **How many rows are there?** (2) **Has the number of counters changed?** (no) Say: **We now have two rows of five counters. Since the number of counters has not changed, there must still be 10 counters.**

- Ask: **Who can come to the board to write a multiplication sentence described by this array?** Choose a child to write the sentence. Expect: 2 × 5 = 10.

- Point to both multiplication sentences: 5 × 2 = 10 and 2 × 5 = 10. Ask: **What do you notice about both multiplication facts?** Accept answers. Explain to the class that, like addition, multiplication can be done in any order.

- Repeat the above activity for a different multiplication, for example, 4 × 10 = 40.

- Give the children mini whiteboards and ask them to arrange counters in four rows of ten on card.

- Choose a child to write the multiplication sentence described by the array. (4 × 10 = 40)

- Ask the children to turn the card a quarter turn and write the multiplication sentence described by the array. (10 × 4 = 40) Say: **Since multiplication can be done in any order, 4 × 10 gives the same answer as 10 × 4. That is 40.**

- Point to the 40 counters arranged in 10 rows of 4. Ask: **Who can tell me a division sentence that is described by this array?** Choose a child to write the division sentence on the board. (40 ÷ 10 = 4)

- Say: **We know multiplication can be done in any order. Let's find out if that is true for division.**

- Point to the number sentence: 40 ÷ 10 = 4. Underneath, write the division calculation: 10 ÷ 40. Say: **The numbers in the division problem have swapped places. Does 10 divided by 40 give the same answer as 40 divided by 10?** Give the children time to discuss the question, then accept answers. Establish that we cannot divide 10 by 40 and get a whole number.

- Write on the board: 40 ÷ 10 does not equal 0 ÷ 40. Say: **Whereas addition and multiplication can be done in any order, division, like subtraction, cannot be done in any order.**

Teaching Activity 1b (15 minutes)

Show that multiplication of 2 numbers can be done in any order (commutative) and division of 1 number by another cannot

- Say: **We are going to create picture models to help us solve multiplication and division problems.**

- Write on the board: **The waiter in a restaurant needs to place 5 plates on each of 7 tables in a restaurant. How many plates is that in total?**

- Ask: **What sort of problem is this, multiplication or division?** (multiplication) **How do you know?** (we need to multiply the number of plates by the number of tables)

- Ask the children to work in pairs and draw a picture that will solve this problem. Say: **Think about the symbol you could use to represent a plate and how the symbols should be arranged to describe the multiplication. What would be a good picture model for this problem?**

- Establish that a good model is to draw plates arranged in rows and columns.

- Ask a child to draw an array that describes the multiplication. Expect: 7 rows of 5 circles where each circle represents one plate. Ask: **How many plates is that?** (35)

- Say: **Who can tell me the multiplication that describes this array?** (7 times/lots of/groups of 5)

- Choose a child to come to the board to write the multiplication sentence described by the array (7 × 5 = 35) Say: **We know that 7 times 5 is 35.**

- Write on the board: **The next day, the same waiter must place 7 plates on each of 5 tables in the restaurant. How many plates is that in total?**

- Choose a child to come to the board to draw an array that describes the multiplication. Expect: 5 rows of 7 circles where each circle represents one plate. Ask: **How many plates is that?** (35) Ask children to explain how they worked out the answer.

- Say: **Who can tell me the multiplication that describes this array?** (5 times/lots of/groups of 7)

- Choose a child to come to the board to write the multiplication sentence described by the array (5 × 7 = 35) Say: **We know that 5 times 7 is 35.**

- Point to both multiplication sentences: 7 × 5 = 35 and 5 × 7 = 35. Ask: **What do you notice about both multiplication facts?**

- Explain to the class that, like addition, multiplication can be done in any order. Say: **It doesn't matter whether we decide to multiply 5 by 7 or 7 by 5, the answer will still be the same. That is 35.**

- Point to the drawing that represents 35 plates arranged in 5 rows of 7. Ask: **Who can tell me a division sentence that describes this array?** Choose a child to write the division sentence on the board. (35 ÷ 5 = 7)

- Say: **We know multiplication can be done in any order. Let's find out if that is true for division.**

- Point to the number sentence: 35 ÷ 5 = 7. Underneath, write the division calculation: 5 ÷ 35. Say: **The numbers in the division problem have swapped places. Does 5 divided by 35 give the same answer as 35 divided by 5?** Give the children time to discuss the question then accept answers. Establish that we cannot divide 5 by 35 and get a whole number.

- On the board, write: 35 ÷ 5 does not equal 5 ÷ 35. Say: **Whereas addition and multiplication can be done in any order, division, like subtraction, cannot be done in any order.**

Unit 15: Solve problems involving multiplication and division, using materials, arrays, repeated addition, mental methods, and multiplication and division facts, including problems in contexts

Content domain reference: 2C8

Prerequisites for learning

Recognise and write number facts using the symbols x, ÷ and =

Be familiar with the concept of arrays

Know multiplication and related division facts for the 2, 5 and 10 multiplication tables

Learning outcomes

Solve problems involving multiplication and division, using materials, arrays, repeated addition, mental methods, and multiplication and division facts, including problems in contexts

Key vocabulary

array, multiply, multiple, multiplication table, times table, divide, share, number fact

Resources

Resource 3: Multiplication and division problems (1); Resource 4: Multiplication and division problems (2)

Background knowledge

- In order to solve number problems effectively, children need to be taught specific strategies. They also need to be taught to identify keywords that provide clues to what a problem is asking them to do and to select relevant information. Providing guided examples of how to construct a pictorial model to describe a word problem will also prove effective in developing competency in problem-solving.

Teaching Activity 1a (25 minutes)

Solve problems involving multiplication and division, using materials, arrays, repeated addition, mental methods, and multiplication and division facts, including problems in contexts

- Write on the board: 'repeated addition and subtraction', 'arrays', 'mental methods' and 'number facts'.
- Display **Resource sheet 3: Multiplication and division problems (1)**. Split the children into four equal groups and name the groups according to the methods on the board. Discuss the different methods as follows:
  - **Repeated addition:** Read out Problem 1. Ask: **Is this a multiplication or division problem?** (multiplication) **How do you know?** (we need to find 6 lots of 10p) Say: **If I were to solve this problem by adding one 10p at a time, up to six 10ps, how would I write this as an addition problem?** Choose a child to come to the board and write and solve the problem as a repeated addition. Expect: 10p + 10p + 10p + 10p + 10p + 10p = 60p.
  - **Arrays:** Read out Problem 3. Say: **You will remember from Unit 14 that arrays, objects arranged in rows and columns, can be used to help solve multiplication problems.** Ask: **Who can come to the board and draw an array that will help us solve this problem?** Ask a child to the board to draw a visual model of the problem. Expect: Two rows of ten pictures. Ask the children to explain how they would use the diagram to work out the total number of seeds, for example, counting in 2s or 10s.

    Look at Problem 2. Ask: **How would you use an array to solve this problem?** Establish that the problem could be solved by drawing rows of 5 symbols, representing the flowers in one bunch, until 20 flowers are drawn. The number of bunches can be found by counting the number of rows.
  - **Mental methods:** Remind the children of Problem 1. Ask: **How would you work out this problem in your head?** Establish that the calculation involves an easy multiplication. (6 times 10 is 60) Ask: **What is the answer?** (60p)

Remind the children of Problem 2. Ask: **How would you work out this problem in your head?** Establish that the calculation involves a division. (20 divided by 5 is 4) Ask: **What is the answer?** (4 bunches)

* **Number facts:** Refer to the problems discussed in the previous 'Mental methods' section. Say: **For both calculations knowing multiplication and division facts off by heart will mean that problems can be solved quickly.** Refer to Problem 1. Ask: **Knowing which multiplication fact will help to solve the problem?** (6 × 10 = 60) Refer to Problem 2. Ask: **Knowing which division fact will help to solve the problem?** (20 ÷ 5 = 4)

• Ask the children, in each group, to solve problems 4 and 5 using the method they have been allocated. Once the groups have worked on both problems, bring them together to confirm the answers. Ask each group in turn to choose a problem and demonstrate the solution.

• Swap the children around so that they are in different groups. Ask each group to solve problems 6 and 7 using the method they have been allocated. Once the groups have worked on both problems, bring them together to confirm the answers. Ask each group in turn to choose a problem and demonstrate the solution.

Teaching Activity 1b (15 minutes)

Solve problems involving multiplication and division, using materials, arrays, repeated addition, mental methods, and multiplication and division facts, including problems in contexts

• Write on the board: 'repeated addition and subtraction', 'arrays', 'mental methods' and 'number facts'. Display **Resource 4: Multiplication and division problems (2)**.

• Split the children into four equal groups and name the groups according to the methods on the board. Discuss the different methods as follows:

* **Repeated addition:** Read out Problem 1. Ask: **Is this a multiplication or division problem?** (multiplication) **How do you know?** (we need to find 6 lots of 5 minutes) Say: **If I were to solve this problem by adding one lot of 5 minutes at a time, up to six lots of 5 minutes, how would I write this as an addition problem?** Choose a child to come to the board and write and solve the problem as a repeated addition. Expect: 5 min + 5 min + 5 min + 5 min + 5 min + 5 min = 30 minutes.

* **Arrays:** Read out Problem 3. Say: **You will remember from Unit 14 that arrays, objects arranged in rows and columns, can be used to help solve multiplication problems.** Ask: **Who can come to the board and draw an array that will help us solve this problem?** Ask a child to the board to draw a visual model of the problem. Expect: Two rows of ten pictures. Ask the children to explain how they would use the diagram to work out the total number of owls, for example, counting in 2s or 10s.

* Remind the children of Problem 2. Ask: **How would you use an array to solve this problem?** Accept the children's ideas. Establish that the problem could be solved by drawing rows of 2 symbols, representing the two heads of one alien, until 16 heads are drawn. The number of aliens can be found by counting the number of rows.

* **Mental methods:** Remind the children of Problem 1. Ask: **How would you work out this problem in your head?** Establish that the calculation involves an easy multiplication. (6 times 5 is 30) **What is the answer?** (30 minutes) Remind the children of Problem 2. Ask: **How would you work out this problem in your head?** Establish that the calculation involves a division. (16 divided by 2 is 8) **What is the answer?** (8 aliens)

* **Number facts:** Refer to the problems discussed in the previous 'Mental methods' section. Say: **For both calculations, knowing multiplication and division facts off by heart will mean that problems can be solved quickly.** Refer to Problem 1. Ask: **Knowing which multiplication fact will help to solve the problem?** (6 × 10 = 60) Refer to Problem 2. Ask: **Knowing which division fact will help to solve the problem?** (16 ÷ 2 = 8) Ask the children in each group to solve problems 4 and 5 using the method they have been allocated. Once the groups have worked on both problems, bring them together to confirm the answers. Ask each group in turn to choose a problem and demonstrate the solution.

• Swap the children around so that they are in different groups. Ask each group to solve problems 6 and 7 using the method they have been allocated. Once the groups have worked on both problems, bring them together to confirm the answers. Ask each group in turn to choose a problem and demonstrate the solution.

Unit 16: Recognise, find, name and write fractions $\frac{1}{3}$, $\frac{1}{4}$, $\frac{2}{4}$ and $\frac{3}{4}$ of a length, shape, set of objects or quantity

Content domain reference: 2F1a

Prerequisites for learning

Know that a fraction is part of a whole

Recognise, find and name a half as 1 of 2 equal parts of an object, shape or quantity

Recognise, find and name a quarter as 1 of 4 equal parts of an object, shape or quantity

Learning outcomes

Recognise, find, name and write fractions $\frac{1}{3}$, $\frac{1}{4}$, $\frac{2}{4}$ and $\frac{3}{4}$ of a shape

Recognise, find, name and write fractions $\frac{1}{3}$, $\frac{1}{4}$, $\frac{2}{4}$ and $\frac{3}{4}$ of a length

Recognise, find, name and write fractions $\frac{1}{3}$, $\frac{1}{4}$, $\frac{2}{4}$ and $\frac{3}{4}$ of a set of objects or quantity

Key vocabulary

part, whole, fraction, half, halves, quarter, third

Resources

paper squares; paper squares marked with lines to divide them into thirds; circular fraction tiles; 40 cm and 60 cm strips of paper; 30 cm strips marked in thirds; circular fraction tiles; paper circles, beads, small cloth bag

Background knowledge

- Throughout this unit, reinforce the meaning of a fraction as part of a whole. Emphasise that the part-whole nature of fractions can be applied to a whole that is a single unit, for example, a pizza; or a group of objects, for example, a tray of cupcakes.

- When teaching fractions of quantities and measures, explain that units of measurement can be ignored until the answer is recorded.

Teaching Activity 1a (20 minutes)

Recognise, find, name and write fractions $\frac{1}{3}$, $\frac{1}{4}$, $\frac{2}{4}$ and $\frac{3}{4}$ of a shape

- Say: **Who can remember what a fraction is?** Remind the children that a fraction is a part of a whole. Give the children paper squares. Say: **Fold your square in half.** Choose children to demonstrate how they folded the paper in half. Check that they know the square has been divided into two halves by asking them to point to the halves of the square. Ask: **How do you know the square has been divided into half?** (the paper is folded into two-equal sized pieces)

- Write 'half' and '$\frac{1}{2}$' on the board. Point to the word and the number and say: **We can write the fraction 'one half' as a word and as a number**. Point to '$\frac{1}{2}$'. Ask: **Who can tell me why we write the fraction like this?**

- Establish that a fraction in numerals is written as two numbers, a top and a bottom number separated by a bar. Point to 2. Say: **The bottom number tells us how many equal parts a whole has been divided into, in this case, two equal parts.** Point to 1. Say: **The top number tells us how many parts we are interested in, in this case, only one part (we are thinking about one half not two halves).**

- Using another square, demonstrate how to fold it into quarters. Use a pencil and ruler to mark the fold lines. Ask: **How many equal pieces has this shape been folded into?** (4) **Who can tell me what each of these four equal pieces is called?** (a quarter) Give out paper squares and ask children to fold them into quarters. Check they are able to fold the shape in half then half again.

- Write 'quarter' and '$\frac{1}{4}$' on the board. Point to the word and the number and say: **We can write the fraction 'one quarter' as a word and as a number**. Point to '$\frac{1}{4}$'. Ask: **Who can tell me why we write a quarter like this?**

- Point to 4. Say: **The bottom number tells us how many equal parts a whole has been divided into, in this case four equal parts.** Point to 1.

Say: **The top number tells us how many parts we are interested in, in this case, only one part (we are thinking about one quarter not two, three or four quarters).**

- On the board, write 'three quarters' and '$\frac{3}{4}$'. Point to the word and the number and say: **We can write the fraction three quarters as a word and as a number.** Point to '$\frac{3}{4}$'. Ask: **Who can tell me why we write three quarters like this?** Point to 4. Say: **The bottom number tells us how many equal parts a whole has been divided into, in this case four equal parts.** Point to 3. Say: **The top number tells us how many parts there are, in this case three parts (we are thinking about three quarters not one, two or four quarters).**

- Fold another paper square into quarters, mark the fold lines and then cut the shape in half. Ask: **How many quarters is this?** (2) Write 'Two quarters' on the board. Ask: **Who can come to the board and write this number as a fraction in numerals?** Ask a child to the board. Expect: $\frac{2}{4}$. Ask: **Who can tell me why we write two quarters like this?** Point to 4. Say: **The bottom number tells us how many equal parts a whole has been divided into, in this case four equal parts.** Point to 2. Say: **The top number tells us how many parts there are, in this case two parts (we are thinking about two quarters not one, three or four quarters).**

- Remind the children that when we talk about fractions, we are thinking about equal parts of a whole. Divide a paper square into three equal parts. Hold up the shape and fold along the marked lines. Open up the shape. Ask: **How many equal pieces are there?** (3) Say: **How would I prove that all the pieces are equal in size?** Establish that we could cut along the lines and overlap the three strips to confirm they are the same size. Cut out and compare the shapes.

- Say: **The square has been divided into three equal parts. What fraction do we use to describe three equal parts of a whole?** Praise any child that says 'thirds'.

- Take one third of the square and attach it to the board. Write 'one third' and '$\frac{1}{3}$'.

Teaching Activity 1b (20 minutes)

Recognise, find, name and write fractions $\frac{1}{3}$, $\frac{1}{4}$, $\frac{2}{4}$ and $\frac{3}{4}$ of a shape

- Say: **Who can remember what a fraction is?** Remind the children that a fraction is a part of a whole.

- Give a pair of children a tray of circular fraction tiles. Say: **Join two halves to make a whole**

circle. Choose a group to demonstrate how they combine two halves to make a whole circle. Check that they know the circle has been divided into two halves by asking them to point to one half of the square and then the other half.

- Ask: **How do you know each piece is a half?** Ask a pair to demonstrate. Expect them to place one half on top of the other. Confirm that the pieces are of equal size. Say: **As fractions are equal parts of a whole, we must be sure that the two parts we consider to be halves are of equal size.**

- Write 'half' and '$\frac{1}{2}$' on the board. Point to the word and the number and say: **We can write the fraction half as a word and as a number.** Point to '$\frac{1}{2}$'. Ask: **Who can tell me why we write one half like this?** Establish that a fraction written in numerals is two numbers, a top and a bottom number separated by a bar.

- Point to 2. Say: **The bottom number tells us how many equal parts a whole has been divided into, in this case two equal parts.** Point to 1. Say: **The top number tells us how many parts we are interested in, in this case one part (we are only thinking about one half not two halves).**

- Say: **Using fraction tiles, make a whole circle from four equal parts.** Choose a pair to demonstrate how they achieve this. Ask: **How many equal pieces is the circle made from?** (4) **Who can tell me what each of these four equal pieces is called?** (a quarter)

- Write 'quarter' and '$\frac{1}{4}$' on the board. Point to the word and the number and say: **We can write the fraction quarter as a word and as a number.** Point to '$\frac{1}{4}$'. Ask: **Who can tell me why we write a quarter like this?** Point to 4. Say: **The bottom number tells us how many equal parts a whole has been divided into, in this case, four equal parts.** Point to 1. Say: **The top number tells us how many parts we are interested in, in this case one part (we are thinking about one quarter not two, three or four quarters).**

- Write 'three quarters' and '$\frac{3}{4}$' on the board. Point to the word and the number and say: **We can write the fraction three quarters as a word and as a number.** Point to '$\frac{3}{4}$'. Ask: **Who can tell me why we write three quarters like this?**

- Point to 4. Say: **The bottom number tells us how many equal parts a whole has been divided into, in this case four equal parts.** Point to 3. Say: **The top number tells us how many parts we are interested in, in this case three parts (we are thinking about three quarters not one, two or four parts).**

- Say: **Now use your fraction tiles to make three quarters of a circle. How many pieces did you need?** (3) **What fraction is each piece?** (a quarter) Say: **We have looked at two fractions that involve quarters, one quarter and three quarters. Are there any other fractions that can be made from quarters?** (two quarters and four quarters) Say: **If we were to put four quarter pieces together, what would we get?** (one whole circle)

- On the board, write: $\frac{4}{4}$. Say: **This is the fraction four quarters, equivalent to one whole circle.** Ask: **What fraction would we get if we changed the top number from a 4 to a 2?** (two quarters) Ask the children to use the tiles to model 'two quarters'.

- Say: **Look at your fraction tiles. Is it possible to make a whole from three equal parts?** Choose a child to demonstrate how a circle can be formed from three equal parts.

- Ask: **Does anyone know what we call a shape or object that has been divided into three equal-sized pieces?** Praise any child that says 'thirds'. Ask: **How many of these pieces would be one third of a circle?** (1) Ask the children to hold up one third of the circle.

- Take one third of a paper circle and attach it to the board. Write 'one third' and '$\frac{1}{3}$'.

Teaching Activity 2a (20 minutes)

Recognise, find, name and write fractions $\frac{1}{3}$, $\frac{1}{4}$, $\frac{2}{4}$ and $\frac{3}{4}$ of a set of objects or quantity

- Choose two children to stand in front of the group. Present them with a tray of 10 beads and ask the group how the beads could be shared equally between the two children.

- Ask a third child to stand up and share the beads equally between the children. Ask: **How many beads does each child get?** (5)

- Say: **We began with 10 beads, the whole amount. Then we divided the beads evenly between the two children so that each child received an equal part of the beads. What fraction would we use to describe each part?** (a half) Say: **Each child received half of the beads. That is 5 beads out of 10. So half of ten is five. Or, in other words, five is half of ten.**

- Choose four children to stand in front of the group. Present them with a tray of 12 beads and ask the group how the beads could be shared equally between the four children.

- Ask another child to stand up and share the beads equally between the children. Ask: **How many beads does each child get?** (3)

- Say: **We began with 12 beads, the whole amount. Then we divided the beads evenly between the four children so that each child received an equal part of the beads. What fraction would we use to describe one part out of four equal parts?** Prompt the children by reviewing the fraction that describes one equal part of a shape divided into four equal parts. (a quarter) Say: **Each child received a quarter of the beads, that is, 3 beads out of 12. So a quarter of 12 is 3. Or, in other words, three is a quarter of 12.**

- Establish that we find one quarter (5) and then multiply by three to find three quarters. (15)

- Choose three children to stand in front of the group. Present them with a tray of 9 beads and ask the group how the beads could be shared equally between the three children.

- Ask another child to stand up and share the beads equally between the children. Ask: **How many beads does each child get?** (3)

- Say: **We began with 9 beads, the whole amount. Then we divided the beads evenly between the three children so that each child received an equal part of the beads. What fraction would we use to describe one part out of three equal parts?** Prompt the children by reviewing the fraction that describes one equal part of a shape divided into three equal parts. (a third) Say: **Each child received a third of the beads. That is 3 beads out of 9. So a third of 9 is 3. Or, in other words, three is a third of 9.**

Teaching Activity 2b (20 minutes)

Recognise, find, name and write fractions $\frac{1}{3}$, $\frac{1}{4}$, $\frac{2}{4}$ and $\frac{3}{4}$ of a set of objects or quantity

- Draw two rows of five circles on the board. Say: **Each circle represents a cupcake. There are ten cupcakes in total. How could we split the cupcakes into two equal groups?** Ask a child to draw a circle around the cupcakes to divide them into groups. Ask: **How many cupcakes are in each group?** (5)

- Say: **The 10 cupcakes, the whole amount of cupcakes, is divided into two equal groups. What fraction would we use to describe each group?** (a half) Say: **Each group represents half of the cupcakes. That is 5 cupcakes out of 10. So half of ten is five. Or, in other words, five is half of ten.**

- Repeat with 16 cupcakes. Ask: **How many cupcakes are there in each group?** (8) **What fraction of the whole amount, 16 cupcakes, is 8 cupcakes?** (a half) **So what is half of 16?** (8)

- Draw three cupcakes on the board. Say: **This is one half of a set of cupcakes. How many would be in the whole set?** (6) **How do you know?** Prompt the children by asking them to complete the sentence: 'Because 3 is one half of …(6)'

- Draw on the board four rows of three circles. Say: **We have 12 cupcakes. How could we split the cupcakes into four equal groups?** Ask a child to come to the board and draw circles to divide the cupcakes into groups. Ask: **How many cupcakes are in each group?** (3)

- Say: **The 12 cupcakes, the whole amount of cupcakes, is divided into four equal groups. What fraction would we use to describe each group?** Prompt the children by reviewing the fraction that describes one equal part of a shape divided into four equal parts. (a quarter) Say: **Each group represents a quarter of the cupcakes. That is, 3 cupcakes out of 12. So a quarter of 12 is 3. Or, in other words, 3 is a quarter of 12.**

- Ask: **How would you find three quarters of the amount of cupcakes?** Establish that we find one quarter (5) and then multiply by three to find three quarters (15).

Teaching Activity 3a (15 minutes)

Recognise, find, name and write fractions $\frac{1}{3}$, $\frac{1}{4}$, $\frac{2}{4}$ and $\frac{3}{4}$ of a length

- Provide pairs of children with a 40 cm strip of paper. Explain that we can find a fraction of a length in a similar way to how we found a fraction of a number.

- Say: **We are going to find fractions of a 40 cm paper strip. Let's start by finding one half of the strip**. Fold the strip in half and choose a child to measure the length. Ask: **What is the length of half of the strip?** (20 cm) Say: **So one half of 40 is 20.**

- Say: **Now let's find the length of one quarter of the strip.** Ask the children to predict the length of the strip when folded into quarters. Fold the strip in quarters and choose a child to measure the length. Ask: **What is the length of half of the strip?** (10 cm) Say: **So one quarter of 40 is 10. Was your prediction correct?**

- Ask: **How would you find the length of three quarters of a strip?** Establish that we could fold the strip into quarters, unfold it and measure the distance from the edge of the strip to the three

quarters fold line. Fold the strip in quarters and choose a child to measure the length. Ask: **What is the length of three quarters of the strip?** (30 cm) Say: **So three quarters of 40 is 30.**

- Provide each group with a 30 cm strip previously marked in thirds. Say: **Now let's find the length of one third of the strip.** Ask the children to predict the length of the strip when folded into thirds. Fold the strip and choose a child to measure the length. Ask: **What is the length of a third of the strip?** (10 cm) Say: **So one third of 30 is 10. Was your prediction correct?**

Teaching Activity 3b (15 minutes)

Recognise, find, name and write fractions $\frac{1}{3}$, $\frac{1}{4}$, $\frac{2}{4}$ and $\frac{3}{4}$ of a length

- Provide pairs of children with a 60 cm strip of paper. Explain that we can find a fraction of a length in a similar way to how we found a fraction of a number.

- Say: **We are going to find fractions of a 60 cm paper strip. Let's start by finding one half of the strip.** Fold the strip in half and choose a child to measure the length. Ask: **What is the length of half of the strip?** (30 cm)

- Ask: **Is there an easier way to find one half of 60 centimetres?** Establish that, as double 30 is 60, we know that a half of 60 is 30. Say: **Instead of measuring we can calculate the answer.**

- Ask: **How would you find the length of one quarter of the strip?** Establish that we could fold the strip into quarters and measure the length of one quarter, but an easier way would be to calculate the answer.

- Choose a pair of children to state the answer and explain how they worked it out. (15 cm) Establish that one method is to halve 60 (30) and then halve again (15).

- Ask: **How would you find the length of one third of the strip?** Establish that calculating the answer is preferable to attempting to fold a strip of paper into thirds. Ask the children to calculate the answer. (20 cm) Say: **Since 6 divided by 3 is 2, it follows that the answer to 60 divided by three will be three times bigger. That is 20 cm.**

Unit 17: Write simple fractions, for example, $\frac{1}{2}$ of 6 = 3 and recognise the equivalence of $\frac{2}{4}$ and $\frac{1}{2}$

Content domain reference: 2F1b/2F2

Prerequisites for learning

Know that a fraction is part of a whole

Recognise, find, name and write $\frac{1}{3}$, $\frac{1}{4}$, $\frac{2}{4}$ and $\frac{3}{4}$ of a set of objects or quantity

Learning outcomes

Write simple fractions, for example, $\frac{1}{2}$ of 6 = 3

Recognise the equivalence of $\frac{2}{4}$ and $\frac{1}{2}$

Key vocabulary

part, whole, fraction, half, halves, quarter, third, equivalent fractions

Resources

identical sets of fruit (real or plastic); paper squares; circles and regular hexagons

Background knowledge

• Try to make extensive use of manipulatives when teaching fractions. The use of manipulatives is important in helping children construct mental images that enable them to perform fraction calculations meaningfully.

Teaching Activity 1a (15 minutes)

Write simple fractions, for example, $\frac{1}{2}$ of 6 = 3

• Draw three rows of 4 circles on the board. Say: **I have drawn a set of circles in rows and columns. Who can remember what we call this type of arrangement?** (an array)

• Ask: **How many rows are there?** (3) **How many columns?** (4) **How many circles are there in total?** (12) Discuss their strategies.

• Say: **You will remember that we can write multiplication and division facts to describe an array. Who can write a number fact to describe the array of 12 circles?** (Expect: 3 × 4 = 12, 4 × 3 = 12, 12 ÷ 4 = 3, 12 ÷ 3 = 4)

• Say: **Arrays can be used to help find fractions of amounts. Who can draw rings around the circles to divide them into two equal groups?** Choose a child to identify the two equal sets. Ask: **How many are in each set?** (6) **What fraction of the 12 circles does each set of 6 circles represent?** (a half) Say: **So we can say that a half of 12 is 6. Or, in other words, 6 is a half of 12.** Write on the board: $\frac{1}{2}$ of 12 = 6.

• Ask: **Is it possible to split the circles into four equal sets?** Ask a child to draw rings around the circles to divide them into four equal groups. Ask: **How many circles are there in each set?** (3) **What fraction of the 12 circles does each set of 3 circles represent?** (a quarter)

• Say: **We found that a set of 6 circles is a half of a set of 12 circles and wrote the fraction sentence, 'one half of 12 is 6'. Now we know that a set of 3 circles is a quarter of a set of 12 circles, how would we write this?** (one quarter of 12 is 3) Write: $\frac{1}{4}$ of 12 is 3.

• Give whiteboards to pairs of children and ask them to draw three rows of 4 circles. Say: **We found that one quarter of a set of 12 circles is 3 circles. How many circles would be in three quarters of the set? Draw a ring around the circles to show me three quarters of the set.**

• Confirm that three quarters of 12 circles is 9 circles. Demonstrate that three quarters of 12 circles can be found by combining three quarter sets (3 lots of 3 circles) together.

• Ask: **Is it possible to divide the circles into three equal groups?** Ask a child to draw rings around the circles to divide them into three equal groups. Ask: **How many circles are there in each set?** (4) **What fraction of the 12 circles does each set of 4 circles represent?** (a third)

• Say: **Give me a fraction sentence that has 12, 4 and a third in it.** (one third of 12 is 4) Write: $\frac{1}{3}$ of 12 is 4.

Teaching Activity 1b (15 minutes)

Write simple fractions, for example, $\frac{1}{2}$ of 6 = 3

- Say: **You will remember from Unit 16 that we found fractions of sets of objects or quantities by dividing them into equal groups.**

- Choose two children to stand in front of the group. Give each child a basket. Arrange a set of 12 identical fruit on the table, for example, apples, and ask the group how the apples could be shared equally between the two children.

- Ask a third child to stand up and share the apples equally between the children. Ask: **How many apples does each child get?** (6)

- Say: **We began with 12 apples, then we divided the apples evenly between the two children so that each child received an equal part. What fraction would we use to describe each part?** (a half) **Each child received half of the apples. So we can say that a half of 12 is 6. Or, in other words, 6 is a half of 12.** Write on the board: $\frac{1}{2}$ of 12 = 6.

- Place the apples back on the table. Ask: **Is it possible to split the 12 apples evenly between four children?** Ask four children to stand up and give each a basket and a fifth child to share the apples equally between the children. Ask: **How many apples does each child get?** (3)

- Write: $\frac{1}{4}$ of 12 = 3.

- Ask: **How many apples would there be in three quarters of a set of 12 apples?** Establish that, since we know a quarter of the set is 3, then three quarters of the set must be 9. Demonstrate this by asking three children each holding a quarter of the apples to stand together and count three sets of three apples. (9 apples)

- Place the apples back on the table. Ask: **Is it possible to split the 12 apples evenly between three children?** Ask three children to stand up and give each a basket and a fourth child to share the apples equally between the children. Ask: **How many apples does each child get?** (4)

- Write: $\frac{1}{3}$ of 12 = 4.

Teaching Activity 2a (10 minutes)

Recognise the equivalence of $\frac{2}{4}$ and $\frac{1}{2}$

- Give two paper squares to each child. Say: **You will remember that in Unit 16, we folded squares into halves and quarters.** Discuss what they notice about the fractions two quarters and a half.

- Ask them to fold one paper square in half and the other into quarters. Say: **Carefully cut the first square into halves and the second square into two quarters. What do you notice?** (they are the same size)

- Ask the children how they would prove that the two fractions are the same size. Establish that the two shapes could be placed one on top of the other and the sizes compared. The children compare the shapes and confirm that they are the same size. Write on the board $\frac{2}{4} = \frac{1}{2}$. Say: **Two fractions that are the same size are called 'equivalent fractions'. Two quarters and one half are an example of equivalent fractions.**

Teaching Activity 2b (10 minutes)

Recognise the equivalence of $\frac{2}{4}$ and $\frac{1}{2}$

- Draw 4 rows of 2 circles on the board. Ask a child to the board to draw a ring around one half of the set of circles. Ask: **How many circles are in half of the set?** (4)

- Draw another set of 8 circles, again arranged in 4 rows of 2. Invite a child to the board to draw a ring around one quarter of the set of circles. Ask: **How many circles are in a quarter of the set?** (2)

- Say: **I want to find two quarters of the set. How could I do that?** Establish that two quarter sets could be circled and the total found. Ask: **How many is that?** (4)

- Point to the half set of circles in the first array and the two quarters set of circles in the second array. Ask: **What do you notice about each fraction?** (the sets have the same number of circles)

- Repeat, finding $\frac{1}{2}$ and $\frac{2}{4}$ of the sets of 12 (3 rows of 4) and 16 (4 rows of 4) circles. Confirm that the number of circles in each fraction of the set, $\frac{1}{2}$ and $\frac{2}{4}$, are the same.

- Write on the board $\frac{2}{4} = \frac{1}{2}$. Say: **Two fractions that are the same size are called 'equivalent fractions'. Two quarters and one half are an example of equivalent fractions.**

Unit 18: Choose and use appropriate standard units to estimate and measure length/height in any direction (m/cm) and mass (kg/g) to the nearest appropriate unit, using rulers and scales

Content domain reference: 2M2

Prerequisites for learning

Compare and describe measurements: lengths and heights using vocabulary long/short, longer/shorter, tall/short, double/half; mass using vocabulary heavy/light, heavier/lighter, heaviest/lightest; and capacity of different containers using vocabulary more/less, most/least

Learning outcomes

Choose and use appropriate standard units to estimate and measure length/height in any direction (m/cm)

Choose and use appropriate standard units to estimate and measure mass (kg/g)

Key vocabulary

estimate, measure, centimetres, metres, ruler, height, centimetres, metres, kilogram, weighing scales, mass, heavy, light

Resources

five lengths (whole numbers of centimetres between 10 cm and 150 cm) of coloured tape or string fixed to the classroom or main hall floor; 30 cm rulers; metre rulers; tape measures; children's height chart marked in metres and centimetres; food items and drink items (between 100 g and 1500 g): apple, bag of fruit, bag of sugar, bag of flour, 1-litre bottle of water, 1·5-litre bottle of water; 1 kg, 500 g, 100 g, 50 g, 10 g, 1 g weights; balance scale

Background knowledge

- Children often confuse the words 'weight' and 'mass'. They consider weight to be a measure of how heavy something is, but the correct term for this is 'mass'. Mass is a measurement of how much matter is in an object, whereas weight is a measurement of how hard gravity is pulling on that object. Use the example of an astronaut in space to explain this. The astronaut's weight in space is nothing because there is no pull of gravity. Their mass remains the same as it is on Earth because the amount of matter that makes up that person is the same. It is important to use the correct vocabulary with the children.

Teaching Activity 1a (15 minutes)

Choose and use appropriate standard units to estimate and measure length/height in any direction (m/cm)

- Prior to the lesson, attach five lengths of coloured tape or string to the floor of the classroom or main hall. The strips should be spaced out, aligned at one end and parallel to each other but arranged in a random order of length. Label the strips with letter codes from 'A' to 'E'.
- Gather the children around the strips. Ask questions that encourage the children to use the comparative and superlative language of length. Ask: **Which of these strips do you think is the longest? Which do you think is the shortest? Look at strips A and D,** which do you think is longer? Look at strips **B and E, which do you think is shorter?**
- Say: **To know for sure whether one object is longer or shorter than another, we should measure them. Who can tell me what measuring tools we can use to measure the length of an object?** (a ruler, measuring tape)
- Display a 30 cm ruler, a metre ruler and a tape measure. Ask: **Who can tell me the difference between these rulers?** Establish that the 30 cm ruler is appropriate for measuring shorter lengths or distances and has a scale that is marked in centimetres.

- Say: **A metre rule is also marked out in centimetres.** Explain that since 100 centimetres is equivalent to 1 metre, the metre ruler is useful for measuring lengths and heights up to 1 metre. Extend the measuring tape and say: **The measuring tape has the advantage of measuring lengths and distances much greater than 1 metre.** Demonstrate that the metre rule is marked in both centimetre and metre divisions.

- Point to each strip in turn. Ask the children to decide the most appropriate tool for measuring its length.

- Give out whiteboards to pairs of children and ask them to draw a table with headings 'Estimate' and 'Measurement' and rows 'A' to 'E'. Say: **We made a choice of measuring tool for each strip. To do so, we had to make rough estimates in our head of the length of the strip. For example, we did not select the 30 cm ruler to measure the length of a strip over one metre.** Ask the children to estimate the length of each strip in centimetres. They write their estimates in the table.

- Demonstrate the correct use of a ruler to measure length. Emphasise that one end of the object must be lined up with the zero mark of the ruler. Demonstrate how to read the scale at the other end of the object to the nearest centimetre. Place 30 cm rulers, metre rulers and tape measures centrally. Ask the children to measure the objects and record the lengths in the table.

- When all the groups have completed their measurements, ask: **How accurate were your estimates? Whose estimate was the closest?** Choose children to discuss how close their estimates were to the actual measurements.

- Ask: **What was the length of the longest strip? The shortest strip?**

Teaching Activity 1b (15 minutes)

Choose and use appropriate standard units to estimate and measure length/height in any direction (m/cm)

- Prior to the lesson, attach a height chart to the wall. Choose five children to stand in a line. The children should be chosen to reflect a range of heights and should stand in random order.

- Say: **We are going to measure the height of each of the children standing in the line.** Remind the children that height is a measurement of how tall someone or something is.

- Ask questions that encourage the children to use the comparative and superlative language of height. Ask: **Which of the children do you think is the tallest? Which do you think is the shortest? Compare the height of [name] to the height of [name], who do you think is tallest? Compare the height of [name] to the [name], who do you think is shortest?**

- Say: **To know for sure whether one person is taller or shorter than another, we should measure their heights. Who can tell me which measuring tool we should use?** Discuss the appropriateness of each suggestion.

- Say: **We are going to use three tools to measure height.** Display a 30 cm ruler and a metre ruler. Point to the height chart on the wall.

- Ask: **Who can tell me the difference between these measuring tools?** Establish that the 30 cm ruler has a scale that is marked in centimetres, a metre rule is also marked out in centimetres but is longer and measures lengths and heights up to 1 metre. Write 1 metre = 100 centimetres on the board and explain that a metre is equivalent to 100 centimetres.

- Say: **The height chart has the advantage of measuring heights greater than 1 metre.** Demonstrate that the height chart is marked in both centimetre and metre divisions.

- Ask: **Which measuring tool should we use to measure a person's height?** Agree that the metre rule is better than the 30 cm ruler for measuring heights up to 1 metre and the height chart is best as it is easier to measure standing height.

- Hold the metre rule vertically and ask: **Who is taller than a metre? Who is shorter than a metre?** Remind the children that, if a child is taller than a metre, then their height must be greater than 100 centimetres.

- Give out whiteboards to pairs of children and ask them to draw a table with rows for the names of the five children and columns headed 'estimate' and 'measurement'. Ask the children to estimate how tall each child is in centimetres and record the estimates in the table.

- Compare the estimates with the actual heights. Ask: **How accurate were your estimates? Whose estimate was the closest?**

Teaching Activity 2a (15 minutes)

Choose and use appropriate standard units to estimate and measure mass (kg/g)

- Arrange a set of food and drink items on the table that have a mass ranging from 100 g to 1500 g. Label the items with letter codes from 'A' to 'E'.

- Say: **We are going to measure the mass of each of these items. What do we mean when we talk about the mass of an object?** Agree that mass is a measure of how heavy something is. Ask: **What words do we use to describe the mass of an object?** Agree that we use the words heavy, heavier, heaviest and light, lighter and lightest to describe and compare mass.

- Hold up a 1 kg weight and point to the 'kg' abbreviation. Ask: **Which unit of mass does kg stand for?** (kilogram) Say: **This weight has a mass of 1 kilogram. Give the children the weight to pass around.**

- Hold up a 1 g weight and point to the 'g' abbreviation. Ask: **Which unit of mass does g stand for?** (gram) Say: **This weight has a mass of 1 gram.** Give the children the weight to pass around.

- Ask: **Which unit is bigger, kilogram or gram?** (kilogram)

- Place the weights on the table and introduce 500 g, 100 g, 50 g and 10 g weights. Say: **These weights can be used as benchmarks.** Explain that benchmark weights are objects with a known mass that we can use to compare with other objects.

- Ask the children to compare the mass of the food and drink items with the standard weights. Ask questions that encourage the children to use the comparative and superlative language of mass, for example: **Which is heavier, object A or object B? Which is lighter, object C or object D? Which objects do you think have a mass greater than 100 g? A mass greater than 500 g? Greater than 1 kg? Which object do you think is the heaviest? The lightest?**

- Say: **We are now going to measure the mass of each of the objects. But first, let's estimate.** Draw a table on the board with rows for the letter code of each object and columns for 'estimate' and 'measurement'. Give the children different objects to hold and ask them to estimate the mass. Record the estimates in the table.

- Ask: **What equipment would you use to measure how heavy something is?** (kitchen scales: analogue; bathroom scales: digital) Provide both types of scales and use them to weigh each object in turn. Compare and contrast the reading on the digital scale to that of the kitchen scales. Help the children to read the pointer on the kitchen scales. Record the measurements in the table.

- When all the groups have completed their measurements, ask: **How accurate were your estimates? Whose estimate was the closest?** Choose children to discuss how close their estimates were to the actual measurements. Ask: **Which object was the heaviest? Which object was the lightest?**

Teaching Activity 2b (15 minutes)

Choose and use appropriate standard units to estimate and measure mass (kg/g)

- Arrange a set of food and drink items on the table that have a mass ranging from 100 g to 1500 g. Label the items with letter codes from 'A' to 'E'.

- Say: **In this lesson, we are going to investigate mass. What do we mean when we talk about the mass of an object?** Discuss and then say: **The amount of material that an object is made of is called its mass.** Ask: **Who can tell me the units we use for mass?** Expect the children to mention grams and kilograms.

- Hold a 1 kilogram weight in one hand and a 1-litre bottle of water in the other. Say: **A 1-litre bottle of water weighs about 1 kilogram.** Ask the children to pass around and comment on the mass of the 1 kg weight and the bottle.

- Hold a 1 gram weight in one hand and two paper clips in the other. Say: **Two paper clips weigh about 1 gram.** Ask the children to pass around and comment on the mass of the 1 g weight and the paper clips.

- Introduce a balance scale to the children. Say: **A balance scale is a tool that can be used to compare the mass of two objects.** Place an apple in one pan and a bag of sugar or similar in the other. Say: **The balance scale is similar to a seesaw. When one object is heavier than the other, the scale is unbalanced, and the heavier object drops below the level of the lighter object.**

- Demonstrate that the pan with the bag of sugar drops below the level of the pan with the apple. Ask: **Which object is heavier, the apple or the bag of sugar?** (bag of sugar) **Which object is lighter?** (the apple)

- Place an apple in each of the pans. Say: **When the scale is balanced, we know that the objects on both sides have the same mass.**

- Introduce a set of weights (1 kg, 500 g, 100 g, 50 g, 10 g, 1 g). Discuss the mass of each weight. Say: **We can use these weights as benchmarks. As the mass of the weight is known, we can use it to compare to objects with a mass we don't yet know.**

- Place a 100 g weight in one pan and a bag of fruit in the other. Ask: **What happens to the scales?** (the pan with the bread drops below the level of the pan with the 100 g) **What does this tell us?** (the loaf of bread is heavier than 100 g)

- Hold up a 50 g weight and a bag of flour. Ask: **Which do you think will be lighter, the 50 g weight or the bag of flour?** (the 50 g weight) **How can I check?** (use the balance scales)

- Place the items in the scale pans and demonstrate that the bag of flour is heavier. Say: **What does this tell me about the mass of the bag of flour?** (it is greater than 50 g)

- Ask the children to compare the mass of the food and drink items with the standard weights. Ask questions that encourage the children to use the comparative and superlative language of mass, for example: **Which is heavier, object A or object B? Which is lighter, object C or object D? Which objects do you think have a mass greater than 100 g? A mass greater than 500 g? Greater than 1 kg? Which object do you think is the heaviest? The lightest?**

- Say: **We are now going to measure the mass of each of the objects. But first, let's estimate.** Construct a table on the board with rows for the letter code of each object and columns for 'estimate' and 'measurement'. Give the children different objects to hold and ask them to estimate the mass. Record the estimates in the table.

- Ask: **What equipment would you use to measure how heavy something is?** (kitchen scales: analogue; bathroom scales: digital) Provide both types of scales and use them to weigh each object in turn. Compare and contrast the reading on the digital scale to that of the kitchen scales. Help the children to read the pointer on the kitchen scales. Record the measurements in the table.

- When all the groups have completed their measurements, ask: **How accurate were your estimates? Whose estimate was the closest?** Choose children to discuss how close their estimates were to the actual measurements. Ask: **Which object was the heaviest? Which object was the lightest?**

Unit 19: Choose and use appropriate standard units to estimate and measure temperature (°C) and capacity (litres/ml) to the nearest appropriate unit, using thermometers and measuring vessels

Content domain reference: 2M2

Prerequisites for learning

Compare and describe measurements: lengths and heights using vocabulary long/short, longer/shorter, tall/short, double/half; mass using vocabulary heavy/light, heavier/lighter, heaviest/lightest; and capacity of different containers using vocabulary more/less, most/least

Learning outcomes

Choose and use appropriate standard units to estimate and measure temperature (°C)

Choose and use appropriate standard units to estimate and measure capacity (litres/ml)

Key vocabulary

estimate, measure, capacity, full, empty, litre, millilitre, temperature, thermometer, degrees, Celsius, negative

Resources

1-litre bottle of water, 1.5-litre bottle of water, etc; 1 kg, 500 g, 100 g, 50 g, 10 g, 1 g weights; balance scale; Celsius thermometer; container of cold water; container of warm water; ice cubes; hot air dryer; 1-litre squash bottle; 500 or 250 ml plastic bottle; 5 containers of different sizes labelled 'A' to 'E', for example a plastic milk bottle, glass drinks bottle, squash bottle, plastic bowl, ice cream tub; 100 ml plastic bottle, large (2 litres) measuring jug

Background knowledge

• Some children find it difficult to select the most appropriate measuring vessel when measuring capacity. Discuss the range of measurement vessels available and ask children to estimate the capacity of containers that each vessel may be best suited to measure.

Teaching Activity 1a (10 minutes)

Choose and use appropriate standard units to estimate and measure temperature (°C)

• Hold up a thermometer. Ask: **What is this device and what does it measure?** (thermometer, temperature) Establish that temperature is a measure of how hot or cold something is.

• Explain that the temperature can be below zero. Introduce the negative part of the scale by explaining that numbers continue on the scale below zero, getting smaller.

• Write °C on the board. Point to the symbol and say: **We measure temperature in degrees Celsius and record measurements using a special symbol.**

• Show a container of warm water and a container of cold water. Choose a child to place the thermometer in the container of warm water and help them read the

temperature. Record the temperature on the board using the unit °C. Then measure and record the temperature of the cold water.

• Ask: **Which temperature is higher, the temperature of the warm water or the cold water?** (warm) **Which temperature is lower?** (cold) Ask the children why they think the temperatures vary.

• Say: **I am going to place an ice cube in the warm water. What do you think will happen to the temperature of the water?** Discuss and then place the ice cube in the water. Wait for it to melt then choose a child to measure the temperature of the water. Ask: **What has happened to the temperature?** (it has decreased) **Why?** (the ice has made the water colder, meaning its temperature has dropped)

• Say: **I am now going to blow hot air from a hot air dryer onto the container. What do you think will happen to the temperature?** (it will increase) **Why?** (the hot air will make the water warmer)

Demonstrate that the temperature increases when hot air is blown onto the water. Stop the dryer and choose a child to measure and record the temperature.

Teaching Activity 1b (10 minutes)

Choose and use appropriate standard units to estimate and measure temperature (°C)

- Hold up a thermometer. Ask: **What is this device and what does it measure?** (thermometer, temperature) Establish that temperature is a measure of how hot or cold something is.

- Explain that the temperature can be below zero. Introduce the negative part of the scale by explaining that numbers continue on the scale below zero, getting smaller.

- Write °C on the board. Point to the symbol and say: **We measure temperature in degrees Celsius and record measurements using a special symbol.**

- Show a container of soil, and a container of water to the children. Choose a child to place the thermometer in the container of soil and help them read the temperature. Record the temperature on the board using the unit °C. Then measure and record the temperature of the water.

- Choose a child to read the temperature. Help them read the scale then record the temperature on the board using the unit °C.

Teaching Activity 2a (10 minutes)

Choose and use appropriate standard units to estimate and measure capacity (litres/ml)

- Arrange a set of containers of varying sizes on the table that have a capacity ranging from 100 ml to 2 litres. Label the containers with letter codes from 'A' to 'E'.

- Say: **We are going to measure the capacity of each of these items. What do we mean when we talk about the capacity of something?** Establish that capacity is the amount of liquid a container can hold.

- Hold up a 1-litre plastic squash bottle and point to the 'L' abbreviation. Ask: **Which unit of capacity does L stand for?** (litre) Say: **This bottle has a capacity of 1 litre.** Give the children the bottle to pass around.

- Hold up a 500 ml or 250 ml plastic drinks bottle and point to the 'ml' abbreviation. Ask: **Which unit of capacity does ml stand for?** (millilitres) Say: **This bottle has a capacity of 500/250 ml.** Give the children the bottle to pass around.

- Write on the board: 1 litre = 1000 ml. Say: **Since there are 1000 millilitres in a litre,** **the capacity of this bottle is half/quarter that of the 1-litre bottle**.

- Show the containers labelled 'A' to 'E' to the children. Provide a large water jug, and some cups of identical size.

- Hold up container 'A' and a 100 ml plastic bottle. Ask the children to estimate the number of bottles of water needed to fill container 'A'. Record the estimates on the board.

- Ask the children to measure the number of bottles needed to fill the container and record the number on the board. Ask: **How accurate were your estimates?**

Teaching Activity 2b (10 minutes)

Choose and use appropriate standard units to estimate and measure capacity (litres/ml)

- Arrange a set of containers of varying sizes on the table that have a capacity ranging from 100 ml to 2 litres. Label the containers with letter codes from 'A' to 'E'.

- Say: **We are going to measure the capacity of each of these items. What do we mean when we talk about the capacity of something?** Establish that capacity is the amount of liquid a container can hold. Ask: **What words do we use to describe the capacity of something?** Agree that we use the words full, half full, empty, more and less when we describe capacity.

- Hold up a 1-litre plastic squash bottle and point to the 'L' abbreviation. Ask: **Which unit of capacity does L stand for?** (litre) Say: **This bottle has a capacity of 1 litre**. Give the children the bottle to pass around.

- Hold up a 500 ml or 250 ml plastic drinks bottle and point to the 'ml' abbreviation. Ask: **Which unit of capacity does ml stand for?** (millilitres) Say: **This bottle has a capacity of 500/250 ml.** Give the children the bottle to pass around.

- Write on the board: 1 litre = 1000 ml. Say: **Since there are 1000 millilitres in a litre, the capacity of this bottle is half/quarter that of the 1-litre bottle.**

- Provide a large water jug, cups of identical size and containers labelled 'A' to 'E'. Ask the children to estimate the capacity of each container and record the estimates on the board.

- Give pairs of children a large measuring jug each. Allocate a container to each group and ask the children to measure the capacity of the container.

- They fill the container with water then pour it into the jug. Help them to read the scale, then record the measurement on the board in millilitres. Ask: **How accurate were your estimates?**

Unit 20: Compare and order lengths, mass, volume/ capacity and record the results using >, < and =

Content domain reference: 2M1

Prerequisites for learning

Compare and order lengths, mass, volume/ capacity and record the results using >, < and =

Learning outcomes

Compare and order lengths, mass, volume/ capacity and record the results using >, < and =

Key vocabulary

length, longer, shorter, volume, capacity, greater than/more than, less than

Resources

4 long, narrow objects of varying lengths between 100 cm and 1200 cm labelled A to D; tape measure; sticky notes; 4 classroom objects with a mass between 100 g and 1200 g labelled E to H; weighing scales; 4 containers of varying shapes and sizes with a capacity between 100 ml and 1200 ml labelled J to M

Background knowledge

- In this lesson, the children will use knowledge of place value to support them in making comparisons between measurements. Look out for children who compare numbers based on the value of the digits, instead of place value, for example: writing 89 > 104, because 8 and 9 are greater than 1 and 4.

Teaching Activity 1a (20 minutes)

Compare and order lengths, mass, volume/capacity and record the results using >, < and =

- Place a set of four objects of varying lengths labelled A to D on the table. Hold up objects A and B with their ends aligned. Ask: **Which of these objects do you think is longer? Which is shorter?**

- Extend a tape measure to 2 metres and fix the end points to a table. Ask two children to measure the length of objects A and B. Ensure that they correctly align the end of the object with the zero marker on the scale of the tape measure. Record the measurement, with an arrow pointing up, on sticky notes and attach them to the tape measure, lining up the arrow to correct point on the scale.

- Point to two sticky notes and ask: **Which of the two measurements is greater? How do you know?** Establish that measurements further to the right of zero on the scale are greater.

- Write the symbols <, > on the board. Remind the children that these are inequality symbols and are used to compare two numbers to say which number is greater and which number is smaller. Say: **To tell the difference between the symbols remember that the symbol 'points' to the smaller number.**

- Choose a child to insert the correct symbol of inequality between the length measurements of the objects measured, for example, 73 cm > 47 cm. Demonstrate the alternative way of writing the inequality with the numbers in reversed order (47 < 73).

- Repeat the measurement and comparison activities above for objects C and D. Choose a child to compare the measurements using the symbol < or >.

- Ask: **How would you order the measurements, from shortest to longest?** Agree that this order is given by the positions of the sticky notes along the tape measure. Choose a child to write the order on the board.

- Place a set of four objects labelled E to H on the table. Encourage the children to pick up the objects and compare their weights.

- Ask two children to measure the mass of objects E and F on weighing scales. Help them to read the scale, then record the measurement on a sticky note with an arrow pointing upwards.

- Draw a number line from 0 to 1200 g on the board marked in intervals of 100 g. The children attach the sticky notes to the number line lining up the arrow to correct point on the scale.

- Point to the measurements and ask: **Which of the two measurements is greater? How do you know?**

- Choose a child to record both measurements and insert the correct symbol of inequality between the numbers, for example, 750 g > 450 g. Demonstrate the alternative way of writing the inequality with the numbers in reversed order (450 g < 750 g).
- Repeat the measurement and comparison activities above for objects G and H. Choose a child to compare the measurements using the symbol < or >.
- Ask: **How would you order the measurements, from lightest to heaviest?** Agree that this order is given by the positions of the sticky notes along the number line. Choose a child to write the order on the board.

Teaching Activity 1b (20 minutes)

Compare and order lengths, mass, volume/capacity and record the results using >, < and =

- Place a set of four objects labelled A to D on the table. Hold up objects A and B with their ends aligned. Ask: **Which of these objects to do you think is longer? Which is shorter?**
- Extend a tape measure to 2 metres and fix the end points to a table. Invite two children to the table to measure the length of objects A and B. Ensure that they correctly align the end of the object with the zero marker on the scale of the tape measure. Record the measurements on the board under the letter codes of the objects, for example, (A) 56 cm and (B) 97 cm.
- Ask: **Which object is longer A or B?** (B) **How do you know?** (since 9 tens is greater than 5 tens, I know that 97 is greater than 56)
- On the board, write the symbols <, >. Remind the children that these are inequality symbols and are used to compare two numbers to say which number is greater and which number is smaller. Say: **To tell the difference between the symbols, remember that the symbol 'points' to the smaller number.**
- Choose a child to come to the board to insert the correct symbol of inequality between the length measurements for objects A and B, for example, 97 cm > 56 cm. Demonstrate the alternative way of writing the inequality with the numbers in reversed order (56 cm < 97 cm).
- Repeat the measurement and comparison activities above for objects C and D. Choose a child to compare the measurements using the symbol < or >.

- Ask: **How would you order the measurements from shortest to longest?** Prompt the children to compare the measurements by place value. Remind them that if the hundreds/tens digits of two or more numbers are the same, then they should compare the digits of the next lowest place value until a difference is found. Compare the measurements and order them on the board.
- Place a set of four objects labelled 'J' to 'M' on the table. Say: **We are going to measure the capacity of these containers then compare and order them from the container that holds the least (the smallest capacity) to the container that holds the most (the greatest capacity).**
- Invite the children to the table to estimate and compare the capacity of the containers using the comparative language of capacity, for example, 'I think container J will have a greater capacity/will hold more than container K'.
- Provide a large measuring jug. Invite two children to the table to measure the capacity of containers J and K. They fill the container with water, then pour the contents into the jug. Help them to read the scale, then record the measurements on the board under the letter codes of the objects, for example, (J) 450 ml and (K) 950 ml.
- Ask: **Which container holds more, container J or container K?** (K) **How do you know?** (since 9 hundreds is greater than 4 hundreds, I know that 950 is greater than 450)
- Choose a child to come to the board to record both measurements and insert the correct symbol of inequality between the numbers, for example, 950 ml > 450 ml. Demonstrate the alternative way of writing the inequality with the numbers in reversed order (450 ml < 950 ml).
- Repeat the measurement and comparison activities above for objects L and M. Choose a child to compare the measurements using the symbol < or >.
- Ask: **How would you order the measurements from smallest to greatest capacity?** Prompt the children to compare the measurements by place value. Remind them that, if the hundreds digits of two or more numbers are the same, then they should compare the digits of the next lowest place value until a difference is found. Choose a child to compare the measurements and order them on the board.

Unit 21: Recognise and use symbols for pounds (£) and pence (p); combine amounts to make a particular value

Content domain reference: 2M3a

Prerequisites for learning

Recognise and know the value of different denominations of coins and notes

Know that there are 100 pence in one pound

Learning outcomes

Recognise and use symbols for pounds (£) and pence (p); combine amounts to make a particular value

Key vocabulary

pound, £ symbol, pence, p symbol, coin, note, cost, price

Resources

trays of 1p, 2p, 5p, 10p, 20p and 50p coins for pairs of children; items for a classroom shop with a 'stationery' theme: crayons, pencils, pens, scissors, staplers, calculators, tablet computers, whiteboards

Background knowledge

- Setting up a variety of classroom 'shops' can help to develop children's confidence in handling and computing with money. Role-play, where children take on roles of customer and shopkeeper, also helps to keep their interest for longer.

- Explain to the children that some of the prices in the classroom shop are not real and items would cost more in an actual shop.

Teaching Activity 1a (20 minutes)

Recognise and use symbols for pounds (£) and pence (p); combine amounts to make a particular value

- Hold up different notes and coins and ask the children to identify them. Discuss the different features and symbols of each coin that can be used to identify their value.

- Hold up a 1 pence coin. Ask: **Who knows how to write the value of this coin?** Choose a child to write the value on the board. Expect '1 pence' or '1p'. Ask: **What does the 'p' sign mean?** (pence) Say: **When we write 1 pence, or any other amount in pence, we write the 'p' sign immediately after the value without a space.**

- Hold up a 2 pence coin. Ask: **Who knows how to write the value of this coin?** Choose a child to write the value on the board. (2p) Ask: **How does the value of this coin compare to the one pence coin?** (it is twice/double the value)

- Give pairs of children a whiteboard. Hold up the other coins in turn (5p, 10p, 20p and 50p) and ask the children to write the amount on their whiteboards. Confirm the amount, then ask questions about the value of the coin compared to another, for example: **Fill in the blank. The value of the 10p coin is [blank] times the value of the 1p coin/2p coin/5p coin.** (10 times, 5 times, 2 times)

- Give each pair a tray of coins (1p, 2p, 5p, 10p, 20p and 50p).

- Say: **Use your coins to make 14p. Which coins will you use?** Choose pairs to discuss the coins they used. Establish that one possible combination is two 5p coins and two 2p coins. Ask: **Are there any other combinations of coins we could have used?** Ask the children to demonstrate other combinations. Ask: **How would you make 14p with the least number of coins?** (one 10p and two 2p coins)

- Repeat for other amounts, for example, 27p, 49p, 73p. Choose children to explain how they selected the combination of coins and ask them to demonstrate finding the total of the coins.

- Hold up a £1 coin. Ask: **Which coin is this?** (£1 coin) **Who can come to the board to write this amount?** Choose a child to write the amount. Confirm the amount is written as £1. Point to the '£' sign and say: **What does this symbol mean?** (pound) Say: **When we write 1 pound, or any other amount in pounds, we write the pound sign immediately before the value without a space.**

- Hold up a £2 coin. Say: **I want you to write the value of this coin on your whiteboards.** Choose a child to display how they wrote the amount. Expect: £2.

- Repeat for the notes, £5, £10, £20 and £50. For each note, ask the children to write the amount on their whiteboards. Confirm the amount, then ask questions about the value of the note compared to another, for example: **Fill in the blank. The value of the £50 note is [blank] times the value of the £10 note.** (5 times)

- Say: **Draw the combination of coins and notes that you would use to make to make £7.** Give the children time to select the appropriate coins and notes to make the amount, then choose pairs to discuss how they achieved it. Establish that one possible combination is three £2 coins and one £1 coin. Ask: **Are there any other combinations you could have used?** Ask the children to demonstrate other combinations. Ask: **How would you make £7 with the least number of notes or coins?** (one £5 note, one £2 coin)

- Repeat for £19. Ask: **Which notes and coins did you use? Which combination uses the least number of notes and coins?** (one £10 note, one £5 note, two £2 coins)

- Repeat for other amounts, for example, £28, £43, £86. Choose children to explain how they selected the combination of notes and/or coins.

Teaching Activity 1b (15 minutes)

Recognise and use symbols for pounds (£) and pence (p); combine amounts to make a particular value

- In preparation for the lesson, set up a classroom shop with items for sale, such as pens, pencils, sharpeners, scissors and more expensive items like books and computer tablets. Write price labels for each of the items that range from a few pence up to £50. The prices should be a whole number of pence or pounds, but not both.

- Give pairs of children whiteboards and say: **Write down an item that you want to buy, but it has to be something that costs less than 50 pence.**

- Choose children to show their whiteboard and state the item they wish to buy and its price. Point to the 'p' sign and ask them what the sign means (pence). Say: **When we write any amount in pence, we write the 'p' sign immediately after the value without a space.**

- Choose other children to show their whiteboards and name the item they wish to buy and its price.

- Give each pair a tray of coins (1p, 2p, 5p, 10p and 20p). Say: **Which coins would you use to pay for your item? Select the coins and place them in one corner of your tray.** Discuss the coins they used. Ask: **Are there any other combinations of coins you could have used?** Ask the children to demonstrate other combinations. Ask: **How could you make the amount with the least number of coins?** Discuss the coins used.

- Provide each group with 50p coins and ask them to choose another item from the shop to buy. This time, tell them that the item must cost between 50p and one pound. Discuss the different combinations the children use and how they could pay with the least number of coins.

- Explain that some of the items in the shop are more expensive and priced in pounds. Say: **I want you to choose another item to buy. Write down an item you wish to buy that is priced in pounds.**

- Choose children to show the item they have chosen and its price, for example, a calculator for £9. Ask: **What is the price of this item?** (£9) Point to the '£' sign and say: **What does this symbol mean?** (pound) Say: **When we write 1 pound, or any other amount in pounds, we write the pound sign immediately before the value without a space.**

- Say: **On your whiteboards, draw the combination of coins and notes that you would use to pay for your item.** Discuss the combination they used.

- Ask: **Are there any other combinations of notes and coins you could have used?** Ask the children to demonstrate other combinations. Ask: **How could you make the amount with the least number of notes and coins?** Discuss coins used.

Unit 22: Find different combinations of coins that equal the same amounts of money

Content domain reference: 2M3b

Prerequisites for learning

Recognise and know the value of different denominations of coins

Know that there are 100 pence in one pound

Identify coin combinations of equivalent value, for example, 5 × 1p is the same as 5p

Learning outcomes

Recognise that the same amount of money can be made using different combinations of coins

Key vocabulary

pound, £ symbol, pence, p symbol, coin, note, cost, price

Resources

trays of 1p, 2p, 5p, 10p, 20p and 50p coins; items for a classroom shop with a 'stationery' theme, for example, crayons, pencils, pens, scissors, staplers, calculators, tablet computers

Background knowledge

- Setting up a variety of classroom 'shops' can help to develop children's confidence in handling and computing with money. Role-play where children take on roles of customer and shopkeeper also helps to keep their interest for longer.

- Explain to the children that some of the prices in the classroom shop are not real and items would cost more in an actual shop.

Teaching Activity 1a (15 minutes)

Recognise that the same amount of money can be made using different combinations of coins

- Say: **In this lesson we are going to investigate whether the same amount of money can be made using different combinations of coins. Why might it be useful to know different ways of making the same amount?**

- Establish that, when paying for an item in a shop, we may only have a certain number of coins available. Say: **If we can make the amount from different sets of coins, then it will give us a better chance of having the right coins to pay for the item.**

- Put a tray of coins in front of the children (1p, 2p, 5p, 10p, 20p and 50p). Hold up a 2p coin. Ask: **Are there any coins that we could put together to make the same value as this coin?** Choose a child to select the coins. Agree that 2 × 1p is equivalent to 2p.

- Hold up a 5p coin. Ask: **Are there any coins that we could put together to make the same value as this coin?** Choose a child to select the coins. Agree that 5 × 1p is equivalent to 5p. Ask: **Is there another combination that uses coins with a higher value than 1p?**

Praise anyone who suggests the combination 2 × 2p (4p) and 1p making 5p.

- Hold up a 10p coin. Ask: **Are there any coins that we could put together to make the same value as this coin?** Choose a child to select the coins. Agree that 10 × 1p is equivalent to 10p. Ask: **Is there another combination that uses coins with a higher value than 1p?** Praise anyone who suggests the combination 2 × 5p to make 10p. Ask: **Is there a combination that uses 2ps or 1ps?** (5 × 2ps or a combination of 2ps and 1ps)

- Repeat for 20p and 50p, asking the children to select different combinations of higher and lower value coins.

- Give pairs of children a tray of coins (1p, 2p, 5p, 10p, 20p and 50p). Say: **Use your coins to make 29p. Which coins will you use?** Give the children time to select the appropriate coins to make the amount, then choose pairs of children to discuss the combination they used. Establish that one possible combination is two 10p coins, one 5p coin, two 2p coins.

- Ask: **Are there any other combinations of coins you could have used?** Ask the children to demonstrate other combinations. Ask: **Could you have made most of the amount from 5ps?** Establish that 5 × 5p make 25p and the remaining 3p could be made from 2 × 2p and 1p.

Ask: **How would you make 29p with the least number of coins?** (2 × 10p, 1 × 5p, 2 × 2p)

- Repeat for other amounts, for example, 36p, 53p, 88p. Choose children to explain how they selected the coins and to demonstrate how they found the total.

- Ask the children to select the following coins: 3 × 20p, 2 × 10p, 3 × 5p, 2 × 2p. Write on the board: 49p, 67p, 98p, 76p. Say: **Which of the amounts on the board can you make with the coins you have been given? Which of the amounts is it not possible to make?**

- Give the children time to work on the problem, then choose groups to explain how they made the amounts with coins. Ask: **Which amounts were not possible?** (98p, 76p) **Why?** (for 98p, 95p can be made, but the extra 3p requires a combination of a 2p and a 1p that is not available; for 76p, 75p can be made but the extra 1p is not available)

Teaching Activity 1b (15 minutes)

Recognise that the same amount of money can be made using different combinations of coins

- In preparation for the lesson, set up a classroom shop with a stationery theme. Items for sale might include pens, pencils, sharpeners, scissors and other items that could be priced for under one pound. Write price labels for each of the items that range from a few pence up to 99p.

- Say: **In this lesson, we are going to investigate whether the same amount of money can be made using different combinations of coins. Why might it be useful to know different ways of making the same amount?**

- Establish that, when paying for an item in a shop, we may only have a certain number of coins available. Say: **If we can make the amount from different sets of coins, then it will give us a better chance of having the right coins to pay for the item.**

- Put a tray of coins in front of the children (1p, 2p, 5p, 10p, 20p and 50p). Hold up a 2p coin. Ask: **Are there any coins that we could put together to make the same value as this coin?** Choose a child to select the coins. Agree that 2 × 1p is equivalent to 2p.

- Hold up a 5p coin. Ask: **Are there any coins that we could put together to make the same value as this coin?** Choose a child to select the coins. Agree that 5 × 1p is equivalent to 5p. Ask: **Is there another combination that uses coins with a higher value than 1p?** Praise anyone who suggests the combination 2 × 2p (4p) and 1p making 5p.

- Hold up a 10p coin. Ask: **Are there any coins that we could put together to make the same value as this coin?** Choose a child to select the coins. Agree that 10 × 1p is equivalent to 10p. Ask: **Is there another combination that uses coins with a higher value than 1p?** Praise anyone who suggests the combination 2 × 5p to make 10p.

- Ask: **Is there a combination that uses 2ps or 1ps?** (5 × 2ps or a combination of 2ps and 1ps)

- Repeat for 20p and 50p, asking the children to select different combinations of higher and lower value coins.

- Show the children around the shop. Explain that they will get the chance to go shopping for various items on sale. Ask them to work in pairs and provide each group with a whiteboard. Give each group a tray of coins (1p, 2p, 5p, 10p and 20p).

- Say: **Write down an item that you want to buy, for example, a pen for 38p. Which coins would you use to pay for your item?** Select the coins and place them in one corner of your tray. Give the children time to select the appropriate coins to pay for the item, then choose pairs of children to discuss the combination of coins that they used. Establish that for an item that costs 38p, one possible combination is three 10p coins, one 5p coin, one 2p coin and one 1p coin. Ask: **Are there any other combinations of coins you could have used?** Ask the children to demonstrate other combinations. Ask: **Could you have made most of the amount from 5ps?** Accept comments. Establish that 7 × 5p makes 35p and the remaining 3p could be made from 2p and 1p.

- Ask other groups to explain the coin combinations they used to pay for an item. Ask the children if they can suggest alternative coin combinations. Discuss which combinations use the most/least number of coins.

- Ask the children to select the following coins: 3 × 20p, 2 × 10p, 3 × 5p, 2 × 2p. Write on the board: 49p, 67p, 98p, 76p. Say: **Which of the amounts on the board is it possible to make with the coins you have been given? Which of the amounts is it not possible to make?** Give the children time to work on the problem, then choose groups to explain how they made the amounts. Ask: **Which amounts were not possible?** (98p, 76p) **Why?** (for 98p, 95p can be made but the extra 3p requires a combination of a 2p and a 1p that is not available; for 76p, 75p can be made but the extra 1p is not available)

Unit 23: Solve simple problems in a practical context involving addition and subtraction of money of the same unit, including giving change

Content domain reference: 2M9

Prerequisites for learning

Recognise and know the value of different denominations of coins

Know that there are 100 pence in one pound

Identify coin combinations of equivalent value, for example, 5 × 1p is the same as 5p

Know that change is the difference between what someone paid and how much an item costs

Learning outcomes

Solve problems that involve combining coins and/or notes to make a given value and calculating change

Key vocabulary

change, cost, price, total, pound, pence

Resources

equipment for a classroom shop: money tray, a play till with coins of all denominations; table and chairs; items for sale such as staplers, pencils, exercise books for a stationery store or plastic fruit to be part of a supermarket or grocers; price labels, pens, mini whiteboards, Resource 5: Items to buy

Background knowledge

- Before beginning the activity, remind the children of the mental and informal written strategies they have used to add and subtract numbers, for example, counting forward or back on the number line, partitioning by place value and finding the sum or difference of the place values.

- Ensure that children understand what 'change' is by explaining that when we pay for an item, we might not have the exact coins to make the amount. Instead, we can pay with one or more coins that have a value greater than the cost of the items. We should then expect the shopkeeper to give us back the extra money as change.

Teaching Activity 1a (25 minutes)

Solve problems that involve combining coins and/or notes to make a given value and calculating change

- In preparation for the lesson, set up a classroom shop using the resources. Each item in the shop should be labelled with a price clearly written with a marker pen or printed. The prices should range between 10p and £99 written in a whole number of pounds and pence, but not both.

- Give the children a tray of coins (£2, £1, 50p, 20p, 10p, 5p, 2p, 1p) and plastic notes (£50, £20, £10, £5) they can use to pay for items and whiteboards to write their shopping lists. Say: **Go into the shop and choose an item to buy that is priced in pence only. Write the item and the price on your whiteboard.**

- Ask the children to find the combination of coins that can be used to pay for their item. Choose children to explain the coins they selected.

- Ask a child to take on the role of shopkeeper. The other children tell the shopkeeper the item they wish to buy and pay using the coins they have selected. The shopkeeper finds the total of the coins and confirms whether the customer has paid the correct amount.

- Choose a different child to play the role of shopkeeper. Ask the other children to select a new item to buy that is priced in pence only and to give the shopkeeper the coins they selected. Ensure the shopkeeper is able to keep a running total of the coins as they count them.

- Say: **Now I want you to go into the shop and choose an item to buy that is priced in pounds only. Write the item and the price on your whiteboard.**

- Ask the children to find the combination of notes and coins that can be used to pay.

- Choose a different child to play the role of shopkeeper. Ask the children to select a new item to buy that is priced in pounds only. The children enter the shop and pay for the item.

- Add some new items to the shop priced between 1p and 9p. Give each child a 10p coin and say: **This time, you only have 10 pence to pay for your item. Is this possible?** Discuss and establish that paying with a 10 pence coin means you will spend too much and will need to some money back. Say: **The money we get back when paying too much for an item is called change.**

- Choose an item priced 4p. Ask: **How could I work out the change I should expect to get back? What calculation do I need to do?** Agree that this is a subtraction. Choose a child to write the calculation on the board. Expect: 10p – 4p. Ask: **What is the answer?** (6p)

- Choose a shopkeeper and ask the children to enter the shop and pay for the items. The shopkeeper works out the correct change and hands it to the customer. Remind the customers to check their change.

- Give each child a 20p coin and ask them to pay for an item that costs 19p or less. Encourage them to work out the change they should get before paying for the item.

- Give each child a £10 note and ask them to pay for an item that costs less than £10 (not less than £1). Encourage them to work out the change they should get before paying for the item. Repeat for payments with a £20 note.

Teaching Activity 1b (15 minutes)

Solve problems that involve combining coins and/or notes to make a given value and calculating change

- Display **Resource 5: Items to buy**, a tray of coins of all denominations and whiteboards.

- Choose two items from Resource 5 and write the prices on the board, for example: Jack-in-the-box (17p) and orange juice carton (37p). Ask: **What is the the total cost of these items? How would you work this out?** Establish that a good method is to count on using the number line.

- Draw an unlabelled number line. Ask: **Which number should we start the count with?** (37) **Why?** (starting with the larger number means less counting on) Mark and label 37. Say: **We can split 17 into 10 and 7.** Point to 37. Say: **Let's add 10. How far are we along the number line?** (47)

- Mark 47 on the number line and extend a line from 37 to 47. Ask: **How much more do we need to add?** (7) Establish that we need to

bridge through the next tens barrier. Ask: **How many to 50?** (3) Mark 50 on the number line and extend a line from 47 to 50. Ask: **How much more do we need to add?** (4) Mark and extend a line to 54. Say: **We have the total, 54p.**

- Ask: **Which coins should we use to pay for the two items?** Give the children time to find a combination of coins to make 54p, then choose a group to demonstrate how they would pay the amount.

- Ask the children to choose two different items given in pence. They calculate the cost of both items, then find the combination of coins they would use to pay for them.

- Choose two items from **Resource 5: Items to buy** given in pounds and write the prices on the board, for example: trainers (£46) and umbrella (£18). Draw a number line and use it to calculate the total cost of both items (£64). Then ask the children to suggest a combination of notes and coins that could be used to pay for the items.

- Ask the children to select and record an item to buy that costs less than 10p. Give each child a 10p coin and say: **This time you only have 10 pence to pay for your item. Is this possible?** Discuss and establish that paying with a 10 pence coin means you will spend too much and will need to some money back. Say: **The money we get back when paying too much for an item is called 'change'.**

- Say: **I would like to buy the box of crayons for 4p. How much change should I get back? What calculation do I need to do?** Agree that this is a subtraction. Choose a child to write the calculation on the board. Expect: 10p – 4p. Ask: **What is the answer?** (6p) **How would you give 6p in change?** (5p and 1p) Explain that it is important to be able to add and subtract money in order to give and check change.

- Give each child a 20p coin and ask them to choose an item to buy that costs 19p or less. Ask: **How much change should you receive?** Remind them of strategies for subtraction, such as counting back along the number line or counting forward to find the difference.

- Give each child a £10 note and ask them to pay for an item that costs less than £10 (not less than £1). Choose a pair of children to demonstrate how they worked out the change and the notes and/or coins they would use to give it. Repeat for an item that costs less than £20 and payment with a £20 note.

Unit 24: Compare and sequence intervals of time

Content domain reference: 2M4b

Prerequisites for learning

Know the number of minutes in an hour

Key vocabulary

second, minute, day, week, month, earlier, later

Learning outcomes

Compare and sequence intervals of time

Resources

footballs or sponge balls; stopwatch/ timer; cones; large sheet of paper

Background knowledge

- Children find it difficult to grasp the true size of time units: minutes and hours are too long and seconds are too short for them to comprehend. This problem is not helped by phrases where time units are used inaccurately, for instance, 'just a minute' or 'be there in a second'.
- Although educators tend to focus on how clocks measure time, clocks are not ideal for measuring amounts of time that children can grasp. It is far better to give children opportunities to measure the time taken to complete activities that they are familiar with.

Teaching Activity 1a (20 minutes)

Compare and sequence intervals of time

- Take the children to the playground or hall. Say: **In this lesson, we are going to time how long it takes to complete a ball game.**
- Working in pairs, ask the children to stand facing their partner approximately two metres apart. Give each pair a ball. Say: **I want you to practise throwing a ball backwards and forwards between you and your partner, 50 times in all. The idea is to pass the ball and catch it as quickly as possible.** Tell the children that you will time them so it is important that they try not to drop the ball.
- Give the children a chance to practise before you time them.
- On a large sheet of paper, draw a table with a heading 'Time taken (seconds)' and rows for each group. Allocate alphabetical team names to each group and record these as the group names in the table: Team A, Team B, Team C, and so on.
- Time the first group for 50 throws (each person throwing the ball 25 times). Record the time taken in the table. Repeat for all the groups then return to the classroom
- Point to the recorded times for two groups. Ask: **Who took longer, Team A or Team B? How do you know?** The children compare the times and identify the team that was the slowest.

- Choose two more groups and ask: **Which team was the fastest?**
- Ask: **How would you arrange the times in order, from slowest to fastest?** Discuss and establish that the times could be marked on a number line. Ask: **Where will the faster times be positioned? Since faster times will be shorter/smaller times, these will be positioned towards the left of the number line. Longer times will be positioned towards the right of the number line.**
- Draw a number line on the board and ask a child to mark the positions of the recorded times and team names. Ask: **Which team had the slowest time?** Write the time and team name on the board. Ask: **Which team had the next fastest time?** Insert the team name after the team with the slowest time. Continue ordering until all the teams have been listed. Say: **We have our order.**
- Arrange cones in a circuit around the playground or hall. Time how long it takes for each team to complete two laps of the hall dribbling a football between the cones. Record the time to the nearest minute.
- Back in class, construct a table of the recorded times. Ask the children to compare times to find which team was faster/slower. Use a number line to order the teams from slowest to fastest.

Teaching Activity 1b (20 minutes)

Compare and sequence intervals of time

- Ask the children to work in pairs and give each pair an an analogue clock.

- Say: **I am going to show you two times and I want you to say which one is earlier and which one is later.** Explain that both will be morning times.

- Set one clock to 7 o'clock and the other to half past 7. Ask: **Which of the two times is earlier?** (7 o'clock) **Which is later?** (half past 7) **How do you know?** (the hands of the clock move around the clock face as the time moves forward) Establish that half past the hour is a later time than the o'clock time just gone.

- Ask: **How much time has gone by between the times shown on the clocks?** (30 minutes) **How do you know?** Establish that the minute had has travelled halfway round the clock from 12 (7 o'clock) to 6 (half past 7). Point to each of the small minute divisions around the clock face. Say: **It takes one minute for the minute hand to move between these markers**.

- Explain that between each two consecutive numbers on the dial of a clock, there are five small divisions, and therefore it means the minute hand moves from one number to the next in 5 minutes. Demonstrate that the number of intervals of 5 minutes when the minute hand moves from the 12 to the 6 is equal to 30 minutes.

- Set one clock to quarter past three and the other to ten to four o'clock. Ask: **Which of the two times is earlier?** (quarter past 3) **Which is later?** (4 o'clock) **How do you know?**

- Ask: **How much time has gone by between the times shown on the clocks**? (45 minutes) Give the children time to discuss the question, then choose a pair of children to explain how they worked out the interval. Say: **Let's count in steps of 5 minutes from the numeral 3 to numeral 12: 5 minutes, 10 minutes…40 minutes, 45 minutes.** Confirm that the interval is 45 minutes.

- Say: **Now show me a time that is 15 minutes earlier.** Give the children time to set their clocks then ask: **What is the earlier time?** (5 minutes past 5) Confirm the time by counting backward 15 minutes in three steps of 5 minutes.

- Set the clock to half past ten. Say: **What time is this?** (half past 10) Say: **Show me the time 20 minutes later.** Give the children time to set their clocks then ask: **What is the later time?** (ten to 11) Confirm the time by counting forward 20 minutes on the clock in four steps of 5 minutes.

- Say: **Now show me a time that is 20 minutes earlier**. Give the children time to set their clocks then ask: **What is the earlier time?** (10 minutes past 10) Confirm the time by counting backward 20 minutes in four steps of 5 minutes.

- Show a clock set at the earlier time (ten past 10) and the later time (ten to 11). Ask: **How many minutes have passed between the two times shown?** (40 minutes) Choose a child to demonstrate how they count in steps of five minutes from the earlier time to the later time to calculate the interval.

- Tell the children a story that involves a time interval, for example: **I have booked cinema tickets for five minutes to 6 and the time is now ten minutes past 5. How long have I got before I need to be at the cinema?**

- Give the children time to discuss the problem. Demonstrate how to count in steps of 5 minutes from 5:10 to 5:55. Confirm the answer is 45 minutes.

- Continue with another story: **I am at the library, but need to catch the bus home at twenty-five minutes past 3. The time now is ten past 2. How long have I got until the bus arrives?**

- Accept answers. Demonstrate that the time can be found by counting in intervals of five minutes from 2:10 to 3:00 (50 minutes) then from 3:00 to 3:25 (25 minutes). Write on the board: 50 + 25 =. Ask: **What is the answer?** (75 minutes)

Unit 25: Tell and write the time to five minutes, including quarter past/to the hour and draw the hands on a clock face to show these times

Content domain reference: 2M4a

Prerequisites for learning

Tell and write the time to o'clock and half past

Tell and write the time, quarter to and quarter past the hour

Learning outcomes

Tell and write the time to five minutes, including quarter past/to the hour and draw the hands on a clock face to show these times

Key vocabulary

hour, o'clock, half past, quarter past, minutes past the hour, minutes to the hour

Resources

12-hour analogue clocks; Resource 6: Blank clock faces; Resource 7: 12-hour clock; split pins

Background knowledge

- When teaching children to tell the time, it is important that they see the minute hand and hour hand working together and not each hand in isolation. Move the minute hand between consecutive numbers on the clock face, showing the movement of the hour hand as you proceed. Ensure the children notice that the hour hand gradually moves from one numeral to the next as the minute hand completes the full circle.

Teaching Activity 1a (25 minutes)

Tell and write the time to five minutes, including quarter past/ to the hour and draw the hands on a clock face to show these times

- Hold up a 12-hour analogue clock set to 9 o'clock. Point to each of the small minute divisions around the clock face. Remind the children that it takes one minute for the minute hand to move between these markers and therefore, it means the minute hand moves from one number to the next in 5 minutes.

- Say: **I am going to move the minute hand from 12 to 1**. Move the hand. Ask: **How many minutes is that?** (5 minutes) Say: **When the minute hand points to 1, we call this time '5 minutes past' or '5 past'. The time on the clock shows 5 minutes past 9.**

- Move the minute hand to 2. Ask: **How many minutes past the hour is this?** (10 minutes) Say: **When the minute hand points to 2 we call this time '10 minutes past' or '10 past'.** Ask: **What does the time say now?** ('10 minutes past 9' or 'ten past 9')

- Move the minute hand to 3. Ask: **How many minutes past the hour is this?** (15 minutes) Ask: **What is the time shown?**

Do we say '15 minutes past 9'? Establish that, although the minute hand points to 3 and the time is 15 minutes past the hour, we usually say 'quarter past'.

- Count around the clock from 20 minutes past to 25 minutes past and explain that we refer to these times as '20 minutes past' (or '20 past') and '25 minutes past' or ('25 past').

- Move the minute hand to 6. Ask: **How many minutes past the hour is this?** (30 minutes) Ask: **What is the time shown? Do we say '30 minutes past 9'?** Establish that, although the minute hand points to 6 and the time is 30 minutes past the hour, we usually say 'half past'.

- Set the time to 3 o' clock and count around the clock from 5 minutes past to half past, reading the time together.

- Set the clock to different 'minutes past' times, for example, 5/10/20/25 and ask the children to say the time.

- Give pairs of children a 12-hour analogue clock. Say: **I am going to say a time and want you to set the hands of your clock to show this time.** Call out different 'minutes past' times and ask the children to model them on their clocks: 5 minutes past 4, 25 minutes past 6, 20 past 12. Ask the children to show their clocks and confirm the time.

- Display an enlarged copy of **Resource 6: Blank clock faces** on the board. Say: **I am going to say a time and I want someone to come to the board and draw the hands on a clock face to show this time.** Begin with 'Show me 20 past 4'. Choose a child to draw the hands on the clock. Repeat for 'ten past 8' and '25 past 7'.

- Set the clock to 3:30. Say: **The time is half past 3. I am going to move the hands of the clock to show the time 5 minutes later.** Move the hands forward five minutes. Ask: **What time is this?** Explain that up to half way through an hour, 30 minutes, we describe 'minutes past' the hour; but when we are beyond 'half past' we talk about 'minutes to' the next hour.

- Point to the clock showing 3:35. Ask: **How many minutes to the hour is this time?** Count the intervals of 5 minutes to the hour and confirm that when the minute hand is pointing to 7, the time is 25 minutes to the next hour. Say: **We could read this time as 35 minutes past 3 but for times between half past and o'clock, we usually read this as 'minutes' to. This time shown is '25 minutes to 4' or '25 to 4'.**

- Move the minute hand in 5-minute intervals around the clock to 4 o'clock while the class reads the time in 'minutes to' the hour: '25 minutes to 4', '20 minutes to 4', 'quarter to 4', '10 minutes to 4', '5 minutes to 4'.

- Set the clock to different 'minutes to' times, for example, 5/10/20/25 and ask the children to say the time.

- Say: **I am going to say a time and want you to set the hands of your clock to show this time.**

- Call out different 'minutes to' times and ask the children to model them on their clocks: 5 minutes to 11, 25 minutes to 5, 10 minutes to 8. Ask the children to show their clocks and confirm the time.

- Say: **I am going to say a time and I want someone to come to the board and draw the hands on a clock face to show this time.** Begin with '25 to 2'. Choose a child to draw the hands on the clock. Repeat for '10 minutes to 6' and '20 minutes to 12'.

Teaching Activity 1b (15 minutes)

Tell and write the time to five minutes, including quarter past/ to the hour and draw the hands on a clock face to show these times

- Give pairs of children a copy of **Resource 7: 12-hour clock**. The children cut out the pieces and fix the hands on the clock with split pins. Say: **How is this clock different from the clocks you usually see around you?** (it shows the number of minutes for every position of the minute hand)

- Set a 12-hour analogue clock to 7 o'clock. The children set their clocks to show the same time. Ask: **What time is it?** (7 o'clock)

- Move the minute hand to 7:05. Ask: **What time is it now?** If the children have difficulty answering the question, point to each of the small minute divisions around the clock face and remind them that it takes one minute for the minute hand to move between these markers. Say: **This means the minute hand moves from one number to the next in 5 minutes. When the minute hand points to 1, we know the time is '5 minutes past'**

- Establish that the time is read as 'five minutes past seven' or '5 past 7'. Display an enlarged copy of **Resource 6: Blank clock faces** on the board. Choose a child to draw the hands of the clock to show this time. Write the time below the clock.

- Move the minute hand to 7:10. The children model the time on their own clocks. Ask: **What time is this?** ('10 minutes past 7' or '10 past 7') Choose a child to draw the hands of the clock to show this time. Write the time below the clock.

- Repeat for 7:15 (reminding the children that we usually call this time 'quarter past' rather than '15 minutes past'), 7:20, 7:25 and 7:30 ('half past 7').

- Point to the shaded halves of the clock face. Explain that up to halfway through an hour, we describe 'minutes past' the hour. Set the clock to 8:30. Say: **I am going to move the hands of the clock to show the time 5 minutes later.** Move the minute hand to 7. The children model the time on their own clocks.

- Ask: **Which half of the clock is the minute hand in now**? (minutes to) Explain that when the minute hand is beyond 'half past' we talk about 'minutes to' the next hour. Ask: **How many minutes to the nest hour is this time?** (25) **How do you think we read this time?** ('twenty-five minutes to 9' or '25 to 9') Say: **We could read this time as '35 minutes past 8', but for times between half past and o'clock, we usually say 'minutes' to. This time is read as '25 minutes to 9' or '25 to 9'.**

- Move the minute hand in 5-minute intervals around the clock to 9 o'clock while the class reads the time in 'minutes to' form: '25 minutes to 9', '20 minutes to 9', 'quarter to 9', '10 minutes to 9', '5 minutes to 9'.

- Set the clock to different 'minutes to' times, for example, 5/10/20/25 and ask the children to read the time.

Unit 26: Know the number of minutes in an hour and the number of hours in a day

Content domain reference: 2M4c

Prerequisites for learning

Tell and write the time, quarter to and quarter past the hour

Tell and write the time to 5 minutes for minutes past and to the hour

Learning outcomes

Know the number of minutes in an hour and the number of hours in a day

Key vocabulary

minute, hour, day, o'clock, half past, quarter past, minutes past the hour, minutes to the hour

Resources

12-hour analogue clocks; number cards: 12 cards numbered 1–12 on one side to represent the numerals of a clock face, on the flipside the minute interval that corresponds to the numeral (5, 10, 15…55, 60)

Background knowledge

- As an introduction to the lesson, encourage the children to make a list of activities that take approximately one minute, one hour and one day. Compare the units of time and discuss which unit is larger and which is smaller. Guide them to understand that the larger the unit of time, the fewer units needed for the same measurement, for example, 60 minutes compared to one hour.

Teaching Activity 1a (20 minutes)

Know the number of minutes in an hour and the number of hours in a day

- Hold up a 12-hour analogue clock. Remind the children that it takes a minute for the minute hand to move between each of the small divisions on the clock face and five minutes to move between each consecutive numeral.

- Say: **Let's count in steps of five minutes to find the number of minutes in one hour.** Lead a count from 12 round the clock, pausing at every numeral to say the next step in the sequence: **5, 10, 15…55, 60.**

- Ask: **How many minutes are there in an hour?** (60) Write on the board: 60 seconds = 1 minute. Say: **It takes 60 minutes for the minute hand to make one complete turn of the clock.**

- Draw a number line on the board from 0 to 600, marked out to give ten divisions. Write '0' at the left-most marker and '600' at the right-most. Say: **We are going to use this number line to convert between hours and minutes.**

- Lead the children in a skip-count of multiples of 60. As the chant proceeds, ask a child to label the number line with the multiples: 60, 120, 180, and so on. Ask: **60 minutes makes how many hours?** (1) Write '1' below 60. Ask: **120 minutes makes how many**

hours? (120) Continue, until the number of hours is written below each multiple of 60.

- Ask the children questions that involve converting between hours and minutes. Remind them to use the number line to convert between the units. Ask: **How many minutes are there in 3 hours?** (180) **10 hours?** (600) **5 hours?** (300)

- Ask questions that involve converting fractions of one hour into minutes. Ask: **How many minutes are there in half an hour?** (30) **Quarter of an hour?** (15) **Three quarters of an hour?** (45)

- Write on the board: 'Seconds, minutes, hours, _____' Say: **We can order time units from smallest to largest. The order begins with seconds, the smallest unit, then minutes, then hours. Which unit comes next?** Agree and record the next largest unit: 'day'.

- Hold up a 12-hour analogue clock. Ask: **What time is it when a new day begins?** (12 o'clock midnight) Set the clock to 12 o'clock. Ask: **What are we usually doing at this time of day?** (sleeping) Ask the children about events that take place in the morning and model the time of these events on the clock.

- Ask: **Who can tell me what time the afternoon begins?** Explain that the morning is made up of 12 hours, the time it takes for the hour hand to make one full turn of the clock from 12 to 12.

Say: **The afternoon begins at 12 o'clock, but this time is 12 hours later than midnight.**

- Explain that we refer to 12 o'clock when the afternoon begins as '12 noon' or just 'noon' so not to be confused with midnight. Ask: **What are we usually doing at this time of day?** (we are about to have lunch) Ask the children about events that take place in the afternoon and evening, and model the time of these events on the clock.

- Say: **We know that morning is the time from midnight to 12 noon. How many hours is that?** (12) **We also know that the afternoon and evening is the time from 12 noon to midnight. How many hours is that?** (12) Ask: **Can you work out how many hours that is?** (24) Write on the board: 12 + 12 = 24. Confirm that there are 24 hours in a day and that the hour hand would go twice around the clock.

- Ask: **How many hours would there be in 2 days?** Confirm the answer is 48 hours. Choose a child to explain the strategy they used to find the answer. Repeat for 3 days. (72 hours)

Teaching Activity 1b (15 minutes)

Know the number of minutes in an hour and the number of hours in a day

- In preparation for the lesson, create a set of cards that display the numbers 1 to 12, representing the numerals of a clock face on the front and the minute interval that corresponds with that numeral on the back, for example: 1 and 5, 2 and 10, 3 and 15, and so on.

- Give a set of cards to pairs of children and ask them to lay the cards in order, from 1 to 12. Say: **These are the numerals of a clock face.**

- Then ask each pair to turn over the cards to reveal the order: 5, 10, 15 …55, 60. Ask: **What do you notice about this sequence of numbers?** (the sequence is a skip-count in 5s)

- Ask: **What is the connection between the numbers on this side of the cards and the numbers on the other side?** Prompt the children by telling them that the sequence is connected to the clock face. Praise any child who makes the connection between the numeral of the clock and the interval of five minutes.

- Hold up a 12-hour analogue clock. Remind the children that it takes a minute for the minute hand to move between each of the small divisions on the clock face, and five minutes to move between each consecutive numeral.

- Say: **Let's count in steps of five minutes to find the number of minutes on one hour.** Lead a count from 12 round the clock,

pausing at every numeral to say the next step in the sequence: 5, 10, 15…55, 60.

- Ask: **How many minutes are there in one hour?** (60) On the board, write: 60 seconds = 1 minute. Say: **It takes 60 minutes for the minute hand to make one complete turn of the clock.**

- Write on the board: 'Seconds, minutes, hours, _____' Say: **We can order time units from smallest to largest. The order begins with seconds, the smallest unit, then minutes, then hours. Which unit comes next?** Agree and record the next largest unit: 'day'.

- Hold up a 12-hour analogue clock. Ask: **What time is it when a new day begins?** (12 o'clock midnight) Set the clock to 12 o'clock. Ask: **What are we usually doing at this time of day?** (sleeping) Ask the children about events that take place in the morning and model the time of these events on the clock.

- Ask: **Who can tell me what time the afternoon begins?** Explain that the morning is made up of 12 hours, the time it takes for the hour hand to make one full turn of the clock from 12 to 12. Say: **The afternoon begins at 12 o'clock but this time is 12 hours later than midnight.** Explain that we refer to 12 o'clock, when the afternoon begins, as '12 noon' or just 'noon' so not to be confused with midnight. Ask: **What are we usually doing at this time of day?** (we are about to have lunch) Ask the children about events that take place in the afternoon and evening and model the time of these events on the clock.

- Say: **We know that morning is the time from midnight to 12 noon. How many hours is that?** (12) **We also know that the afternoon and evening is the time from 12 noon to midnight. How many hours is that?** (12) Ask: **Can you work out how many hours that is?** (24) Write on the board: 12 + 12 = 24. Confirm that there are 24 hours in a day and that the hour hand would go twice around the clock.

- Draw a timeline on the board and label each end '12 midnight'. Mark out 24 divisions and label the middle division '12 noon'. Number each half of the number line from 1 to 11 and label the halves 'morning' and 'afternoon/evening' respectively.

- With the children assisting, label the timeline with events that happen throughout the morning, afternoon and evening. Ask questions that require the calculation of time intervals, for example: **How many hours' difference is there between the start of school and the beginning of lunchtime?**

Unit 27: Identify and describe the properties of 2-D shapes, including the number of sides, and line symmetry in a vertical line

Content domain reference: 2G2a

Prerequisites for learning

Find and identify common 2-D shapes, for example: circle, square, oblong, triangle, hexagon

Learning outcomes

Identify and describe the properties of 2-D shapes, including the number of sides and vertices

Identify vertical lines of symmetry in 2-D shapes

Key vocabulary

2-D shape, corner, side, circle, square, oblong, triangle, hexagon, regular shape, irregular shape, symmetry, line of symmetry

Resources

trays of 2-D shapes including: circle, square, oblong, triangle, pentagon, hexagon and octagon; geostrips and fasteners; paper shapes: circles, squares, oblongs, equilateral triangles, isosceles triangles, scalene triangles, regular and irregular pentagons, regular and irregular hexagons and octagons; mirrors

Background knowledge

- The children should learn to identify regular and irregular 2-D shapes in any form, size or orientation. The focus of the lesson is the geometrical properties of 2-D shapes, rather than their attributes. These properties should include the number of sides, number of vertices, straight or curved sides, and equal side length.

- Help the children acquire mathematical language by modelling the correct mathematical vocabulary themselves. For example, use the term 'vertex' rather than 'corner' to describe the point at which two straight sides meet.

Teaching Activity 1a 20 minutes

Identify and describe the properties of 2-D shapes, including the number of sides

- Give pairs of children trays of 2-D shapes given in the resources. Remind the children that 2-D shapes are flat shapes – flat like a piece of paper. Hold up a square. Ask: **What shape is this?** (square) Draw a square on the board and say: **2-D shapes are the easiest shapes to draw.**

- Ask the children to compare drawing a square to that of a solid shape such as a box. Establish that a square can be constructed from four straight lines, whereas the drawing of a cube would involve many more lines in many different directions.

- Point to the sides of the square. Ask: **What are these parts of the shape called?** (sides) Remind the children that a side is one of the straight lines that make a 2-D shape.

- Ask the children to hold up a square and identify a side. Ask: **How many sides does a square have?** (4) **What do you notice about the sides of a square?** (they are all the same length) Say: **A square is a 2-D shape that has four sides all the same length.**

- Point to the vertices. Ask: **What are these parts of the shape called?** The children are likely to use the word 'corner'. Say: **Although some people use the word 'corner' to describe this part of a shape, a better, more mathematical word is 'vertex'.**

- Ask the children to hold up a square, point to a vertex and say the word out loud. Say: **If there is more than one vertex, then we use the word 'vertices'. How many vertices does a square have?** (4)

- Say: **Look at the shapes in your tray. Are there any shapes with four sides that are not squares?** Ask the children to hold up the shape(s). Expect the children to identify oblongs.

Ask: **What is the name of this shape?** Expect many of the children to describe the shape as a 'rectangle'.

- Say: **We often hear people use the word 'rectangle' to describe this shape but it is in fact an oblong.** Explain that 'rectangle' is a collective term for both oblongs and squares. Say: **A square is a 'special' rectangle that has all sides equal; an oblong is a rectangle that has two sides longer than the other two sides. If you get confused, just think of the word 'oblong'. The 'long' part of the word tells you that it has longer and shorter sides.**

- Hold up a triangle. Ask: **What shape is this?** (triangle) **How many sides does a triangle have?** (3) **How many vertices?** (3) Ask the children to select shapes from their trays to make a set of triangles. Choose a group to share the set. Ask: **How do you know these shapes are all triangles?** (they all have three sides and three vertices)

- Point to the remaining shapes and elicit that the pentagon has five sides, the hexagon has six sides and the octagon has eight sides. Elicit that all 2-D shapes have the same number of vertices as sides.

- Hold up an irregular hexagon for the children to see. Ask: **How many sides does this shape have?** (6) **How many vertices?** (6) **What shape is this?** Establish that, since the shape has six straight sides, it must be a hexagon. Hold a regular and an irregular hexagon side by side. Say: **All six-sided shapes are hexagons, but not all hexagons have sides of equal length.** Hold up the regular hexagon. Say: **This is an example of a regular hexagon. We use the word 'regular' to describe a shape that has sides all the same length.** Hold up the irregular hexagon. Say: **This is an example of an irregular hexagon. We use the word 'irregular' to describe a shape that has sides of different lengths.**

- Compare and contrast the sides of a regular and an irregular pentagon, and the sides of a regular and an irregular octagon.

- Hold up a circle. Ask: **What shape is this?** (circle) **How is this shape different from the other shapes we have looked at?** Establish that a circle does not have straight sides or vertices. Say: **A circle is a 2-D shape that has no sides or vertices.** Point to the edge of the circle and say: **We can describe a circle as having a curved edge but cannot describe it as having a curved side since all sides are straight lines.**

Teaching Activity 1b 20 minutes

Identify and describe the properties of 2-D shapes, including the number of sides

- Give pairs of children geostrips and fasteners.

- Say: **I want you to join four strips of the same length together to make a shape that has four corners, like the corners of a book.**

- The children construct the shape and hold it up for the group to see. Ask: **What shape have you made?** (square) Say: **A square is an example of a 2-D shape.** Remind the children that 2-D shapes are flat shapes – flat like a piece of paper. Draw a square on the board and say: **2-D shapes are the easiest shapes to draw**.

- Ask the children to compare drawing a square to that of a solid shape such as a box. Establish that a square can be constructed from four straight lines, whereas the drawing of a cube would involve many more lines in many different directions.

- Construct a square from geostrips. Point to the sides and ask: **What are these parts of the shape called?** (sides) Remind the children that a side is one of the straight lines that make a 2-D shape.

- Ask the children to hold up a square and identify a side. Ask: **How many sides does a square have?** (4) **What do you notice about the sides of a square?** (they are all the same length) Say: **A square is a 2-D shape that has four sides all the same length.**

- Point to the four vertices of the square. Ask: **What are these parts of the shape called?** The children are likely to use the word 'corner'. Say: **Although some people use the word 'corner' to describe this part of a shape, a better, more mathematical word is 'vertex'.** Ask the children to hold up a square, point to a vertex and say the word out loud. Say: **If there is more than one vertex, then we use the word 'vertices'. How many vertices does a square have?** (4)

- Say: **I want you to construct another shape with four sides, but this time, use two strips of one length and two strips of a different length. Make sure that your shape has corners like the corners of a book.**

- The children construct the shape and hold it up for the group to see. Ask: **What is the name of this shape?** Expect many of the children to describe the shape as a 'rectangle'. Say: **We often hear people use the word 'rectangle' to describe this shape but it is in fact an oblong.**

- Explain that 'rectangle' is a collective term for both oblongs and squares. Say: **A square is a 'special' rectangle that has all sides equal; an oblong is a rectangle that has two sides longer than the other two sides. If you get confused, just think of the word 'oblong'. The 'long' part of the word tells you that it has longer and shorter sides.**

- Say: **Now construct a shape that has three sides only.** The children construct the shape and hold it up for the group to see. Ask: **What shape is this?** (triangle) **How many sides does a triangle have?** (3) **How many vertices?** (3)

- Use geostrips to construct an isosceles triangle. Say: **What shape is this?** (triangle) **How do you know?** (it has three sides and three vertices) **Establish that any shape that has three straight sides and three vertices is a triangle.**

- Ask the children to construct a 5-sided shape, a 6-sided shape and an 8-sided shape from strips of the same length. Remind the children that a 5-sided shape is called a pentagon, a 6-sided shape is a hexagon and an 8-sided shape is an octagon. Elicit that all 2-D shapes have the same number of corners as sides.

- Construct and hold up an irregular hexagon for the children to see. Ask: **How many sides does this shape have?** (6) **How many vertices?** (6) **What shape is this?** Establish that, since the shape has six straight sides, it must be a hexagon. Hold a regular and an irregular hexagon side by side. Say: **All six-sided shapes are hexagons, but not all hexagons have sides of equal length.**

- Hold up the regular hexagon. Say: **This is an example of a regular hexagon. We use the word 'regular' to describe a shape that has sides all the same length.** Hold up the irregular hexagon. Say: **This is an example of an irregular hexagon. We use the word 'irregular' to describe a shape that has sides of different lengths.**

- Compare and contrast the sides of a regular and an irregular pentagon, and the sides of a regular and an irregular octagon.

- Hold up a circle. Ask: **What shape is this?** (circle) **Is it possible to construct a circle from geostrips?** (no) **Why not?** Establish that a circle does not have straight sides or vertices. Say: **A circle is a 2-D shape that has no sides or vertices.** Point to the edge of the circle and say: **We can describe a circle as having a curved edge, but cannot describe it as having a curved side since all sides are straight lines.**

Identify vertical lines of symmetry in 2-D shapes

- Say: **In this lesson, we are going to look at shapes that have symmetry.** Fold a paper circle in half and hold the shape so that the fold line is vertical. Say: **A circle is an example of a shape that has symmetry. When I fold the shape in half, both sides fold neatly over the top of one another. This is because the two parts are the same size and shape. This tells us that the shape has symmetry.**

- Ask: **What other shapes are symmetrical?** Confirm the suggestions are symmetrical. Agree that a butterfly has symmetry because the wings are the same on each side. Fold a piece of paper in half, draw the wings of a butterfly and cut out the shape. Open it up and demonstrate the symmetry of the figure. Point to the fold line and say: **This is the line that divides the figure into two parts. Since the line goes up and down, not from side to side, we call it a 'vertical line'. When we fold the paper across the line we get two matching parts. When this happens we call the fold line a vertical line of symmetry.** Explain that a line of symmetry that goes from side to side is called a 'horizontal line of symmetry'.

- Give pairs of children paper squares, oblongs, isosceles triangles and regular hexagons and a scalene triangle.

- Say: **Let's investigate these shapes to see if they have a vertical line of symmetry.**

- Hold up an oblong and fold it along a vertical line that is to the right or left of the mid-way point. Ask: **Does the folded shape look the same on both sides of the fold line?** (no) **Is this a line of symmetry?** (no) Ask: **Who can help me find a vertical line of symmetry for this oblong?** Choose a child to fold the shape along its mid-way point and confirm that the folded sides are the same size and shape. Say: **As we have found a line of symmetry, we can say that an oblong is symmetrical.**

- Ask the children to fold other shapes to find vertical lines of symmetry. Give them time to investigate, then choose pairs to demonstrate how they folded shapes to find vertical lines of symmetry. Confirm that squares, oblongs, isosceles triangles and regular hexagons are all symmetrical. Say: **Show me a shape that does not have symmetry.** Expect the children to select a scalene triangle. Ask: **How do you know these shapes do not have symmetry?** Agree that it is impossible to fold the shape so that there are matching parts.

Teaching Activity 2b (15 minutes)

Identify vertical lines of symmetry in 2-D shapes

- Say: **In this lesson, we are going to look at shapes that have symmetry.** Fold a paper circle in half and hold the shape so that the fold line is vertical. Say: **A circle is an example of a shape that has symmetry. When I fold the shape in half, both sides fold neatly over the top of one another. This is because the two parts are the same size and shape. This tells us that the shape has symmetry.**

- Ask: **What other shapes are symmetrical?** Confirm the suggestions are symmetrical. Agree that a butterfly has symmetry because the wings are the same on each side.

- Fold a piece of paper in half, draw the wings of a butterfly and cut out the shape. Open it up and demonstrate the symmetry of the figure. Point to the fold line and say: **This is the line that divides the figure into two parts. Since the line goes up and down, not from side to side, we call it a 'vertical line'. When we fold the paper across the line we get two matching parts. When this happens we call the fold line a vertical line of symmetry.** Explain that a line of symmetry that goes from side to side is called a 'horizontal line of symmetry'.

- Hold up a mirror. Say: **Another way to confirm if a shape is symmetrical is to use a mirror.** Line up the mirror down the central vertical line of the butterfly and show that what is reflected in the mirror is what we see on the other side. Point to the line and say: **The mirror image confirms that the figure has symmetry.**

- Give pairs of children a mirror and a tray of shapes: squares, oblongs, equilateral triangles, isosceles triangles, scalene triangles, regular and irregular pentagons, hexagons and octagons.

- Say: **Let's investigate these shapes to see if they are symmetrical.**

- Place a regular hexagon on the table. Line the mirror up vertically with the midpoint of the shape and say: **I place my mirror along a line that I think might be a vertical line of symmetry. Then I look to see if the other half of the shape matches the reflection. If they match, then the shape is symmetrical and the line is a vertical line of symmetry.** Confirm that the hexagon is symmetrical.

- Ask the children to use a mirror to investigate shapes to find vertical lines of symmetry. Give them time to complete the activity, then choose pairs to demonstrate how they tested for symmetry. Confirm that squares, oblongs, isosceles triangles and regular pentagons, hexagons and octagons all have vertical lines of symmetry.

- Say: **Show me a shape that does not have symmetry.** Expect the children to select examples of scalene triangles or an irregular pentagon, hexagon or octagon. Ask: **How do you know these shapes do not have symmetry?** Agree that it is impossible to find a mirror image along a line of the shape that creates the whole shape.

Unit 28: Identify and describe the properties of 3-D shapes, including the number of edges, vertices and faces

Content domain reference: 2G2b

Prerequisites for learning

Begin to name and describe three-dimensional shapes with mathematical vocabulary, such as sphere, cube and cylinder

Understand that shapes can also be related to real-world examples, for example, a sphere and a ball have the same shape

Learning outcomes

Identify and describe the properties of 3-D shapes, including the number of edges, vertices and faces

Key vocabulary

vertex (vertices), edge, face, sphere, cone, cylinder, cube, cuboid, triangular prism, square pyramid

Resources

trays of 3-D shapes: sphere, cone, cylinder, cube, cuboid, triangular prism, square pyramid; trays of objects that are examples of 3-D shapes: football (sphere), ice-cream cornet (cone), kitchen roll tube (cylinder), large dice (cube), cereal packet or tissue box (cuboid), chocolate packaging (triangular prism), pyramidal-shaped chocolate (square pyramid)

Background knowledge

- In preparation for this lesson, children should have had experience in handling 3-D shapes and discussing their properties. Through constructive practical play experiences, such as construction building, they will acquire an informal understanding of the properties of each shape.

Teaching Activity 1a (15 minutes)

Identify and describe the properties of 3-D shapes, including the number of edges, vertices and faces

- Give pairs of children trays of 3-D shapes. Explain that 3-D shapes are shapes that are represented in 3 dimensions rather than just flat. Say: **3-D shapes are solid shapes – they are fat, not flat like a piece of paper.** Hold up a cube. Ask: **What shape is this?** (cube)

- Say: **Like 2-D shapes, 3-D shapes have their own properties. We can use these properties to help identify a 3-D shape.** Ask the children to find a cube and point to a face. Address any misconceptions at this stage.

- Say: **A face is the flat surface on a solid shape. Let's count the number of faces on a cube.** Lead a count pointing to each face in turn. Establish that a cube has six faces. Ask: **What is the shape of each face?** (square)

- Point to an edge. Say: **This is an edge. An edge is where two faces meet. Let's count the number of edges on a cube.**

Lead a count pointing to each edge in turn. Establish that a cube has 12 edges.

- Point to a vertex. Say: **The vertex of a 2-D shape is the point where two sides meet. For a 3-D cube shape, a vertex is the point where three edges meet. Let's count the number of vertices on a cube.** Establish that a cube has 8 vertices.

- Draw a table on the board with columns headed 'Name of shape', 'Number of faces', 'Number of vertices' and 'Number of edges' and complete a row of the table for a cube.

- Hold up a cuboid. Ask: **What shape is this?** (cuboid) Ask children to count the number of faces, vertices and edges. Agree the number and complete a row in the table for a cuboid. (6, 8, 12)

- Ask: **Look at the numbers for the cube and the cuboid. What do you notice?** (they are the same) Say: **From the numbers in the table, it looks like the cube and the cuboid are the same shape. How do we tell them apart?** Establish that the shapes of the faces are different. Say: **A cube has square faces but a cuboid has rectangular faces, some or all will be oblongs.**

- Hold up a triangular prism. Say: **This shape is a type of prism.** Explain that a prism is a solid shape with identical faces at each end, known as bases, connected together by flat sides. Ask: **What do you think the name of this prism is?** (triangular prism)

- Ask the children to count the number of faces, vertices and edges for a triangular prism. Agree the number and complete a row in the table for this shape. (5, 6, 9)

- Hold up a square pyramid. Say: **This shape is a type of pyramid.** Explain that a pyramid is a solid shape with a base that connects to a point at the top of the shape by triangular sides. Demonstrate that the triangular sides taper from the base to a common point. Explain that pyramids are named according to the shape of their base. Ask: **What do you think the name of this pyramid is?** (square pyramid)

- Ask the children to count the number of faces, vertices and edges. Agree the number and complete a row in the table for a square pyramid. (5, 5, 8)

- Display three shapes on the table: a sphere, a cone and a cylinder. Ask the children to name the shapes. Say: **These shapes are different from the other solid shapes we have looked at.** Point out that the sphere is really just one curved surface, and the cone and cylinder are a mix of flat circular surfaces and curved surfaces.

- Explain that since the definitions of vertices, edges and faces are based on shapes with straight edges and flat surfaces bound by straight lines, they do not apply to these shapes.

Teaching Activity 1b (15 minutes)

Identify and describe the properties of 3-D shapes, including the number of edges, vertices and faces

- Give pairs of children objects which are examples of 3-D shapes. Say: **Today we are going to look at different 3-D shapes.** Explain that 3-D shapes are shapes that are represented in 3 dimensions rather than just flat. Say: **3-D shapes are solid shapes – they are fat, not flat like a piece of paper.**

- Hold up the large dice. Ask: **What shape is this?** (cube) Ask: **What other examples of cubes can you find?** Give the children the opportunity to look around the classroom for real-life examples of cubes.

- Say: **Let's take a look at the faces of the dice.** Hand out dice to the children. Ask the children to point to a face. Address any misconceptions at this stage.

- Say: **A face is the flat surface on a solid shape. Let's count the number of faces on this cube.** Lead a count pointing to each face in turn. Establish that a cube has six faces. Ask: **What is the shape of each face?** (square)

- Point to an edge. Say: **This is an edge. An edge is where two faces meet. Let's count the number of edges on this cube.** Lead a count pointing to each edge in turn. Establish that a cube has 12 edges.

- Point to a vertex. Say: **The vertex of a 2-D shape is the point where two sides meet. For a 3-D cube shape, a vertex is the point where three edges meet. Let's count the number of vertices on this cube.** Lead a count pointing to each edge. Establish that a cube has 8 vertices.

- Draw a table on the board with columns headed 'Name of shape', 'Number of faces', 'Number of vertices' and 'Number of edges' and complete a row of the table for a cube.

- Hold up a tissue box or cereal packet. Ask: **What shape is this?** (cuboid)

- Ask the children to count the number of faces, vertices and edges. Agree the number and complete a row in the table for a cuboid. (6, 8, 12)

- Hold up an example of a triangular prism, for example, chocolate packaging. Say: **This shape is a type of prism.** Explain that a prism is a solid shape with identical faces at each end, known as bases, connected together by flat sides. Explain that prisms are named according to the shape of their base. Ask: **What do you think the name of this prism is?** (triangular prism)

- Ask the children to count the number of faces, vertices and edges. Agree the number and complete a row in the table for a triangular prism. (5, 6, 9)

- Hold up a real-life example of a square pyramid, for example, a chocolate-shaped mint. Say: **This shape is a type of pyramid.** Explain that a pyramid is a solid shape with a base that connects to a point at the top of the shape by triangular sides. Demonstrate that the triangular sides taper from the base to a common point. Explain that pyramids are named according to the shape of their base. Ask: **What do you think the name of this pyramid is?** (square pyramid)

- Ask the children to count the number of faces, vertices and edges. Agree the number and complete a row in the table for a square pyramid. (5, 5, 8)

Unit 29:   Identify 2-D shapes on the surface of 3-D shapes, [for example, a circle on a cylinder and a triangle on a pyramid]

Content domain reference: 2G3

Prerequisites for learning

Understand the terms face, edge and vertex
Identify common 2-D shapes

Key vocabulary

vertex (vertices), edge, face, sphere, cone, cylinder, cube, cuboid, triangular prism, square pyramid

Learning outcomes

Identify 2-D shapes on the surface of 3-D shapes, [for example, a circle on a cylinder and a triangle on a pyramid]

Resources

trays of 3-D shapes: sphere, cone, cylinder, cube, cuboid, triangular prism, square pyramid; paint and paint trays

Background knowledge

- In preparation for this lesson, children should have had experience in handling 3-D shapes and discussing their properties. Through constructive practical play experiences, such as construction building, they will acquire an informal understanding of the properties of each shape.

Teaching Activity 1a (15 minutes)

Identify 2-D shapes on the surface of 3-D shapes, [for example, a circle on a cylinder and a triangle on a pyramid]

- Place a tray of 3-D shapes on the table. Say: **I am going to show you one face of a solid shape and I want you to try to guess what the shape is.**

- Show the children just the base of a cylinder. Ask: **Which 2-D shape can you see?** (circle) **What do you think the solid shape could be?** Agree that it could be a cone or a cylinder. Ask: **Why could it not be a sphere?** (the surface of a sphere is curved) Give the children an extra clue to help them decide whether the shape is a cone or a cylinder. Say: **The solid shape has two circular bases identical to this shape. What is the shape?** (cylinder)

- Repeat for a cube, revealing only one square face. Ask: **Which 2-D shape can you see?** (square) **What do you think the solid shape could be?** Establish that there are several possibilities, including a cube, cuboid and square pyramid. Ask: **Why might the shape be a cuboid and not a cube?** (cuboids can have a mix of square and oblong faces) **Why would it not be a cone?** (a cone does not have any square faces)

- Give the children an extra clue to help them decide whether the shape is a cube, cuboid or square pyramid. Say: **The shape has six identical square faces. What is the shape?** (cube)

- Say: **You have seen that the shape of the faces of a 3-D solid gives a clue to its identity. Let's look at the faces of some more shapes to see if we can identify them.**

- Show the children just the end of a triangular prism. Ask: **Which 2-D shape can you see?** (triangle) **What do you think the solid shape could be?** Establish that there are several possibilities, including a pyramid and a triangular prism. Ask: **Why would it not be a cone?** (a cone does not have a flat triangular face) Give the children an extra clue to help them decide whether the shape is a prism or a pyramid. Say: **The faces at both ends of this shape have the shape that you can see. What is the shape?** (triangular prism)

- Give pairs of children a tray of 3-D shapes. Say: **Take turns to select a shape when your partner is not looking. Show them one face or surface and ask your partner to guess which shape you are holding. If your partner has selected several possible shapes, then provide a clue that will help them decide.**

- Give the children time to play the game, then choose two children to demonstrate the shapes they chose and the clues they provided.

Teaching Activity 1b (15 minutes)

Identify 2-D shapes on the surface of 3-D shapes, [for example, a circle on a cylinder and a triangle on a pyramid]

- Prepare a tray with paint. Place it on a table with a set of 3-D shapes. Say: **I am going to turn around, dip one face or surface of a shape into the paint and print it on paper**.

- Make sure the children cannot see, then dip the circular end of a cylinder into the paint. Press the end of the cylinder on a piece of paper. Hold up the paper and ask: **Which 2-D shape can you see?** (circle) **Which shape do you think made this print?** Agree that it could be a cone or a cylinder. Ask: **Why would it not be a sphere?** (the surface of a sphere is curved)

- Give the children an extra clue to help them decide whether the shape is a cone or a cylinder. Say: **The solid shape has two circular bases identical to this shape. What is the shape?** (cylinder)

- Repeat for a cube, printing one square face. Ask: **Which 2-D shape can you see?** (square) **What do you think the solid shape could be?** Establish that there are several possibilities, including a cube, cuboid and square pyramid. Ask: **Why might the shape be a cuboid and not a cube?** (cuboids can have a mix of square and oblong faces) **Why would it not be a cone?** (a cone does not have any square faces)

- Give the children an extra clue to help them decide whether the shape is a cube, cuboid or square pyramid. Say: **The shape has six identical square faces. What is the shape?** (cube)

- Say: **You have seen that the shape of the faces of a 3-D solid gives a clue to its identity. Let's look at the faces of some more shapes to see if we can identify them.**

- Repeat for a triangular prism, using paint to print one of its triangular faces.

- Ask: **Which 2-D shape can you see?** (triangle) **What do you think the solid shape could be?** Establish that there are several possibilities, including a pyramid and a triangular prism. Ask: **Why would it not be a cone?** (a cone does not have a flat triangular face)

- Give the children an extra clue to help them decide whether the shape is a prism or a pyramid. Say: **The faces at both ends of this shape have the shape that you can see. What is the shape?** (triangular prism)

- Give pairs of children a paint tray and a set of 3-D shapes. Say: **Take turns to select a shape when your partner is not looking. Print one of the faces or surfaces of the shape on paper. Show it to your partner and ask them to guess which shape you used to make the print. If your partner has selected several possible shapes, then provide a clue that will help them decide.**

- Give the children time to play the game, then choose two children to demonstrate the shapes they chose and the clues they provided.

Unit 30: Compare and sort common 2-D and 3-D shapes and everyday objects

Content domain reference: 2G3

Prerequisites for learning

Describe the properties of 2-D shapes: circle, triangle, square, oblong, pentagon, hexagon and octagon

Describe the properties of 3-D shapes: sphere, cone, cylinder, cube, cuboid, triangular prism, square pyramid

Learning outcomes

Compare and sort common 2-D shapes and everyday objects

Compare and sort common 3-D shapes and everyday objects

Key vocabulary

side, vertex (vertices), edge, face

Resources

trays of 2-D shapes; trays of 3-D shapes: sphere, cone, cylinder, cube, cuboid, triangular prism, square pyramid (include a tetrahedron and a range of pyramids and prism); Venn diagram mat; mirror

Background knowledge

- Establish the difference between 'side' and 'face' by constructing 2-D and 3-D shapes, using construction materials such as straws and plasticine. Show that 'side' is only used to describe properties of 2-D shapes compared to 'face' that describes a property of solid shapes.

Teaching Activity 1a (15 minutes)

Compare and sort common 2-D shapes and everyday objects

- Draw a Carroll diagram on a large piece of paper with columns labelled: 'Fewer than 4 sides' and '4 sides or more' and rows labelled 'Sides of the same length', 'Sides of different length'. Say: **This is a type of sorting diagram called a Carroll diagram.**

- Hold up a square. Say: **I need to decide which box to put this shape in.** Start with the top left box and say: **To go in the box, the shape must have fewer than 4 sides and the sides must be all the same length.** Establish that it is easier to think of each property as a question, for example: 'Does the shape have fewer than 4 sides?' and 'Does the shape have sides of the same length?' Explain that if we are able to answer 'yes' to both questions, then the shape can be placed in the box.

- Ask: **Does the shape have fewer than 4 sides?** (no) Say: **Since the answer to the question is 'no' there is no point asking the questions in the rows as the shape cannot be placed in this column.**

- Say: **We move to the column to the right and ask the question: 'Does the shape have 4 sides or more?'** (yes) Explain that the shape will only go in this box if we can answer 'yes' to the question in the first row. Say: **Does the shape have sides of the same length?** (yes) Explain that, since we have answered yes to both questions, the shape can be placed in the box for '4 sides or more' and 'Sides of the same length'.

- Repeat the question process for another shape, for example, an isosceles triangle. Start with the top left box and say: **To go in the box, we must be able to answer yes to two questions, 'Does the shape have fewer than 4 sides?' and 'Does the shape have sides of the same length?'** Ask: **Is the answer 'yes' to both questions?** (no) **For which question is the answer 'no'?** (does the shape have sides of the same length?) Say: **As we were able to answer 'yes' to the column question but not the first row question, we move to the second row question and ask: 'Does the shape have sides of different length?' What is the answer?** (yes) Explain that since we have answered yes to both questions, the shape can be placed in the box for 'Fewer than 4 sides' and 'Sides of different length'.

Teaching Activity 1b (15 minutes)

Compare and sort common 2-D shapes and everyday objects

- Display a Venn diagram sorting mat.
- On whiteboards, write two properties to sort the shapes by: 'Has 4 sides or more' and 'Has a vertical line of symmetry' and place each whiteboard next to a set circle.
- Point to the diagram and say: **A Venn diagram is a way of sorting objects with the same properties. In this Venn diagram, we have two sets that are labelled with the properties to sort by.** Point to the overlap section. Say: **The overlap section is where an object goes that belongs to both sets. We call the overlap section the 'intersection'.** Explain that there is also a space outside the circles where objects that do not fit any of the properties can go.
- Hold up a square. Say: **Where does this go? Let's start with the intersection.** Ask: **What shapes go here?** Agree that shapes that have 4 sides or more and a vertical line of symmetry go here. Ask: **Does the square have 4 sides or more?** (yes) **Does the square have a vertical line of symmetry?** (yes) Say: **Since the square belongs to both sets, we place it in the intersection.**
- Hold up an isosceles triangle. Ask: **Does this triangle go in the intersection?** (no) **Why not?** (the shape has a vertical line of symmetry but it does not have 4 sides or more) Explain that since the shape has only one of the sorting properties, we can place it in one set. Point to the area of the diagram for shapes that have a vertical line of symmetry but do not have 4 sides or more. Place the triangle in this area.

Teaching Activity 2a (10 minutes)

Compare and sort common 3-D shapes and everyday objects

- Draw a Carroll diagram on a large piece of paper with columns labelled: 'Has a curved surface' and 'Does not have a curved surface' and rows labelled: 'Has a circular surface' 'Does not have a circular surface'.
- Hold up a cube. Say: **I need to decide which box to put this shape in.** Start with the top left box and say: **To go in the box, the shape must have a curved surface and a circular surface.** Ask: **Does the shape have a curved surface?** (no) Say: **As the answer is 'no' there is no point asking the questions in the rows as the shape cannot be placed in this column.**

- Say: **We move to the column to the right and answer 'yes' as the shape does not have a curved surface.** Explain that the shape will only go in this box if we can answer yes to the question in the first row. Say: **Does the shape have a circular surface?** (no) Explain that we move to the next row and answer 'yes' to the question as it does not have a circular surface. Explain that since we have answered yes to both questions, the shape can be placed in the box for 'Does not have a curved surface' and 'Does not have a circular surface'.

Teaching Activity 2b (10 minutes)

Compare and sort common 3-D shapes and everyday objects

- Display a Venn diagram sorting mat.
- On whiteboards, write two properties to sort the shapes by: '6 or more faces' and '6 or more edges' and place each whiteboard next to a set circle.
- Hold up a cube. Say: **I need to decide which set to put this shape in. Let's start with the intersection.** Ask: **What shapes go here?** Agree shapes that have 6 or more faces and 6 or more edges. Ask: **Does the shape have 6 faces or more?** (yes) **Does the shape have 6 or more edges?** (yes) Say: **Since the shape belongs to both sets, we place it in the intersection.**
- Hold up a triangular prism. Ask: **Does this shape go in the intersection?** (no) **Why not?** (the shape has only 5 faces) **Does the shape have 6 or more edges?** (yes) Explain that since the shape has one, but not both of the sorting properties, we can place it in one set but not the other. Point to the area of the diagram for shapes that have 6 or more edges but do not have 6 faces or more. Place the triangular prism in this area.
- Hold up a triangular pyramid. Say: **Does anyone know its name?** Praise anyone who identifies the shape as a triangular pyramid. Lead the children in a count of the number of faces, vertices and edges. Say: **A tetrahedron is a solid shape with four faces, which are all triangles, 6 edges and 4 vertices.**
- Ask: **Does this shape go in the intersection?** (no) **Why not?** (the shape has 6 or more edges but it only has 4 faces) Explain that since the shape has one but not both of the sorting properties, we can place it in one set but not the other. Point to the area of the diagram for shapes that have 6 or more edges but do not have 6 or more faces. Place the pyramid in this area.

Unit 31: Order and arrange combinations of mathematical objects in patterns and sequences

Content domain reference: 2P1

Prerequisites for learning

Identify 2-D and 3-D shapes and know some of their properties

Understand the language of order and sequencing, e.g. before, after, next

Understand ordinal numbers, e.g. first, second, third, fourth

Key vocabulary

order, before, after, next, pattern, sequence, repeating unit

Resources

2-D shape sets; blank cards; 3-D shape sets; model 'action' figure; large 5 by 5 grids

Learning outcomes

Order and arrange combinations of mathematical objects in patterns and sequences

Background knowledge

- Some children have difficulty identifying the repeating unit of a pattern. For example, for a square-circle pattern they fail to identify the 'square-circle' unit and instead, extend the pattern by alternating a square followed by a circle. Difficulty at this level may limit their ability to work with patterns at higher levels.

- Practising extending and creating a simple pattern comprising two shapes, such as coloured paper clips or cubes, will help to develop their confidence. Ask them to break the paper clip or bead pattern into parts so that each part is exactly the same. Identifying the repeating unit and how many times it is repeated, will help the children to describe many repeating patterns.

Teaching Activity 1a (15 minutes)

Order and arrange combinations of mathematical objects in patterns and sequences

- Say: **What do we mean when we talk about a pattern?** Establish that a pattern is a repeating symbol, shape, object or picture.

- Using 2-D shapes, lay down the beginning of a pattern: square, triangle, circle, square, triangle, circle in front of the children.

- Ask: **Who can tell me what the first shape in the sequence is?** (square) **Which shape is second in the sequence?** (triangle) Repeat for the shapes in the third, fourth, fifth positions to check that the children understand ordinal numbers and the language of sequence.

- Ask: **Who can tell me the shape that comes next in the sequence?** (square) **How do you know?** Agree that the next shape in the sequence is a square.

- Establish that the pattern repeats after the third shape. Ask: **Which set of shapes repeat in the sequence?** (square, triangle, circle) Say: **The repeating set of shapes is square-triangle-circle. We call this the 'repeating unit' of the pattern.** Explain that knowing the repeating unit of a sequence helps to find the next shape in the sequence.

- Say: **Patterns follow certain rules. By working out the rule we can predict the next shape or object in the sequence.**

- Ask the children to predict the shapes that come next. Agree that the next shapes will be: triangle, circle, and then the sequence repeats.

- Arrange the following sequence: circle, hexagon, hexagon, triangle, circle, hexagon, hexagon, triangle. Lay three blank cards to the right of the last triangle and explain that they represent the next three shapes in the sequence.

- Say: **Before I ask you what the next shape in the sequence, let's sing the sequence.** Explain that, by singing a sequence, children might discover the rule for the pattern. Lead the children in a song or chant that follows a familiar beat or tune: 'circle, hexagon, hexagon, triangle …circle, hexagon, hexagon, triangle', and so on. Continue singing beyond the number of objects on the table.

- Point to the first blank card and repeat the song. Stop when you get to the blank card and ask the children the shape that was just mentioned in the song. (circle) Continue until the next two shapes are known. (hexagon, hexagon)

Teaching Activity 1b (15 minutes)

Order and arrange combinations of mathematical objects in patterns and sequences

- Say: **What do we mean when we talk about a pattern?** Establish that a pattern is a repeating symbol, shape, object or picture.

- Draw a 5 by 5 grid on a large piece of paper. Make a 'pathway' of shapes that lead up to the grid: square, triangle, circle, square, triangle, circle.

- Fill the cells in each column of the grid with 2-D shapes. Each column must have a square, circle, triangle, pentagon and hexagon. Create a pathway across the grid from the next five shapes in the sequence: square, triangle, circle, square, triangle. Each of these shapes should be horizontally or diagonally to the right of the previous shape in the sequence.

- Point to the shape 'pathway' and the grid and tell the children that this is a shape problem that they must solve. Say: **Pretend that you are explorers. You have come to a cave seeking treasure and are greeted by a wizard who tells you that you must solve a problem to gain the treasure.** Place a model 'action' figure at the beginning of the 'pathway'.

- Continue the story, revealing that the treasure is on the far side of the grid. Point to the path and explain that the shapes represent a sequence that must be continued across the grid in order to reach the treasure. Say: **Unfortunately, if the explorer selects an incorrect shape they will disappear forever!**

- Say the sequence: square, triangle, circle, square, triangle, circle. Move the figure to the last circle in the path.

- Ask: **Who can tell me what the first shape in the sequence is?** (square) **Which shape is second in the sequence?** (triangle) Repeat for the shapes in the third, fourth, fifth positions to check that the children understand ordinal numbers and the language of sequence.

- Say: **The next shapes in the sequence are hidden in the grid. You need to find the pathway of shapes across the grid to get to the treasure.**

- Ask: **Who can tell me the shape that comes next in the sequence?** (square) **How do you know?** Accept the children's comments. Establish that the pattern repeats after the third shape. Ask: **Which set of shapes repeat in the sequence?** (square, triangle, circle). Say: **The repeating set of shapes is square-triangle-circle. We call this the 'repeating unit' of the pattern.** Explain that knowing the repeating unit of a sequence helps to find the next shape in the sequence. Say: **Patterns follow certain rules. By working out the rule we can predict the next shape or object in the sequence.**

- Choose a child to place the figure on the square in the first column of the grid.

- Ask the children to predict the shape that comes next. Agree that the next shape will be a triangle. Place the figure on the triangle in the second column of the grid.

- Continue until all five shapes in the sequence have been identified (circle, square, triangle).

- Say: **The explorer has got to the other side of the grid and can now claim the treasure!**

- Create a new 'treasure pathway' using the following sequence: circle, hexagon, hexagon, triangle, circle, hexagon, hexagon, triangle. Arrange the shapes in the grid to continue the sequence.

- Ask: **For this sequence, what is the repeating unit – in other words, the set of shapes that repeat?** (circle, hexagon, hexagon, triangle) Choose two children to use the rule of the pattern to establish the next shapes in the sequence and get the figure to the other side of the grid.

Unit 32: Use mathematical vocabulary to describe position, direction and movement, including movement in a straight line and distinguishing between rotation as a turn and in terms of right angles for quarter, half and three-quarter turns (clockwise and anti-clockwise)

Content domain reference: 2P2

Prerequisites for learning

Describe position and movement using everyday language: above, below, in front of, behind, between, left, right, closest, farthest, forwards, backwards

Distinguish between turns of different sizes

Learning outcomes

Use mathematical vocabulary to describe position

Use mathematical vocabulary to describe direction

Identify quarter, half and three quarter turns as clockwise or anticlockwise

Key vocabulary

Position, point, grid, compass, north, south, east, west, quarter turn, half turn, three-quarter turn, clockwise, anti clockwise

Resources

Sorting bears: red, green, yellow, blue; Resource 8: Treasure map; Resource 9: Blank treasure map; cones of different colours, analogue clocks, large arrows

Background knowledge

- When teaching rotation, provide a range of models and comparative examples. An object that experiences a full turn finishes in the same position and faces in the same direction from which it started. A half turn will turn an object to a position opposite to which it started. A quarter turn can be linked to the amount of turn made by the minute hand of a clock from, for example, 12 o'clock to quarter past 12.

Teaching Activity 1a (15 minutes)

Use mathematical vocabulary to describe position

- Say: **What do we mean when we talk about the position of something?** Say: **Position is the language we use to describe where something is by comparing it to where other objects are.**

- Give pairs of children a set of coloured sorting bears. Say: **I am going to give you instructions to follow. The instructions will tell you where to position bears of different colours**.

- The children move the bears according to the following instructions:

- Say: **Place the bears in a row with the green bear to the right of the blue bear and the red bear to the left of the blue bear.** Check that the children remember their right and left. A useful way for children to remember this is for them to hold out their palms, fingers together and the thumbs sticking out. The inner outline of the fingers and thumb on the left hand makes the letter 'L', standing for 'left'. Ask: **Who can describe the position of the blue bear?** (it is in the middle of/between the red and green bears)

- Say: **Place the bears so that the red bear is in front of the green bear and the green bear is in front of the blue bear**. Ask: **Who can describe the position of the blue bear?** (it is behind the green bear)

- Say: **Hold a green bear in the air. Then hold a red bear above the green bear** Ask your partner to hold a blue bear above the red bear. Ask: **Who can describe the position of the red bear?** (it is below the blue bear) **The position of the green bear?** (it is below the red bear)

- Ask each group to stand four bears in a row in the following order: green, blue, red, yellow

- Ask questions such as:
  - **What colour is the bear in front of/ behind the blue bear?** (green, red)
  - **Which bears are closest to the red bear?** (blue, yellow)
  - **Which bear is farthest from the blue bear?** (yellow)
  - **Which bear is between the green and red bears?** (blue)
  - **Which bear is closest to the yellow one?** (red)
  - **Which bear is farthest from the green one?** (yellow)

Teaching Activity 1b (20 minutes)

Use mathematical vocabulary to describe position

- Say: **What do we mean when we talk about the position of something?** Say: **Position is the language we use to describe where something is by comparing it to where other objects are.**

- Attach an enlarged copy of **Resource 8: Treasure map** to the board.

- Point to the first map. Say: **Pretend you are a pirate. This is a map you have drawn reminding you of where you have buried all your treasure**. Continue the story and explain that the map is divided into grid squares where each square is identified by a letter and a number.

- Say: **To find the position of any grid square we move left or right along the letters at the bottom of grid, then up or down the numbers along the side of the grid**.

- Point to the sword. Say: **The position of the sword is C3.** Trace a finger or pointer along the horizontal axis to column C. Say: **The sword is in column C.** Trace a finger up the vertical axis to row 3. Say: **The sword is in row 3. So, the position of the sword is C3**. Repeat for a different treasure object.

- **Ask the children questions that require the location of treasure objects, for exampleWhich treasure object is in square D1?** (gems) **C5?** (ring) **B3?** (treasure chest)

- Say: **Another way to find objects on the grid is to describe where they are compared to the position of other objects.** Ask questions such as:
  - **Which square lies one square above/below the potion in square E2 and which treasure object is there**? (E3, bag of gold; E1, key)
  - **Which square lies between squares E3 and G3 and which treasure object is there?** (F3, 1 silver piece)
  - **Which square lies one square to the left of C3 and which treasure object is there?** (B3, treasure chest)

- Give pairs of children a copy of **Resource sheet 8: Treasure maps.** Say: **Ask your partner questions about the position of treasure objects on your map.** Give the children examples: 'Which square is the treasure chest in?', 'Which treasure object is in square D4?' or 'Which treasure object is above/below/ to the left of/right of the key in square E1?'

- Point to the blank grid on **Resource 9: Blank treasure map.** Say: **I am going to give you instructions to follow. The instructions will tell you where to position treasure items**.

- The children draw the position of treasure objects according to the following instructions:
  - Say: **Draw a telescope in square A1, a hat in square A3 and an eye patch in square A4.** Ask: **Which object is closest to the hat?** (eye patch) **Which object is farthest from the hat?** (telescope)
  - Say: **Draw a treasure chest in square D3 then draw a sword in the square to the right and a diamond in the square to the left**. Check that the children remember their right and left. A useful way for children to remember this is for them to hold out their palms, fingers together and the thumbs sticking out. The inner outline of the fingers and thumb on the left hand makes the letter 'L', standing for 'left'. Ask: **Who can describe the position of the treasure chest compared to the sword and the diamond?** (it is in the middle of/between the sword and the diamond)

Teaching Activity 2a (20 minutes)

Use mathematical vocabulary to describe direction

- In preparation, mark a 7 by 7 grid on the playground. Label the columns A to G along the horizontal axis and the rows 1 to 7 up the vertical axis. Alongside the grid draw a compass and label the points 'North', 'South, 'East' and 'West'.

- Take the children to the playground. Ask them to stand in front of the large grid. Position a red cone in square C3.

- Say: **The grid is divided into squares where each square is identified by a letter and a number. To find the position of any grid square we move left or right along the letters at the bottom of grid, then up or down the numbers along the side of the grid. Let's find the position of the red cone.** Walk along the horizontal axis and stop at column C. Say: **The cone is in column C.** Walk up to meet the cone. Say: **The cone is in row 3. So, we know that the position of the red cone is C3.**

- Ask the children questions that require the location of cones of different colours, for example: 'In which square is the yellow cone?'

- Say: **Another way to find objects on the grid is to use directions. What do we mean when we talk about directions?.** Say: **A direction is that path along which something moves or the point toward which something faces. For example, when you face forward and move, forward is the direction you are moving.**

- Point to the compass. Say: **Compasses are used to show the direction of places on grids or maps.** Point to the compass point 'N'. Say: **'N' stands for north. On most grids or maps, north points to the top of the grid.** Point to 'S'. Say **'S' stands for south. South will be in the opposite direction to north.** Explain that 'E' stands for East and 'W' for West. Say: **You can remember where the points of a compass are by remembering a rhyme 'Never Eat Slimy Wellies'.**

- Remove all the cones from the grid. Place a green cone at A3, red cone at D3 and a yellow cone at G3. Demonstrate that to walk over to the yellow cone from the red cone, one would have to go east. Ask them which direction you would walk to go over to the green cone? (west)

- Introduce the idea of directions between two points. Remove all the cones from the grid. Place a green cone at E7, red cone at E4 and a yellow cone at E2. Ask a child to stand by the red cone. Say: **Face the green cone. Which direction are you facing?** (north) Ask the child to walk north to the green cone. Ask: **How many squares was that?** (3) Say: **The instruction that takes a person from the red cone to the green cones is 'walk three squares north'.**

- The child returns to the red cone. Say: **Face the yellow cone. Which direction are you facing?** (south) Ask the child to walk south to the yellow cone. Ask: **How many squares was that?** (2) Say: **The instruction that takes a person from the red cone to the yellow cone is 'walk two squares south'**

- Repeat the above activity for cones in different grid squares. Ask the children for the instruction that will take a person from one cone to the other. Ensure they state the correct direction and the number of squares.

Teaching Activity 2b (10 minutes)

Use mathematical vocabulary to describe direction

- Return to the map in **Resource 8: Treasure map.** Say: **Another way to find objects on the grid is to describe where they are compared to the position of other objects.**

- Point to the diamond in square G3. Ask: **What is the position of the diamond compared to the key in E1? In other words, how would we get from the key to the diamond?** Point to the key and say: **To find the location of the diamond we need to move two squares to the right of the key** (trace a finger 3 squares to the right to meet column G) then 2 squares up to meet row 3. Say: **We can say that the diamond is 2 squares to the right and 2 squares up from the key.**

- Point to the pearls in square D4. Say: **How would you describe the position of the pearls compared to the position of the pirate flag in square A5?** Demonstrate that the pearls are 3 squares to the right of square A5 and then 1 square down to D4. Say: **We can say that the pearls are 3 squares to the right and 1 square down from the pirate flag.**

- Continue to pose questions that require the children to find the location of an object compared to another, for example: **Where is the treasure chest compared to the sword?** (the treasure chest is 4 squares to the left and 2 squares down from the sword)

- Give pairs of children a copy of **Resource 8: Treasure maps.** Say: **Ask your partner questions about the position of treasure objects compared to others.** Choose groups to demonstrate how they posed and answered questions.

Teaching Activity 3a (15 minutes)

Identify quarter, half and three quarter turns as clockwise or anticlockwise

- Say: **In this lesson we are going to practise moving in quarter, half and three quarter turns.** Remind the children that the word turn is a movement around a point.

- Ask the children to stand in the centre of a large space, such as the hall. Put hoops around the centre of the room. Ask the children to stand in a hoop and all face the same wall. Label the wall 'N' for 'North' and, in a clockwise direction, the three remaining walls 'E', 'S' and 'W' for 'East', 'South' and 'West' to match the compass points.

- Tell them to stretch out their right arms and point towards the wall they are facing. Say: **Follow me as I move around the hall. Rotate your body and use your outstretched finger to trace a circular path around the hoop**. Walk around the hall in a clockwise direction to face East, making sure the children are rotating correctly. Ask: **Can you describe the turn you have made?** (a quarter turn) **How do you know?** (my arm has moved a quarter of the way around the hoop)

- Repeat the movement but this time in an anti-clockwise direction. Ask: **What is the effect of a quarter turn to the right and then a quarter turn to the left?** Agree that the rotation returns one back to the starting position.

- Say: **We are now going to move a half turn. Which compass point do you think we will face?** (South) Walk around the hall in a clockwise direction to face south making sure the children are rotating correctly. Ask: **Were you right?** Establish that all the children now point in the opposite direction from where they started – having moved from north to south. Ask: **How many quarter turns is this the same as?** (2) Ask: **What movement would return use back to our starting point?** (quarter turn to the left) Ask the children to complete the turn back to North.

- Say: **If we were to combine three quarter turns to the right, which compass point do you think we would face?** (west) Walk around the hall in a clockwise direction to face west. Making sure the children are rotating correctly. Ask: **Can you describe the turn you have made?** (a three-quarter turn) **How do you know?** (my arm has moved three-quarters of the way around the hoop)

- Place a clock on the floor near each hoop. The clocks should have second hands. Say: **We are now going to practise moving in clockwise and anticlockwise directions. Look at the second hand of the clock and the direction in which it moves**. Explain that the term 'clockwise' means travelling in the same direction as the hand on a clock, and 'anticlockwise' means the opposite direction.

- Give the children instructions to move in different combinations of quarter, half and three quarter turns in clockwise and anticlockwise directions.

- Play a few rounds of asking the children to predict the compass point they will face after completing a particular turn, for example: 'a quarter turn clockwise' 'a half turn anticlockwise, 'a three quarter turn clockwise'.

Teaching Activity 3b (15 minutes)

Identify quarter, half and three quarter turns as clockwise or anticlockwise

- Say: **In this lesson we are going to practise moving in quarter, half and three quarter turns**. Remind the children that the word turn is a movement around a point.

- Provide each group with a large arrow or show them how to cut one out of a piece of paper.

- Find a large space and ask the children to face in the same direction. They place the arrow on the floor and align it so that it faces directly ahead.

- Say: **If the arrow was to make a quarter turn to the right, where would the arrow be pointing?** Remind the children that a quarter turn is a movement equivalent to one quarter of a circle. Ask the children to turn the arrow and confirm that all the arrows point in the same direction.

- Now ask the children the direction the arrow would point if it made a half turn to the right. Choose a child to demonstrate the half turn. Repeat for a half turn to the left. Ask: **Does it matter which direction the arrow turns?** (no) Finally, ask the children to place the arrow facing forward again and ask the children to demonstrate a three quarter turn to the right. Establish that a three=quarter turn has the same effect as three quarter turns.

- Place a clock on the floor near each hoop. The clocks should have second hands. Say: **We are now going to practise moving in clockwise and anticlockwise directions. Look at the second hand of the clock and the direction in which it moves**. Explain that the term 'clockwise' means travelling in the same direction as the hand on a clock, and 'anticlockwise' means the opposite direction.

- Give the children instructions to move in different combinations of quarter, half and three quarter turns in clockwise and anti-clockwise directions.

- Working in pairs, ask the children to practise calling out turning instructions to each other.

Unit 33: Interpret and construct simple pictograms, tally charts, block diagrams and tables

Content domain reference: 2S1

Prerequisites for learning

Sort objects into groups and compare different groups

Learning outcomes

Interpret and construct simple pictograms

Interpret and construct tally charts, tables and block diagrams

Key vocabulary

pictogram, tally chart, table, block diagram

Resources

Resource 10: Pictogram; interlocking cubes; large grid paper; Resource 11: Tally chart

Background knowledge

- Many children at this age find it difficult to interpret graphs that are unfamiliar to them. It is therefore important that children are actively involved in the collection of data and its presentation in graphical form.

Teaching Activity 1a (10 minutes)

Interpret and construct simple pictograms

- Attach an enlarged copy of **Resource 10: Pictogram** to the board. Say: **A teacher has asked her class what their favourite colour is and the children answered the question by drawing a smiley face next to that colour.**

- Point to the pictogram. Ask: **Who knows what we call this type of diagram?** (pictogram) Say: **A pictogram is a way of showing information using pictures or symbols.** Point to a row of faces. Say: **Each smiley face represents the choice of one person.**

- Point to the votes for 'blue'. Say: **To find the number of children who prefer blue, we simply look across the row labelled blue and count the faces. How many children is that?** (7)

- Say: **Let's make our own pictogram.** Draw a grid on the board and label rows for 'red', 'green', 'blue, 'yellow' and 'purple'. Ask the children to draw a face next to the colour they prefer. Ask: **How many children prefer red? Purple? Green?**

- Next to the pictogram, write: 'Key: 1 face = 1 child'. Say: **A key tells us what the symbol on a pictogram means. For this pictogram, we know that each face means the vote of one child.**

- Change the text to '1 😊 = 2 children'. Tell the children that now each smiley face now represents 2 children. Ask: **How many children prefer blue? Yellow?**

Teaching Activity 1b (15 minutes)

Interpret and construct simple pictogram

- In preparation for the lesson, construct towers of cubes to represent the results of a survey about favourite zoo animals. Use a different colour of cube to represent each animal: tiger (6 cubes), lion (8 cubes), monkey (10 cubes), rhino (4 cubes), giraffe (7 cubes). Label the towers with the name of the animal.

- Point to the towers and say: **The children in a class were asked the question, 'What is your favourite zoo animal?'** Explain that the children voted for their favourite animal by placing a cube next to the animal name. Ask: **How many children voted for lion?** (8) **Giraffe?** (7)

- Say: **I am going to present this information in a diagram.** Attach a large piece of grid paper to the board and construct the framework of a pictogram on it. Label the rows with names of the zoo animals. Beside the animal name, draw enough paw prints to represent the number of votes for that animal.

- Ask: **Who can tell me the name of this type of diagram?** (pictogram) Say: **A pictogram is a way of showing information using pictures or symbols.** Point to a row of paw prints. Say: **Each paw print represents one person's vote.**

- Point to the votes for 'tiger'. Say: **To find the number of children who prefer tigers, we simply look across the row labelled 'tiger' and count the paw prints. How many children is that?** (6)

- Say: **Let's make our own pictogram.** Draw a grid on the board and label the rows with the names of the zoo animals. Ask the children to draw a paw print next to the animal they prefer. Ask: **How many children voted for lion? Monkey? Rhino?**

- Next to the pictogram, write: 'Key: 1 paw print = 1 child'. Say: **A key tells us what the symbol on a pictogram means. For this pictogram, each paw print means the vote of one child.**

- Change the text to '1 🐾 = 2 children'. Say: **A pictogram symbol can be used to represent any amount of things.** Ask: **How many children voted for giraffe? Tiger?**

Teaching Activity 2a (15 minutes)

Interpret and construct tally charts, tables and block diagrams

- Attach an enlarged copy of **Resource Sheet 11: Tally Chart** to the board. Point to the table. Say: **The table shows the responses of a class of children to the question, 'What is your favourite pet?' Each child has voted by making a mark next to the name of their favourite pet.** Point to the row for 'rabbit'. Ask: **How many children voted for rabbit?** (4)

- Point to the row for 'dog'. Say: **In the tally system, every fifth mark is made as a diagonal line thorough the previous four to make a symbol called a 'gate'. Knowing that each gate represents 5 helps us to count the tally marks quickly.**

- Ask: **How many children voted for 'cat'?** Lead a count, skip-counting in 5s for the gate symbols and in 1s for the individual marks: 5, 10, 15, 16. Say: **There are 16 marks. This means that there were 16 votes for 'cat'.**

- With the help of the children, count up the tally marks in each row and write the total in the column 'Number'. Ask: **How many children voted for hamster?** (6)

- Attach a large piece of grid paper to the board. Draw a vertical axis numbered 1 to 20, writing each number in a separate grid square, then label the horizontal axis writing the names of the pets in one grid square of each column. Ask: **How many children voted for 'dog'?** (13) Colour the equivalent number of blocks in the column for 'dog'. Repeat for the other pets, choosing a different colour for each pet. Point to

the column for 'cat'. Ask: **Why have I coloured this number of blocks?** (the number of blocks represents the number of votes for cat, that is 16)

Teaching Activity 2b (15 minutes)

Interpret and construct tally charts, tables and block diagrams

- In preparation for the lesson, draw a frequency table on the board with columns for 'Vehicle', 'Tally', 'Number of children' and rows for 'bike', 'scooter', 'skateboard' and 'roller blades'. Ask: **What is your favourite wheeled vehicle? You will have a choice of 'bike', 'scooter', 'skateboard' and 'roller blades'.**

- Point to the table on the board. Say: **We are going to use a table divided into rows and columns to record our responses to the question.** Point to the first column. Say: **Instead of using pictures to record our results, we will use a set of marks called tally marks.**

- Explain that a mark is made next to the thing that a person prefers or votes for. Draw three marks next to 'bike'. Say: **The three marks mean that three children voted for 'bike'.** Add another mark for 'bike'. Say: **Now we have four marks representing the votes of four people. Let's add a fifth mark.** Draw a diagonal line through the four marks. Say: **For every fifth vote, instead of drawing another vertical tally mark we draw a diagonal line through the previous four marks to make a 'gate'. Knowing that each gate represents 5 helps us to count the tally marks quickly.**

- Draw 12 tally marks for 'scooter': two gates and two single marks. Ask: **How many marks is this?** Lead a count, skip-counting in 5s for the gate symbols and in 1s for the individual marks: 5, 10, 11, 12. Say: **There are 12 marks. This means that there were 12 votes for 'scooter'.**

- Complete a tally for 'skateboard' (11) and 'roller blades' (7). With the help of the children, count up the tally marks in each row and write the total in the column 'Number of children'.

- Attach a large piece of grid paper to the board. Draw a vertical axis numbered 1 to 15, writing each number in a separate grid square then label the horizontal axis writing the names of the vehicles in one grid square of each column. Ask: **How many children voted for 'scooter'?** Colour the equivalent number of blocks in the column for 'scooter'. Repeat for the other vehicles choosing a different colour for each vehicle. Point to the column for 'skateboard'. Ask: **Why have I coloured this number of blocks?** (the number of blocks represents the number of votes for skateboard)

Unit 34: Ask and answer simple questions by counting the number of objects in each category and sorting the categories by quantity

Content domain reference: 2S2a

Prerequisites for learning

Sort objects into groups and compare different groups

Construct and interpret a pictogram and a block diagram

Learning outcomes

Ask and answer questions from the information displayed in pictograms and block diagrams

Key vocabulary

pictogram, tally chart, table, block diagram

Resources

Resource 12: Rainy days 1; Resource 13: Rainy days 2; bag of counters: red, blue, green, yellow and purple; large blank grids

Background knowledge

- You may decide to work with children to create pictograms and block diagrams where symbols and blocks represent more than a single unit of measurement at a time. For example, children can use double units or any other combination of units to represent their data. Alternatively, you may devise data collection and presentation activities where children are required to go to other classrooms for survey data.

Teaching Activity 1a (10 minutes)

Ask and answer questions from the information displayed in pictograms and block diagrams

- Attach an enlarged copy of **Resource 12: Rainy days 1** and **Resource 13: Rainy days 2** to the board. (both pictogram and block diagram) Explain that a Year 2 class in a different school began working on a weather topic.

- Say: **For a project, they decided to record the number of rainy days each month. The class then constructed a pictogram and a block diagram to present the data. What do we mean when we talk about data?** Say: **Data is the information we get from counting things, like the number of birds in a tree, the number of seeds that grew into flowers or the colour of each chocolate in a bag of sweets.**

- Point to the pictogram. Ask: **What does each umbrella symbol represent?** (2 rainy days) **What do you think each half umbrella symbol represents?** (1 rainy day)

- Ask: **How many rainy days were there in March?** (13 rainy days) **How do you know?** (there are 6 whole umbrellas representing 12 rainy days and 1 half umbrella representing 1 rainy day. 12 + 1 = 13)

- Ask: **How many rainy days were there in April?** (16 rainy days) **How do you know?** (there are 8 whole umbrellas. Since each umbrella represents 2 rainy days, 8 umbrellas must represent 16 rainy days)

- Ask: **How would you work out which month had the highest rainfall?** Establish that we look at the pictogram and find the month with the greatest number of umbrellas. Ask: **What is the answer?** (May) **What about the month with the lowest rainfall?** (February) **How do you know?** (February has the fewest umbrellas)

- Attach an enlarged copy of **Resource 13: Rainy days 2** to the board Say: **Let's look at the block diagram.** Remind the children that the data used to construct the block diagram is the same data that was used to construct the pictogram.

- Ask: **How many rainy days were there in January?** (17) **How do you know?** (since there are 17 blocks for January, and each block represents 1 rainy day, the number of rainy days must be 17)

- Ask: **How many rainy days were there in June?** (10) **How do you know?** (since there are 10 blocks for June, and each block represents 1 rainy day, the number of rainy days must be 10)

- Ask: **Out of the months January, February and March, which month had the greatest number of rainy days?** (January) **How do you know?** (it is the tallest column) Establish that since the blocks used to construct the graph are of equal size, the tallest column indicates the month with the largest number of rainy days.

- Ask: **Out of the months April, May and June, which month had the fewest number of rainy days?** (June) **How do you know?** (it is the shortest column) Establish that since the blocks used to construct the graph are of equal size, the shortest column indicates the month with the fewest number of rainy days.

- Working in pairs, ask children to pose questions to their partner using the data in the pictogram and/or the block diagram. The questions should be of the form: **How many rainy days were there in [month]? Out of [names of three months], which month received the greatest/least amount of rain?**

Teaching Activity 1b (20 minutes)

Ask and answer questions from the information displayed in pictograms and block diagrams

- In preparation for the lesson, prepare a bag of counters containing mixed numbers of red, blue, green, purple and yellow. There should be 15 or fewer of each colour.

- Hold up the bag and say: **The bag contains counters of 5 different colours.** Explain that since you scooped up the counters at random you have no idea of the numbers of each colour.

- Ask the children to pretend they are the managers of a café and that each counter represents a coloured plate.

- Say: **10 plates of the same colour must be placed on each table. I want you to count the number of each colour plate and use a tally chart to record the data.** Remind the children that data is the information that we get from counting things.

- Say: **We will then present the data in a pictogram and a block diagram and use the information to decide whether we have at least 10 of each colour plate.**

- Draw a table on the board with headings for 'colour', 'tally' and 'total' and rows for each of the five colours of plate.

- Allocate pairs of children a colour. Spread the counters on a table and ask the groups to count the number of counters (plates) of their chosen colour.

- Say: **Each time you count a counter (plate) of your colour, add a mark to the tally chart.** Remind the children that they need to cross through every fifth mark to make 'gates' to make the counting easier.

- When the tallies are complete, ask each group to add up the number of marks for their colour and write a total in the leftmost column.

- Attach two large blank grids to the board. Draw the layout for a pictogram on one of the grids. With the children assisting, decide on a key for the pictogram, for example: one circle to represent one plate, or one circle to represent two plates and a half circle to represent one plate. Ask the children to add the correct number of circles of their chosen colour to the rows of the pictogram.

- Point to the pictogram. Ask the children questions of the form: **How many red plates are there? Do we have enough red plates for the whole table? What about green plates, do we have enough of them for one table?**

- Ask: **How would you work out which plate colour is most common?** Establish that we look for the colour with the greatest number of circles (plates). Confirm the correct answer. Ask: **What about the plate colour that is least common? How would you find this information?** Establish that we look for the colour with the fewest number of circles (plates). Confirm the correct answer.

- Draw the axes, scale and labels for a block diagram. Ask the children to colour the number of grid squares corresponding to the number of coloured plates. Remind the children that the data used to construct the block diagram is the same data that was used to construct the pictogram.

- Ask the children questions of the following forms: **How many blue plates are there? How do you know?** (the number of blocks on the diagram is equal to the number of plates) **Do we have enough blue plates for the whole table? What about yellow plates, do we have enough of them for one table?** Confirm the correct answers.

- Finally, confirm the colours of plates that can be used in the café.

- Ask the children, in each pair, to pose questions to their partner using the data in the pictogram and/or the block diagram. The questions should be of the form: **How many colour plates are there? Out of [names of three colour plates] which colour plate is most common? Least common?**

Unit 35: Ask-and-answer questions about totalling and comparing categorical data

Content domain reference: 2S2b

Prerequisites for learning

Sort objects into groups and compare different groups

Construct and interpret a pictogram and a block diagram

Learning outcomes

Ask and answer questions about totalling and comparing categorical data

Key vocabulary

pictogram, tally chart, table, block diagram

Resources

Resource 14: Buses; large blank grid

Background knowledge

- As the children become more experienced using block diagrams, encourage them to read off the number of blocks indicated from the number on the axis rather than count them up.

Teaching Activity 1a (10 minutes)

Ask and answer questions about totalling and comparing categorical data

- Attach an enlarged copy of **Resource 14: Buses**. Explain that the pictogram shows the number of buses that were made by a company for the first six months of the year.

- Point to the pictogram. Ask: **What does each bus symbol represent?** (2 buses built) **What do you think each half bus symbol represents?** (1 bus built)

- Ask questions that require reading and comparison of the data:

  ◆ **How many buses were made in April?** (17)

  ◆ **How many buses were made in January?** (9)

  ◆ **In which month were most buses built?** (June)

  ◆ **In which month were the fewest buses built?** (January)

  ◆ **In which month were a greater number of buses built, February or May?** (February)

  ◆ **In which month were fewer buses built, March or April?** (March)

- Say: **Pretend that you work for the bus company. The manager of the company wants you to work out how many more buses were built in February than May. How would you do that?** Discuss and ask: **Is this an addition or subtraction problem?**

Establish that since we need to find the difference between two values, the question is a subtraction. Ask: **What is the calculation we need to solve?** Choose a child to write the subtraction on the board. Expect: 16 – 10. Ask: **How do you know?** (subtract the number of buses built in May from the number built in February to give the difference. This is how many more buses were built in February than May) Ask: **What is the answer?** (6)

- Give the children another task that involves comparing numbers of buses built each month, for example: **The manager of the company wants you to work out how many fewer buses were built in January than April. What is the answer?** Establish that the calculation is 17 – 9. (8 fewer buses)

- Say: **The manager of the company wants you to work out how many buses were built in March and June altogether. How would you do that?** Discuss and ask: **Is this an addition or subtraction problem?** Establish that the word 'altogether' tells us we must add values to find a total. Ask: **What is the calculation we need to solve?** Choose a child to write the addition on the board. Expect: 14 + 18. Ask: **How do you know?** (add the number of buses built in March to the number built in June to find the total number of buses built in both months) Ask: **What is the answer?** (32)

- Give the children another task that involves finding the total numbers of buses built over two months, for example: **The manager of the company wants you to work out how many buses were built in April and May altogether. What is the answer?** Establish that the calculation is 17 + 10. (27 buses)

- Ask the children to work in pairs and pose questions to their partner using the data in the pictogram. The questions should be of the form:

  - How many more/fewer buses were built in [month] than [month]?

  - How many buses were built in the months [month] and [month] altogether?

- Choose groups to give the answer and explain their solution.

Teaching Activity 1b (15 minutes)

Ask and answer questions about totalling and comparing categorical data

- Write on the board: 'There is more chance of throwing a 1 or a 2 on a dice than throwing a 3 or a 4, or a 5 or a 6.'

- Say: **Whether we believe this statement is true or not, how could we test it?** Discuss and establish that we could throw a dice several times, find the number of times the dice lands on each number, then find totals for throwing 1 or 2, 3 or 4, 5 or 6 and compare them.

- Ask the children to work in pairs. Say: **We will throw the dice and record the score each time. How many times do you think we should throw the dice?** Agree on a sensible number, for example, 30.

- Ask each group to draw a tally chart to record the data. Choose a child to throw the dice and call out the score. Say: **Make a tally of the numbers called out. When the dice has been thrown 30 times we will stop and count up the number of times the dice landed on each number.**

- The child begins throwing the dice and calling out the number landed. They repeat this for 30 times then the groups find the total for each dice score. Ask: **Do we all agree on the number of times each score was recorded?** The children say the totals and compare them. Confirm that all the groups agree on the numbers.

- Attach a blank grid to the board. Draw the axes, scale and labels for a block diagram. Ask the children to colour the number of grid squares corresponding to the number of times each score on the dice was thrown.

- Say: **Before we use the information in the graph to decide whether the statement on the board is true or not, let's use the graph to answer some other questions about the dice scores:**

  - **How many times did the dice give a score of 3?**

  - **How many times did the dice give a score of 5?**

  - **Which score occurred the most?**

  - **Which score occurred the least?**

  - **Which scored occurred a greater number of times, 1 or 4?**

  - **Which score occurred a fewer number of time, 2 or 6?**

- Ask the children a question that requires them to work out how many more times a score was thrown than another. Establish that the question involves a subtraction. Choose a child to write the calculation on the board and solve it.

- Ask the children a question that requires them to work out the total number of times two scores occurred. Establish that the question involves an addition. Choose a child to write the calculation on the board and solve it.

- Say: **Now let's return to the statement on the board.**

- Ask: **How many times did the scores 1 or 2 occur? How would you work this out? Establish that the total is found by adding the number of times '1' was rolled to the number of times '2' was rolled**. Choose a child to write the addition calculation on the board and solve it.

- Repeat for scores 3 or 4, then 5 or 6. Ask: **Do our results agree with the statement?** Prompt them to offer a reason for why the results agree/disagree with the statement. Conclude the discussion with a comment on the randomness of dice throws and how over a large number of throws the frequency of the scores should become increasingly similar.

100 square

1	2	3	4	5	6	7	8	9	10
11	12	13	14	15	16	17	18	19	20
21	22	23	24	25	26	27	28	29	30
31	32	33	34	35	36	37	38	39	40
41	42	43	44	45	46	47	48	49	50
51	52	53	54	55	56	57	58	59	60
61	62	63	64	65	66	67	68	69	70
71	72	73	74	75	76	77	78	79	80
81	82	83	84	85	86	87	88	89	90
91	92	93	94	95	96	97	98	99	100

Addition questions

$5 + 3 =$

$4 + 4 =$

$10 + 80 =$

$30 + 40 =$

$4 + 6 =$

$7 + 1 =$

$40 + 60 =$

$1 + 8 =$

$70 + 10 =$

$20 + 50 =$

$3 + 4 =$

$50 + 30 =$

$5 + 3 =$

$2 + 5 =$

Multiplication and division problems (1)

1. A bag of crisps costs 10p. How much do 6 bags cost?

2. Daffodils are sold in bunches of 5. Billy buys 20 daffodils. How many bunches does he buy?

3. Ria plants seeds in 2 rows of 10. How many seeds does she plant altogether?

4. Matt arranged 35 bean bags in 5 equal rows in the hall. How many bean bags will there be in each row?

5. Nina buys 12 packets of stickers. If each packet holds 2 stickers, how many stickers does she have altogether?

6. Packets contain 10 pencils. How many packets will contain 90 pencils?

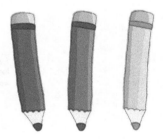

7. Liam arranges 5 books on each shelf in bookcase that has 8 shelves. How many books does he arrange in total?

Multiplication and division problems (2)

1. It takes 5 minutes for the minute hand on a clock to move from one number to the next. How many minutes pass as the minute hand moves from 12 to 6?

2. One alien has 2 heads. How many aliens are in a group if there are 16 heads?

3. 10 owls sit on each branch of a tree. If the tree has 2 branches, how many owls are there altogether?

4. The minute hand on a clock moves 45 minutes. How many groups of 5 minutes is that?

5. Magazines are sold with 2 free gifts. How many free gifts will 12 magazines have?

6. Soldiers stand 10 in a row. If 110 soldiers stand together, how many rows will there be?

7. Aliens have 5 legs. If there are 12 aliens, how many legs will they have altogether?

Items to buy

Blank clock faces

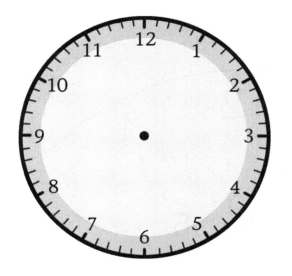

12-hour clock

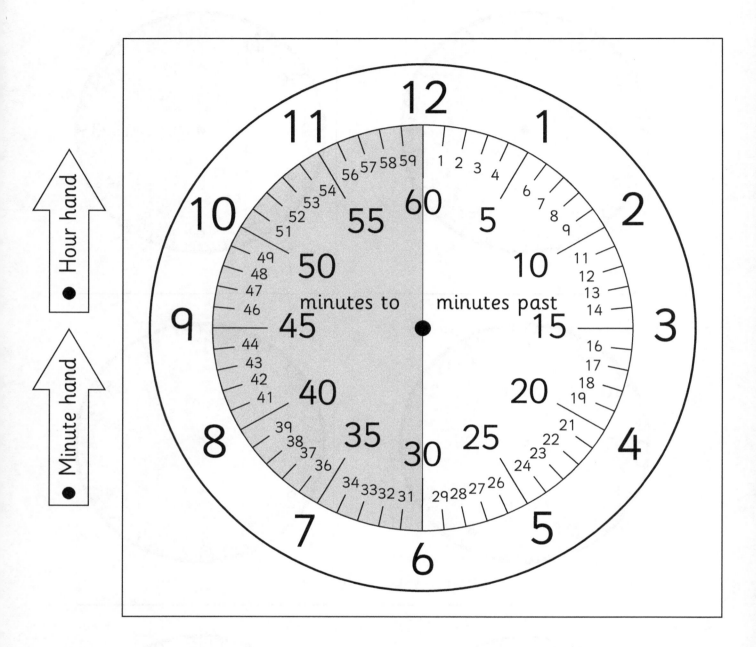

Treasure map

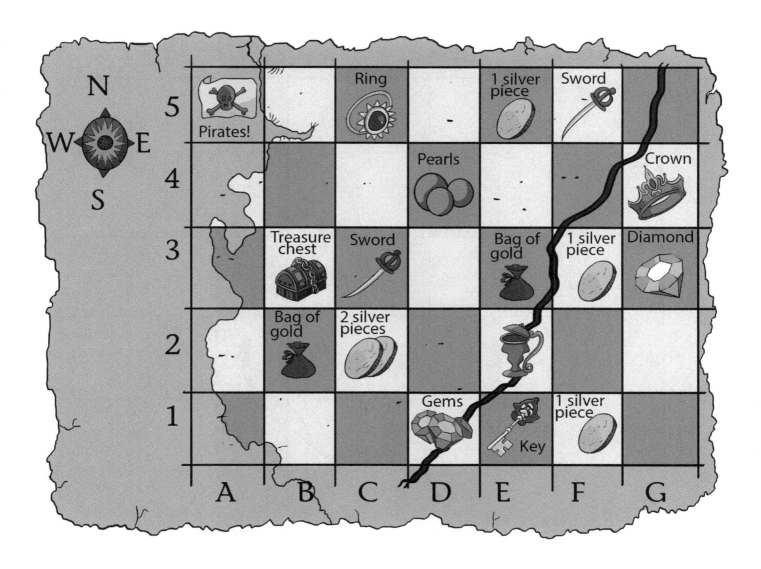

Blank treasure map

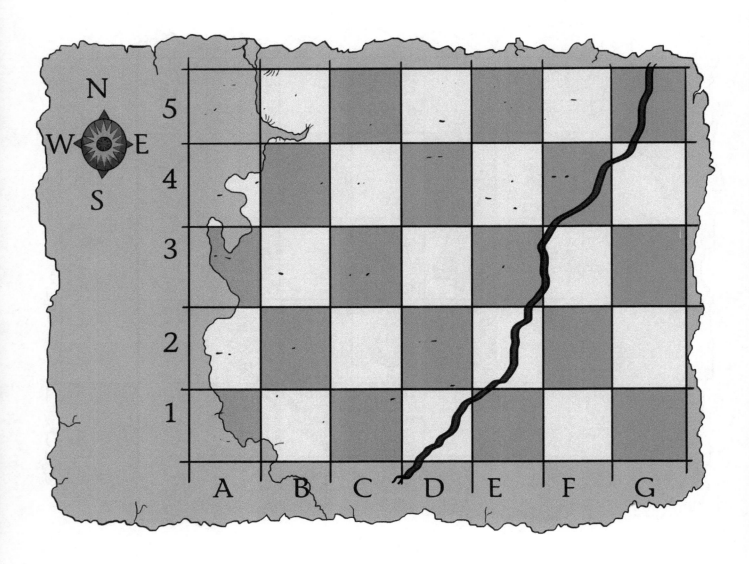

Pictogram

Survey: What is your favourite colour?

red	😊 😊 😊
blue	😊 😊 😊 😊 😊 😊 😊
green	😊 😊 😊 😊
yellow	😊 😊 😊 😊 😊 😊
purple	😊 😊
orange	😊 😊 😊 😊 😊
brown	😊

Tally chart

Favourite pets		
Pet	**Tally marks**	**Number**
dog	卌 卌 |||	
rabbit	||||	
cat	卌 卌 卌		
hamster	卌		

Rainy days

Pictogram: Number of rainy days each month

January	☂ ☂ ☂ ☂ ☂ ☂ ☂ ☂ ⚐
February	☂ ☂ ☂
March	☂ ☂ ☂ ☂ ☂ ☂ ⚐
April	☂ ☂ ☂ ☂ ☂ ☂ ☂
May	☂ ☂ ☂ ☂ ☂ ☂ ☂ ☂ ☂ ⚐
June	☂ ☂ ☂ ☂ ☂

Key ☂ = 2 rainy days

Rainy days 2

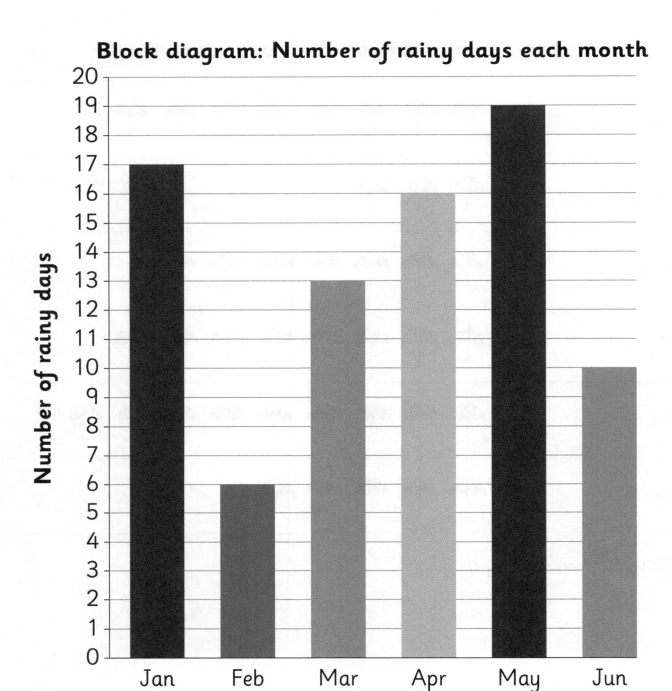

Block diagram: Number of rainy days each month

 Buses

Pictogram: Number of buses built each month

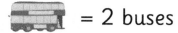 = 2 buses

Jan	🚌 🚌 🚌 🚌 🚌
Feb	🚌 🚌 🚌 🚌 🚌 🚌 🚌 🚌
Mar	🚌 🚌 🚌 🚌 🚌 🚌
Apr	🚌 🚌 🚌 🚌 🚌 🚌 🚌 🚌 🚌
May	🚌 🚌 🚌 🚌 🚌
Jun	🚌 🚌 🚌 🚌 🚌 🚌 🚌 🚌

Pupil Resource Pack Answers

Unit 1

1. **a)** 2s: 0, 2, 4, 6, 8, 10, 12, 14, 16, 18, 20, 22, 24
   3s: 0, 3, 6, 9, 12, 15, 18, 21, 24
   b) 0, 6, 12, 18, 24
2. **a)** 5s: 50, 45, 40, 35, 30, 25, 20, 15, 10, 5, 0
   10s: 50, 40, 30, 20, 10, 0
   b) 50, 40, 30, 20, 10, 0
3. 3s 0, 3, 6, 9, 12, 15
   5s 0, 5, 10, 15, 20, 25, 30
   10s 0, 10, 20, 30
4. 260, 270, 280, 290, 300
   360, 370, 380, 390, 400
   460, 470, 480, 490, 500

Unit 1 Quick test

1. **a)** 12, 15, 18
   b) 80, 90, 100
   c) 8, 10, 12
   d) 20, 25, 30
2. **a)** 10, 25, 35,
   b) 6, 10, 12, 18
   c) 100, 110, 150, 170
   d) 24, 21, 15, 9, 6
3.

Start number	Count in:	I say the number:	True/False
0	3s	34	False
0	5s	75	True
80	10s	130	True
0	2s	53	False

Unit 2

1. Children's own answers
2.

Tens	Ones	Number
10 10	1 1 1	23
10 10 10 10	1 1 1 1 1 1	46
10 10 10	1 1 1 1 1	35
10 10 10 10 10 10 10 10	1 1 1 1	84

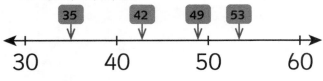

10 10 10 10 10	1 1 1 1 1 1 1	57

3. **a)** 16/36/46/86/96
   b) 81/83/84/86/89
   c) 98
   d) 13
   e) 93
   f) 14

Unit 2 Quick test

1. **a)** 3, 9
   b) 60
   c) 8, 4
   d) 70, 6
2. **a)** 46, **b)** 19, **c)** 13, 24, 35, 46, 57, 68, 79,
   d) 15, 26, 37, 48, 59,
3. Tom: 38 Mia: 68

Unit 3

1. 46 and 23
2.

33

T	O
3 tens	3 ones

55

T	O
5 tens	5 ones

70

T	O
7 tens	0 ones

89

T	O
8 tens	9 ones

3. **a)** 35, 42, 49, 53

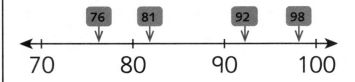

b) 81, 92, 76, and 98.

Unit 3 Quick test

1.

Numeral	Words	Base ten (blocks)
52	fifty-two	5 tens, 2 ones
17	seventeen	1 ten, 7 ones
74	seventy-four	7 tens, 4 ones
28	twenty-eight	2 tens, 8 ones
39	thirty-nine	3 tens, 9 ones
96	ninety-six	9 tens, 6 ones
41	forty-one	4 tens, 1 one
50	fifty	5 tens

2. **a)** $34 = 30 + 4$ **b)** $67 = 60 + 7$
   c) $91 = 90 + 1$ **d)** $79 = 70 + 9$
   e) $12 = 10 + 2$ **f)** $88 = 80 + 8$

3. **a)**

Amount	Number of 10p coins	Number of 1p coins
13p	1	3
62p	6	2
38p	3	8
45p	4	5

   b) 61p   72p   83p   94p

Unit 4

1. **a)** [32] is greater than [23]   [23] is less than [32]
     [32] > [23]
   b) [59] is greater than [57]   [57] is less than [59]
     [59] > [57]
2. **a)** [87] is greater than [78]   [78] is less than [87]
     [87] > [78]
   b) [65] is greater than [61]   [61] is less than [65]
     [65] > [61]
3. Children's own answers
4. **a)** Order: 22, 26, 42, 51
   b) Order: 24, 28, 31, 33

Unit 4 Quick test

1. **a)** 72 [<] 7 tens and 3 ones
   b) 6 tens and 6 ones [>] 65
   c) 8 tens and seven ones [>] 78
   d) 59 [<] 9 tens and 5 ones
   e) 80 [>] 7 tens and 9 ones
   f) 3 tens and 5 ones [<] 53
2. **a)** 46 < [?] < 49   47, 48
   b) 78 < [?] < 81   79, 80
   c) 32 > [ ] > 28   29, 30, 31
   d) 100 > [ ] > 96   97, 98, 99
3. Order: 13, 22, 31
4. **a)** Order: 17, 28, 37, 73
   b) Order: 34, 43, 52, 55
   c) Order: 68, 69, 80, 84, 86
   d) Order: 41, 46, 48, 52, 53

Unit 5

1. Children's own answers
2. **b)** 44 forty-four, **c)** 71 seventy-one, **d)** 59 fifty-nine,
   e) 88 eighty-eight, **f)** 12 twelve

Unit 5 Quick test

1.

Number (words)	Number (numeral)
thirty-eight	38
seventeen	17
eighty-one	81
sixty-three	63
ninety	90
seventy-seven	77

2.

Number (numeral)	Number (words)
40	Forty
68	Sixty eight
13	Thirteen
96	Ninety six
55	Fifty five
14	Fourteen

3.

	27 Twenty seven				63 Sixty three	
36 Thirty six	37 Thirty seven	38 Twenty eight		72 Seventy two	73 Seventy three	74 Seventy four
	47 Forty seven				83 Eighty three	

Unit 6

1. **a)** 76, **b)** 50
2. **a)** 34, 35, 37, 41, 43
   b) 63, 68, 78, 86, 87

Unit 6 Quick test

1. **a)** £45, £46, £47   **b)** 70 cm, 69 cm, 68 cm
   c) 68 days, 70 days, 72 days
   d) 10 hours, 7 hours, 4 hours
2. **a)** 40, **b)** 79, **c)** 36, **d)** 48
3. **a)** 13, 14, 23, 24, 42 (23)
   b) 42, 44, 45, 50, 54 (45)
   c) 57, 60, 67, 75, 77, 78, 87 (75)
   d) 81, 86, 89, 90, 91, 93, 98 (90)

Unit 7

1. **a)** 39 centimetres, **b)** 56 litres, **c)** 76p, **d)** 99 grams
2. **a)** 25 centimetres, **b)** 23 litres, **c)** 36p
3. **a)** 59, **b)** 99, **c)** 13

Unit 7 Quick test

1. **a)** 75 centimetres, **b)** 79 litres, **c)** 79p, **d)** 99 grams
2. **a)** 26 centimetres, **b)** 21 litres, **c)** 51p, **d)** 22 grams
3. **a)** 68, **b)** 99, **c)** 21, **d)** 54
4. **a)** 13, **b)** 59, **c)** 31, **d)** 95

Unit 8

1. **a)** 20 + 10 = 30, **b)** 30 + 20 = 50, **c)** 30 + 40 = 70,
   d) 10 + 50 = 60, **e)** 70 + 20 = 90, **f)** 40 + 40 = 80
2. **a)** 50 − 40 = 10, **b)** 70 − 20 = 50, **c)** 60 − 50 = 10,
   d) 80 − 40 = 40, **e)** 70 − 30 = 40, **f)** 90 − 70 = 20

Unit 8 Quick test

1. **a)** 7, **b)** 11, **c)** 14, **d)** 14, **e)** 18, **f)** 20, **g)** 19,
   h) 16, **i)** 20
2. **a)** 3, **b)** 6, **c)** 1, **d)** 9, **e)** 5, **f)** 7, **g)** 9, **h)** 8, **i)** 6
3. **a)** 6 + 2 = 8, 60 + 20 = 80
   b) 3 + 5 = 8, 30 + 50 = 80
   c) 5 + 4 = 9, 50 + 40 = 90
   d) 8 + 2 = 10, 80 + 20 = 100
   e) 1 + 7 = 8, 10 + 70 = 80,
   f) 3 + 6 = 9, 30 + 60 = 90
   g) 7 − 2 = 5, 70 − 20 = 50
   h) 8 − 4 = 4, 80 − 40 = 40
   i) 9 − 7 = 2, 90 − 70 = 20
   j) 6 − 5 = 1, 60 − 50 = 10
   k) 9 − 8 = 1, 90 − 80 = 10
   l) 10 − 4 = 6. 100 − 40 = 60
4. **a)** 60, **b)** 10, **c)** 30, **d)** 40, **e)** 50, **f)** 90

Unit 9

Children's own answers

Unit 9 Quick test

1. **a)** 15, **b)** 37, **c)** 59, **d)** 49, **e)** 86, **f)** 78, **g)** 33, **h)** 58,
   i) 97, **j)** 62, **k)** 84, **l)** 81
2. **a)** 22, **b)** 42, **c)** 62, **d)** 34, **e)** 51, **f)** 73, **g)** 44, **h)** 66,
   i) 88, **j)** 43, **k)** 47, **l)** 16
3. **a)** 43, **b)** 77, **c)** 76, **d)** 79, **e)** 89, **f)** 88, **g)** 41, **h)** 53,
   i) 63, **j)** 92, **k)** 83, **l)** 98
4.

5	9	3	17
6	8	8	22
4	1	7	12
15	18	18	

Unit 10

1. **a)** 3 + 5 = 8
      8 = 5 + 3
      3 = 8 − 5
      5 − 8 ≠ 3
   b) 7 + 12 = 19
      19 = 12 + 7
      7 = 19 − 12
      12 − 19 ≠ 7
   c) 10 + 50 = 60
      60 = 50 + 10
      10 = 60 − 50
      50 − 60 ≠ 10
   d) 70 + 20 = 90
      90 = 20 + 70
      20 = 90 − 70
      70 − 90 ≠ 20
2. 12 + 5 = 17, 5 + 12 = 17, 17 − 5 = 12,
   17 − 12 = 5, 12 − 7 = 5, 12 - 5 = 7

Unit 10 Quick test

1. 11 + 7 = 18 and 18 = 7 + 11
2. **a)** 77, **b)** 97, **c)** 89, **d)** 78, **e)** 96, **f)** 89
3. 14 + 5 = 19   5 + 14 = 19
   19 − 5 = 14   5 − 19 ≠ 14

4.

Calculations	Same answer (yes/no)
7 − 4 and 4 − 7	no
9 + 28 and 28 + 9	yes
45 + 54 and 54 + 45	yes
86 − 19 and 19 − 86	no

Unit 11

1. **a)**

13	
9	4

b)

21	
12	9

c)

19	
12	7

d)

28	
15	13

2. **a)** 35 + 14 = 49

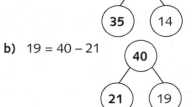

   b) 19 = 40 − 21

3. **a)** 26 − 19 = 7
   b) 8 + 17 = 25
   c) 42 − 16 = 26

Unit 11 Quick test

1. **a)** 6, b) 11, c) 16, d) 17
2. **a)** 8, **b)** 8, **c)** 14, **d)** 24, **e)** 14, **f)** 16, **g)** 5, **h)** 13,
   i) 12, **j)** 93, **k)** 24, **l)** 32
3. **a)** 19 − 5 = 14 (or 19 − 14 = 5),
   b) 8 + 6 = 14 (or 6 + 8 = 14)
   c) 37 − 11 = 26 (or 37 − 26 = 11),
   d) 53 + 22 = 75 (or 22 + 53 = 75)
4. Incorrect: **c)**, **d)**, **f)**

Unit 12

1. **a)** 8, 8 × 2 = 16
   b) 8 hops of two would get the space-hopper
      from 0 to 16.
      The number line between 0 and 16 can be
      divided into 8 steps of 2.
      16 ÷ 8 = 2
2. **a)** 6
      6 × 5 = 30
   b) 6 hops of five would get the space-hopper
      from 0 to 30.
      The number line between 0 and 30 can be
      divided into 6 steps of 5.
      30 ÷ 6 = 5

Unit 12 Quick test

1. **a)** 6, 12, 18
   b) 15, 25, 40
   c) 40, 50, 80
2. **a)** 12, **b)** 20, **c)** 24, **d)** 25, **e)** 35, **f)** 55, **g)** 40,
   h) 80, **i)** 120
3. **a)** 4 × 10, **b)** 4 × 5, **c)** 11 × 2, **d)** 7 × 10
4. **a)** 2, **b)** 9, **c)** 7, **d)** 12

Unit 13

1. **a)** $3 \times 2 = 6$, $6 \div 3 = 2$
   b) $3 \times 5 = 15$, $15 \div 5 = 3$
   c) $2 \times 8 = 16$, $16 \div 8 = 2$
2. **a)** $5 \times 2 = 10$, $10 \div 5 = 2$
   b) $6 \times 5 = 30$, $30 \div 6 = 5$
   c) $3 \times 10 = 30$, $30 \div 10 = 3$
   d) $7 \times 2 = 14$, $14 \div 7 = 2$

Unit 13 Quick test

1. **a)** $2 + 2 + 2 + 2 = 8$
      $4 \times 2 = 8$
   b) $5 + 5 + 5 + 5 + 5 + 5 = 30$
      $6 \times 5 = 30$
   c) $10 + 10 + 10 + 10 + 10 = 50$
      $5 \times 10 = 50$
   d) $5 + 5 + 5 + 5 + 5 + 5 + 5 + 5 = 40$
      $8 \times 5 = 40$
2. **a)** $6 \times 2 = 12$ $12 \div 6 = 2$
   b) $3 \times 5 = 15$ $15 \div 3 = 5$
   c) $7 \times 10 = 70$ $70 \div 7 = 10$
   d) $12 \times 2 = 24$ $24 \div 12 = 2$
   e) $9 \times 5 = 45$ $45 \div 9 = 5$
   f) $11 \times 10 = 110$ $110 \div 11 = 10$
3. **a)** $5 \times 10 = 50$ is greater than $9 \times 5 = 45$
   b) i) £35, $7 \times 5 = 35$
      ii) Sienna, $5 \times £10 = 50$ is greater than $7 \times £5$

Unit 14

1. **a)** $4 \times 2 = 8$, $2 \times 4 = 8$. The answers are the same. The questions share the same numbers but in a different order.
   b) $6 \times 4 = 24$, $4 \times 6 = 24$. The answers are the same. The questions share the same numbers but in a different order.
2. $5 \times 3 = 15$. Since $5 \times 3 = 15$, I also know that $3 \times 5 = 15$ as multiplication can be done in any order. Therefore, the same number of books will be on the second set of shelves (15)
3. $5 \times 8 = 40$ $40 \div 8 = 5$
   $8 \times 5 = 40$ $40 \div 5 = 8$

Unit 14 Quick test

1. **a)** 4, **b)** 7, **c)** 9, **d)** 2
2.

4×10	9×5	2×7	10×12	5×8	6×2
7×2	2×6	10×4	5×9	12×10	8×5

3. TRUE: $10 \times 5 = 5 \times 10$, $8 \div 2$ does not equal $2 \div 8$
4. **a)** There will be a total of 20 beads in 4 trays. [✓]
   b) 45 beads can be shared evenly between 9 trays. [✓]

Unit 15

1. **a)** 40, **b)** 40, **c)** 8, **d)** 5
2. **a)** $2 + 2 + 2 + 2 + 2 + 2 + 2 + 2 + 2 = 18$ shells
   b) $18 - 2 - 2 - 2 - 2 - 2 - 2 - 2 - 2 - 2 = 0$ 9 groups

3.

5 frogs sit on each lily pad. How many frogs will there be on 7 lily pads?	12p is shared equally between six children. How much does each child get?	Birds have 2 legs. How many legs do 12 birds have altogether?	5 beetles sit on each leaf of a plant. If the plant has 9 leaves, how many beetles are there?

$12 \times 2 = 24$	$5 \times 7 = 35$	$9 \times 5 = 45$	$12 \div 6 = 2$

Unit 15 Quick test

1. **a)** 4, **b)** 35p **c)** 7 **d)** 120 **e)** 11 **f)** 24 litres
2. Children's own answers

Unit 16

1. **a)** two parts shaded, **b)** three parts shaded, **c)** one part shaded, **d)** one part shaded
2. **a)** 4, 2, **b)** 6, 2, **c)** 16, 4, **d)** 8, 6, **e)** 12, 4, **f)** 20, 10,
3. **a)** three quarters, $\frac{3}{4}$, **b)** one third, $\frac{1}{3}$,
   c) one half $\frac{1}{2}$

Unit 16 Quick test

1. **a)** 3, **b)** 6, **c)** 2, **d)** 8, **e)** 4, **f)** 10
2. **a)** 1, **b)** 3, **c)** 2, **d)** 5, **e)** 4, **f)** 6
3. **a)** 2, **b)** 5, **c)** 10, **d)** 30, **e)** 20, **f)** 8
4. **a)** 24, **b)** 15, **c)** 20, **d)** 15, **e)** Only $\frac{1}{2}$ and $\frac{1}{4}$ are possible

Unit 17

1. $\frac{1}{2}$ of $8 = 4$

   $\frac{1}{4}$ of $8 = 2$

   $\frac{3}{4}$ of $8 = 6$

   $\frac{1}{2}$ of $16 = 8$

   $\frac{1}{4}$ of $16 = 4$

   $\frac{3}{4}$ of $16 = 12$

   $\frac{1}{2}$ of $12 = 6$

   $\frac{1}{4}$ of $12 = 3$

   $\frac{3}{4}$ of $12 = 9$

   $\frac{1}{3}$ of $12 = 4$

   $\frac{1}{2}$ of $24 = 12$

   $\frac{1}{4}$ of $24 = 6$

   $\frac{3}{4}$ of $24 = 18$

   $\frac{1}{3}$ of $24 = 8$

2. **a)** $\frac{1}{2}$, **b)** $\frac{1}{3}$, **c)** $\frac{3}{4}$, **d)** $\frac{1}{4}$

Unit 17 Quick test

1. a) 5, b) 2, c) 3, d) 1, e) 2, f) 6
2. a) 8, b) 5, c) 6, d) 3, e) 6, f) 9, g) 4, h) 3, i) 2
3. TRUE: a), b), e), f)
4. Cross out: a) and b)

Unit 18

1. a) 6 cm, b) 4 cm
2. a) 5 cm, b) 4 cm
3. a) 400 g, b) 900 g, c) 100 g, d) 700 g

Unit 18 Quick test

1.

Object	Unit of measure	Equipment/tool
length of a paper clip	centimetre	30 cm ruler
height of a small teddy bear	centimetre	30 cm ruler or height chart
mass of a mobile phone	gram	weighing scales
height of the classroom	metre	metre ruler or tape measure
length of a car	metre	metre ruler or tape measure
mass of a packed suitcase	kilogram	weighing scales

2. a) 300 g,

b) 200 g A is heavier. 300 g is greater than 200 g.

Unit 19

1. a) 2°C, 40°C
   b) The juice is colder than the tea.
      The tea is hotter than the juice.
2. 200 ml, 1 litre

Unit 19 Quick test

1.

Object	Unit of measure	Equipment/tool
temperature of a person	degrees Celsius	thermometer
capacity of a large bucket	litre	large measuring jug
temperature of the classroom	degrees Celsius	thermometer
capacity of an eggcup	millilitre	small measuring cylinder, cup or jug

2 a) 12°C   b) 16°C   c) 27°C   d) 67°C

Unit 20

1. The straw is 10 cm and the crayon is 5 cm.
   The straw is longer than the crayon.
   The straw is 5 cm longer than the crayon.
2. Children's own answers
3. 100 ml < 100 l   115 ml < 151 ml   63 ml > 36 ml

Unit 20 Quick test

1. a) <, b) >, c) <, d) >, e) <, f) >, g) >, h) <, i) >
2. Order: 60 g, 75 g, 90 g, 115 g, 135 g
3. Order: 65 ml, 85 ml, 105 ml, 120 ml, 135 ml
4. A, B, D, C
5. B 200 ml   C 50 ml   Order: B, A, C

Unit 21

1. Children's own answers
2. Children's own answers

Unit 21 Quick test

1. a) £3, b) 46p, c) 78p, d) £16, e) 89p, f) £63
2.

Coins/Notes	Total
one 20p coin, three 5p coins, one 1p coin	36p
four 10p coins, four 5p coins, one 2p coin, one 1p coin	63p
one 50p coin, three 10p coins, six 2p coins	92p
one £20 note, one £10 note, one £5 note, two £1 coins	£37
six £10 notes, three £5 notes, three £2 coins	£81
one £50 note, two £20 notes, seven £1 coins	£97

3. Combinations could include: 50p, 20p, 10p (80p) or 50p, 20p, 5p (75p) or 20p, 10p, 5p (35p) or 50p, 10p, 5p (65p)
4. No. With four coins it is possible to make 85p but not 87p. At least one other coin would be required to make 87p.

Unit 22

1. Examples:
   2 × 20p, 1 × 10p, 1 × 5p, 1 × 2p
   2 × 20p, 3 × 5p, 1 × 2p
   1 × 20p, 3 × 10p, 1 × 5p, 1 × 2p
   11 × 5p, 1 × 2p
2. Examples:
   25p
       5 coins: 5 × 5p
       4 coins: 1 × 10p, 3 × 5p
       3 coins: 2 × 10p, 1 × 5p
       2 coins: 1 × 20p, 1 × 5p
   30p
       5 coins: 1 × 20p, 1 × 5p, 2 × 2p, 1 × 1p
       4 coins: 2 × 10p, 2 × 5p
       3 coins: 1 × 20p, 2 × 5p
       2 coins: 1 × 20p, 1 × 10p
   40p
       5 coins: 3 × 10p, 2 × 5p
       4 coins: 1 × 20p, 1 × 10p, 2 × 5p
       3 coins: 1 × 20p, 2 × 10p
       2 coins: 2 × 20p

Unit 22 Quick test

1. Children's own answers
2. **a)** Not possible: pencil (19p), sticky tape (64p), notepad (84p); **b)** children's own choices

Unit 23

1. **a)** 69p **b)** 72p **c)** 98p **d)** 91p
2. **a)** 1p **b)** 4p **c)** 13p **d)** 29p
3. 63p

Unit 23 Quick test

1. **a)** 22p, **b)** 29p, **c)** 41p
   d) 59p, **e)** 91p, **f)** 95p
2. Warthog
3. **a)** 3p, **b)** 6p, **c)** 14p
   d) 22p, **e)** 34p, **f)** 56p
4. Example combination 1: 3 × 10p, 1 × 5p, 1 × 1p
   Example combination 2: 1 × 20p, 1 × 10p, 3 × 2p
5. Combination 1: 3 × £5, 2 × £2
   Combination 2: 1 × £10, 1 × £5, 1 × £2, 2 × £1

Unit 24

1. **a)** Half past 3, quarter to 4, quarter past 4, half past 4
   b) Quarter to 7, half past 7, quarter to 8, quarter past 8
2. **a)** 9:30, 10:30
   b) 10:05, 10:35
   c) 6:40, 8:20

Unit 24 Quick test

1. **a)** half an hour **b)** one hour **c)** 20mins
   d) three quarters of an hour
2. Clock: 9.30, 10.35, 9.55
3.

Earlier time	Later time	Difference (minutes)
half past 6	quarter to 7	15
quarter past 3	ten to 4	35
five past 9	five to 10	50
twenty past 1	half past 2	70
ten to 5	half past 6	100

Unit 25

1. **a)** quarter past 1, **b)** twenty-five to 7, **c)** twenty past 10, **d)** ten past 3, **e)** five to 6, **f)** half past 7
2. **a)** **b)** **c)**

Unit 25 Quick test

1. **a)** 3:10, **b)** 6:25, **c)** 6:40, **d)** 11:55
2. **a)** twenty-five past 3   **b)** ten to 6
   c) ten past 10   **d)** twenty to 12
3. twenty-five to 9, five past 10

Unit 26

1. 5, 15, 20, 25, 30, 40, 50, 55, 60
2.

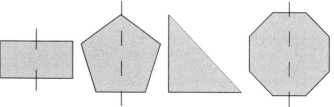

Unit 26 Quick test

1. **a)** 1 hour = 60 minutes   **b)** 1 day = 24hours
   c) half an hour = 30 minutes
   d) half a day = 12 hours
   e) quarter of an hour = 15minutes
   f) 2 days = 48 hours
   g) 2 hours = 120 minutes
   h) 5 days = 120 hours
2. **a)** $\frac{1}{2}$, 30
   b) $\frac{1}{4}$, 15
   c) 1, 60
   d) 2, 120
   e) 1, 24
   f) $\frac{1}{2}$, 12

Unit 27

1. Children to have followed key
2. **a)** oblong, **b)** triangle, **c)** circle, **d)** pentagon
3.

Unit 27 Quick test

1.

Shape	Number of sides	Number of vertices
circle	0	0
triangle	3	3
square	4	4
oblong	4	4
pentagon	5	5
hexagon	6	6
octagon	8	8

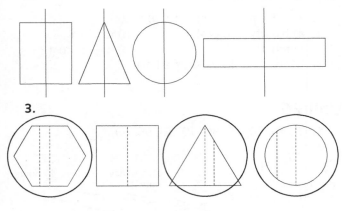

3.

Unit 28

1. Children to have followed key
2. **a)** triangular prism, **b)** cube, **c)** sphere,
   d) square pyramid

Unit 28 Quick test

1.

Shape	Number of faces	Number of vertices	Number of edges
cube	6	8	12
cuboid	6	8	12
triangular prism	5	6	9
square pyramid	5	5	8
sphere	0	0	0

2. **a)** triangular prism, **b)** cube or cuboid,
   c) square pyramid
3. **a)** square pyramid, **b)** cuboid, **c)** cylinder,
   d) triangular prism, **e)** sphere

Unit 29

1. **a)** triangular prism, cuboid
   b) triangular prism, square pyramid
   c) cone, cylinder
   d) cube, cuboid triangular prism
2.

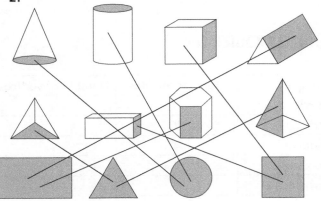

Unit 29 Quick test

1.

Leah draws 6 squares for a cube.

Finn draws 2 triangles and four oblongs for a triangular prism.

Taylor draws 8 oblongs for a cuboid.

Imam draws a square and 3 triangles for a square pyramid.

3 oblongs   6 oblongs   4 triangles

2. **a)** triangle, **b)** rectangle (oblong or square),
   c) square, **d)** circle, **e)** triangle, f) circle
3. triangular pyramid, pentagonal prism, octagonal
   pyramid, hexagonal prism

Unit 30

1. Children's own answers
2. Children's own answers

Unit 30 Quick test

1.

	5 vertices or more	Fewer than 5 vertices
Sides of the same length	regular octagon, regular pentagon	square, equilateral triangle
Sides of different length	irregular pentagon	oblong, scalene triangle, isosceles triangle

2. Flat faces: cube, cuboid, square pyramid, triangular
   prism
   Curved surfaces: sphere
   Both: cylinder, cone
   The 2-D hexagon must sit outside the sets as it
   does not have faces or curved surfaces.

Unit 31

1. **a)** triangle, square, triangle
   b) oblong, oblong, circle
   c) cylinder, sphere, cube
   d) pyramid, cuboid, cuboid
2. Children's own answers

Unit 31 Quick test

1. **a)** triangle (circle)
   b) hexagon (square), square (hexagon)
   c) cube (pyramid)
   d) cone (sphere)
2. **a)** hexagon, **b)** square, **c)** cube

Unit 32

1. **a)** The hot air balloon is above the cat.
   b) The cat is below the hot air balloon and above
   the dog.
   c) The dog is below the cat.
   d) The dog is to the right of the tree and to the
   left of the girl.

2. a) i) snake C3   ii) aeroplane B2   iii) lemon A4
   b) i) 3 squares right, 1 square up
      ii) 2 squares left, 3 squares up
   c) i) west, ii) east
   d) i) Move north 2 squares
      ii) Move west 3 squares

Unit 32 Quick test

1. a) The bridge is below the aeroplane.
   b) The bridge is above the car.
   c) The bridge is in front of the house.
2. a) A quarter turn clockwise
      A three quarter turn anticlockwise
   b) A half turn clockwise
      A half turn anticlockwise
   c) A three quarter turn clockwise
      A quarter turn anticlockwise

Unit 33

1. Children's own answers

Unit 33 Quick test

1.

Flavour	Tally	Number of children
vanilla	𝍢 ⦀	9
strawberry	𝍢 𝍢 ⦀	14
chocolate	𝍢 𝍢 𝍢 ‖	17
cookie dough	𝍢 𝍢 𝍢 ∣	16
bubblegum	𝍢 𝍢 ‖	12

17, 12

2.

☺ = 2 votes

Apple	☺ ☺
Strawberry	☺ ☺ ☺ ☺
Banana	☺ ☺ ☺ ☺ ☺ ☺
Orange	☺ ☺ ☺ ☺ ☺
Melon	☺ ☺ ☺

Unit 34

1. a)

Animal	Tally	Number
goat	𝍢 ⦀	8
horse	‖‖	4
chicken	𝍢 ∣	6
sheep	𝍢 𝍢 ∣	11
cow	𝍢 ‖	7

b) i) 6 **ii)** 11 **iii)** sheep **iv)** horse **v)** goats

Unit 34 Quick test

1. a)

Statement	True	False
On Tuesday, 45 doughnuts were sold.	✓	
On Thursday, 70 doughnuts were sold.		✓
Fewer doughnuts were sold on Tuesday than Wednesday.		✓
More doughnuts were sold on Monday than Wednesday.	✓	
The same number of doughnuts were sold on Monday and Thursday.	✓	
Most doughnuts were sold on Monday.		✓

b) Children's own work

Unit 35

1. Children's own answers

Unit 35 Quick test

1. a) 13 **b)** 9 **c)** 6 **d)** 2
2 a) 65 **b)** 65 **c)** 20 **d)** 20

Notes

Notes

Notes

Notes

Notes

Notes

Notes